A Hallowe'en Anthology

A HALLOWE'EN ANTHOLOGY

ANTHOLOGY

*Literary and Historical
Writings Over the Centuries*

Lisa Morton

McFarland & Company, Inc., Publishers
Jefferson, North Carolina, and London

ALSO BY LISA MORTON
AND FROM McFARLAND

The Halloween Encyclopedia (2003)
The Cinema of Tsui Hark (2001)

Frontispiece: A 1912 postcard

LIBRARY OF CONGRESS CATALOGUING-IN-PUBLICATION DATA

A Hallowe'en anthology : literary and historical writings
over the centuries / [edited by} Lisa Morton.
p.   cm.
Includes bibliographical references and index.

ISBN 978-0-7864-3684-2
softcover : 50# alkaline paper ∞

1. Halloween — Literary collections.
2. Halloween — History — Literary collections.
3. American literature.
4. English literature.
I. Morton, Lisa, 1958–
PS509.H29H33 2008   810.8'0334 — dc22   2007043268

British Library cataloguing data are available

On the cover: Moon and Spiderweb ©2008 Shutterstock;
Witch ©2008 Pictures Now

Manufactured in the United States of America

*McFarland & Company, Inc., Publishers
Box 611, Jefferson, North Carolina 28640
www.mcfarlandpub.com*

Table of Contents

Preface

While researching my earlier book *The Halloween Encyclopedia*, I was continually astonished at the wealth of information relating to Hallowe'en that I was able to locate, some of it dating as far back as the sixteenth century. In pure form, the material was often richer than anything I could have imagined finding; despite sometimes obsolete language, the articles, poems, and calendar entries on Hallowe'en were frequently both very informative and entertaining. Although I felt that *The Halloween Encyclopedia* would fill a significant gap in the study of the holiday's history (in being the first encyclopedic reference on Hallowe'en), I was frustrated at the limitations of the encyclopedic format, which allowed me to use only brief excerpts or synopses of longer pieces.

Which brings us to the current book. *A Hallowe'en Anthology* gathers together some of the most intriguing and useful works I came across while digging for information to use in *The Halloween Encyclopedia*, and even adds a few wonderful new pieces I've found since. Now, for example, I can present William Wells Newell's fascinating 1904 study of the history of jack-o'-lantern legends ("The Ignis Fatuus") in its complex and delightful entirety; likewise, Alexander Montgomerie's oft-quoted 1584 poem "Flyting Against Polwart" (which is also presented here for the first time with extensive annotations that will make it more palatable for the modern reader). If *The Halloween Encyclopedia* filled one gap in the library of works available on the history of the holiday, then *A Hallowe'en Anthology* will fill another, in providing the first collection of complete, original source materials on the history of the holiday.

I have edited a few entries, but only where they overlapped considerably with another entry. I've attempted to adhere as much as possible to the original presentation of these works, complete with obsolete spellings, grammar and punctuation, since I think it's important and valuable to preserve these pieces in their original form as much as possible.

The pieces have been placed in chronological order, according to their original date of publication, since this should serve to provide some idea of how Halloween grew and transformed over time. I've provided commentaries at the beginning of each piece that will provide readers with further background.

Accompanying footnotes are the original authors' except where indicated otherwise in my introductory comments. Only one entry, "Halloween: A Threefold Chronicle" from *Harper's Magazine*, includes illustrations that accompanied the original publication of the work; in all other cases, I have chosen the illustrations on the basis of their appropriateness to the piece.

1

I hope this anthology will prove useful to the academic and entertaining to the Halloween fan; but most especially I hope it will provide further insight into and appreciation of the roots and history of this mysterious and rich celebration.

And now, as the Manx people would say: "*Noght oie howney hop-dy-naw*"! ("This is Hollantide Eve").

"Three Celtic Samhain Myths"

800 B.C.–A.D. 500,
adapted by Lady Gregory

The Celts, who spread throughout Northern Europe and the British Isles from around 800 B.C. to approximately A.D. 500, celebrated their "summer's end" on October 31st, and it is to them that we owe the date and magical attributes of Hallowe'en.

Although the Celts had a rich mythology, little of it was recorded until nearly the turn of the first millennium A.D., when Christian monks in Ireland began recording Irish traditional legends and history. However, it wasn't until almost a millennium later — when Irish nationalism erupted in the late 19th century — that Celtic mythology was translated into English and published in widely available editions.

Isabella Augusta, Lady Gregory (1852–1932), was a playwright and contemporary of William Butler Yeats, with whom she co-founded the famed Irish Literary Theatre; but it's her folklore work that she is perhaps most known for

"Finn heard far off the first notes of the fairy harp" — illustration by Stephen Reid (from 1910's *The High Deeds of Finn and Other Bardic Romances of Ancient Ireland*).

now. Using a number of written and oral sources, Lady Gregory retold Celtic legends in two English-language collections: *Gods and Fighting Men: The Story of the Tuatha de Danaan and of the Fianna of Ireland* (1904) and *Cuchulain of Muirthemne: The Story of the Men of the Red Branch of Ulster* (1902). These volumes remain possibly the most popular books on traditional Celtic mythology.

Presented here are three of the eeriest tales centering on Samhain, the end of the Celtic year and the ancestor of the modern Hallowe'en. The first tale, "Cruachan," taken from *Cuchulain of Muirthemne*, sets up the classic lore of the fairy hills that open only on Samhain (later Hallowe'en), and also paints an unnerving picture of corpses returning to life on this special day.

In "The Coming of Finn" (Finn is the legendary Celtic leader sometimes known as Fionn mac Cumhaill or Finn McCool), Lady Gregory mentions both the yearly Samhain gathering of the Celtic leaders and the story of Aillen, a fairy (or member of the *sidhe*) who laid waste to the Celts' capitol city each year on Samhain; in some versions of this story, Finn is only ten years old, and Aillen has ravaged Teamhair for the past 23 years.

The last story, "The Cave of Cruachan," is once again set in Cruachan, which is an actual location in Ireland; to this day the Cave of Cruachan (also known as "Owenagcat") is known as "the hell-gate of Ireland."

Compare these stories to later folk-tales such as "The Young Man in the Fairy Knoll" and "November Eve," both of which also deal with malicious fairies stealing forth on Halloween to create (somewhat less destructive) mischief.

Excerpt from *Cuchulain of Muirthemne*: "Cruachan"

One night at Samhain, Ailell and Maeve were in Cruachan with their whole household, and the food was being made ready.

Two prisoners had been hanged by them the day before, and Ailell said: "Whoever will put a gad round the foot of either of the two men on the gallows, will get a prize from me."

It was a very dark night, and bad things would always appear on that night of Samhain, and every man that went out to try came back very quickly into the house. "I will go if I will get a prize," said Nera, then. "I will give you this gold-hilted sword," said Ailell.

So Nera went out and he put a gad round the foot of one of the men that had been hanged. Then the man spoke to him. "It is good courage you have," he said, "and bring me with you where I can get a drink, for I was very thirsty when I was hanged." So Nera brought him where he would get a drink, and then he put him on the gallows again, and went back to Cruachan.

But what he saw was the whole of the palace as if on fire before him, and the heads of the people of it lying on the ground, and then he thought he saw an army going into the Hill of Cruachan, and he followed after the army. "There is a man on our track," the last man said. "The track is the heavier," said the next to him, and each said that word to the other from the last to the first. Then they went into the Hill of Cruachan. And they said to their king: "What shall be done to the man that is come in?" "Let him come here till I speak with him," said the king. So Nera came, and the king asked him who it was had brought him in. "I came in with your army," said Nera. "Go to that house beyond," said the king: "there is a woman there will make you welcome. Tell her it is I myself sent you to her. And come every day," he said, "to this house with a load of firing."

So Nera went where he was told, and the woman said: "A welcome before you, if it is the king sent you." So he stopped there, and took the woman for his wife. And every day for three days he brought a load of firing to the king's house, and on each day he saw a blind man, and a lame man on his back, coming out of the house before him. They would go on till they were at the brink of a well before the Hill. "Is it there?" the blind man would say. "It is, indeed," the lame man would say. "Let us go away," the lame man would say then.

And at the end of three days, as he thought, Nera asked the woman about this. "Why do the blind man and the lame man go every day to the well?" he said. "They go to know is the crown safe that is in the well. It is there the king's crown is kept." "Why do these two go?" said Nera. "It is easy to tell that," she said; "they are trusted by the king to visit the crown, and one of them was blinded by him, and the other was lamed. And another thing," she said, "go now and give a warning to your people to mind themselves next Samhain night, unless they will come to attack the hill, for it is only at Samhain," she said. "the army of the Sidhe can go out, for it is at that time all the hills of the Sidhe of Ireland are opened. But if they will come, I will promise them this, the crown of Briun to be carried off by Ailell and by Maeve."

"How can I give them that message," said Nera, "when I saw the whole dun of Cruachan burned and destroyed, and all the people destroyed with it?" "You did not see that, indeed," she said. "It was the host of the Sidhe came and put that appearance before your eyes. And go back to them now," she said, "and you will find them sitting round the same great pot, and the meat has not yet been taken off the fire."

"How will it be believed that I have gone into the Hill?" said Nera. "Bring flowers of summer with you," said the woman. So he brought wild garlic with him, and primroses and golden fern.

So he went back to the palace, and he found his people round the same great pot, and he told them all that had happened him, and the sword was given to him, and he stopped with his people to the end of a year.

At the end of the year Ailell said to Nera: "We are going now against the Hill of the Sidhe, and let you go back," he said, "if you have anything to bring out of it." So he went back to see the woman, and she bade him welcome. "Go now," she said, "and bring in a load of firing to the king, for I went in myself every day for the last year with the load on my back, and I said there was sickness on you." So he did that.

Then the men of Connaught and the black host of the exiles of Ulster went into the Hill and robbed it and brought away the crown of Briun, son of Smetra, that was made by the smith of Angus, son of Umor, and that was kept in the well at Cruachan, to save it from the Morrigu. And Nera was left with his people in the hill, and he has not come out till now, and he will not come out till the end of life and time.

Excerpt from *Gods and Fighting Men, Part II, Book I*: "The Coming of Finn"

And after that, Finn being but a young lad yet, made himself ready and went up at Samhain time to the gathering of the High King at Teamhair. And it was the law at that gathering, no one to raise a quarrel or bring out any grudge against another through the whole of the time it lasted. And the king and his chief men, and Goll, son of Morna, that was now Head of the Fianna, and Caoilte, son of Ronan, and Conan, son of Morna, of the sharp words, were sitting at a feast in the great house of the Middle Court; and the young lad came in and took his place among them, and none of them knew who he was.

The High King looked at him then, and the horn of meetings was brought to him, and he put it into the boy's hand, and asked him who was he.

"I am Finn, son of Cumhal," he said, "son of the man that used to be head over the Fianna, and king of Ireland; and I am come now to get your friendship, and to give you my service."

"You are son of a friend, boy," said the king, "and son of a man I trusted."

Then Finn rose up and made his agreement of service and of faithfulness to the king; and the king took him by the hand and put him sitting beside his own son, and they gave themselves to drinking and to pleasure for a while.

Every year, now, at Samhain time, for nine years, there had come a man of the Tuatha de Danaan out of Sidhe Finnachaidh in the north, and had burned up Teamhair. Aillen, son of Midhna, his name was, and it is the way he used to come, playing music of the Sidhe, and all the people that heard it would fall asleep. And when they were all in their sleep, he would let a flame of fire out of his mouth, and would blow the flame till all Teamhair was burned.

The king rose up at the feast after a while, and his smooth horn in his hand, and it is what he said: "If I could find among you, men of Ireland, any man that would keep Teamhair till the break of day to-morrow without being burned by Aillen, son of Midhna, I would give him whatever inheritance is right for him to have, whether it be much or little."

But the men of Ireland made no answer, for they knew well that at the sound of the sweet pitiful music made by that comely man of the Sidhe, even women in their pains and men that were wounded would fall asleep.

It is then Finn rose up and spoke to the King of Ireland. "Who will be your sureties that you will fulfil this?" he said. "The kings of the provinces of Ireland," said the king, "and Cithruadh with his Druids." So they gave their pledges, and Finn took in hand to keep Teamhair safe till the breaking of day on the morrow.

Now there was a fighting man among the followers of the King of Ireland, Fiacha, son of Conga, that Cumhal, Finn's father, used to have a great liking for, and he said to Finn: "Well, boy," he said, "what reward would you give me if I would bring you a deadly spear, that no false cast was ever made with?" "What reward are you asking of me?" said Finn. "Whatever your right hand wins at any time, the third of it to be mine," said Fiacha, "and a third of your trust and your friendship to be mine." "I will give you that," said Finn. Then Fiacha brought him the spear, unknown to the sons of Morna or to any other person, and he said: "When you will hear the music of the Sidhe, let you strip the covering off the head of the spear and put it to your forehead, and the power of the spear will not let sleep come upon you."

Then Finn rose up before all the men of Ireland, and he made a round of the whole of Teamhair. And it was not long till he heard the sorrowful music, and he stripped the covering from the head of the spear, and he held the power of it to his forehead. And Aillen went on playing his little harp, till he had put every one in their sleep as he was used; and then he let a flame of fire out from his mouth to burn Teamhair. And Finn held up his fringed crimson cloak against the flame, and it fell down through the air and went into the ground, bringing the four-folded cloak with it deep into the earth.

And when Aillen saw his spells were destroyed, he went back to Sidhe Finnachaidh on the top of Slieve Fuad; but Finn followed after him there, and as Aillen was going in at the door he made a cast of the spear that went through his heart. And he struck his head off then, and brought it back to Teamhair, and fixed it on a crooked pole and left it there till the rising of the sun over the heights and invers of the country.

And Aillen's mother came to where his body was lying, and there was great grief on her, and she made this complaint:—

"Ochone! Aillen is fallen, chief of the Sidhe of Beinn Boirche; the slow clouds of death are come on him. Och! he was pleasant, Och! he was kind. Aillen, son of Midhna of Slieve Fuad.

"Nine times he burned Teamhair. It is a great name he was always looking for, Ochone, Ochone, Aillen!"

And at the breaking of day, the king and all the men of Ireland came out upon the lawn at Teamhair where Finn was. "King," said Finn, "there is the head of the man that burned Teamhair, and the pipe and the harp that made his music. And it is what I think," he said, "that Teamhair and all that is in it is saved."

Then they all came together into the place of counsel, and it is what they agreed, the headship of the Fianna of Ireland to be given to Finn. And the king said to Goll, son of Morna: "Well, Goll," he said, "is it your choice to quit Ireland or to put your hand in Finn's hand?" "By my word, I will give Finn my hand," said Goll.

And when the charms that used to bring good luck had done their work, the chief men of the Fianna rose up and struck their hands in Finn's hand, and Goll, son of Morna, was the first to give him his hand the way there would be less shame on the rest for doing it.

And Finn kept the headship of the Fianna until the end; and the place he lived in was Almhuin of Leinster, where the white dun was made by Nuada of the Tuatha de Danaan, that was as white as if all the lime in Ireland was put on it, and that got its name from the great herd of cattle that died fighting one time around the well, and that left their horns there, speckled horns and white.

Excerpt from *Gods and Fighting Men: Part II, Book IV*: "The Cave of Cruachan"

Caoilte was one time at Cruachan of Connacht, and Cascorach was with him, and there he saw sitting on a heap of stones a man with very rough grey hair, having a dark brown cloak fastened with a pin of bronze, and a long stick of white hazel in his hand; and there was a herd of cattle before him in a fenced field.

Caoilte asked news of him. "I am steward to the King of Ireland," said the old man, "and it is from him I hold this land. And we have great troubles on us in this district," he said. "What troubles are those?" said Caoilte. "I have many herds of cattle," he said, "and every year at Samhain time, a woman comes out of the hill of the Sidhe of Cruachan and brings away nine of the best out of every herd. And as to my name, I am Bairnech, son of Carbh of Collamair of Bregia."

"Who was the best man that ever came out of Collamair?" said Caoilte. "I know, and the men of Ireland and of Alban know," said he, "it was Caoilte, son of Ronan. And do you know where is that man now?" he said. "I myself am that man and your own kinsman," said Caoilte.

When Bairnech heard that, he gave him a great welcome, and Caoilte gave him three kisses. "It seems to me that to-night is Samhain night," said Caoilte. "If that is so, it is to-night the woman will come to rob us," said Bairnech. "Let me go to-night to the door of the hill of the Sidhe," said Cascorach. "You may do that, and bring your arms with you," said Caoilte.

So Cascorach went then, and it was not long till he saw the girl going past him out of the hill of Cruachan, having a beautiful cloak of one colour about her; a gown of yellow silk tied up with a knot between her thighs, two spears in her hands, and she not in dread of anything before her or after her.

Then Cascorach blew a blast against her, and put his finger into the thong of his spear, and made a cast at the girl that went through her, and that is the way she was made an end of by Cascorach of the Music.

And then Bairnech said to Caoilte: "Caoilte," he said, "do you know the other oppression that is on me in this place?" "What oppression is that?" said Caoilte. "Three she-wolves that come out of the Cave of Cruachan every year and destroy our sheep and our wethers, and we can do nothing against them, and they go back into the cave again. And it will be a good friend that will rid us of them," he said. "Well, Cascorach," said Caoilte, "do you know what are the three wolves that are robbing this man?" "I know well," said Cascorach, "they are the three daughters of Airetach, of the last of the people of oppression of the Cave of Cruachan, and it is easier for them to do their robbery as wolves than as women." "And will they come near to any one?" said Caoilte. "They will only come near to one sort," said Cascorach; "if they see the world's men having harps for music, they will come near to them. And how would it be for me," he said, "to go to-morrow to the cairn beyond, and to bring my harp to me?"

So in the morning he rose up and went to the cairn and stopped on it, playing his harp till the coming of the mists of the evening. And while he was there he saw the three wolves coming towards him, and they lay down before him, listening to the music. But Cascorach found no way to make an attack on them, and they went back into the cave at the end of the day.

Cascorach went back then to Caoilte and told him what had happened. "Go up to-morrow to the same place," said Caoilte, "and say to them it would be better for them to be in the shape of women for listening to music than in the shape of wolves."

So on the morrow Cascorach went out to the same cairn, and set his people about it, and the wolves came there and stretched themselves to listen to the music. And Cascorach was saying to them: "If you were ever women," he said, "it would be better for you to be listening to the music as women than as wolves." And they heard that, and they threw off the dark trailing coverings that were about them, for they liked well the sweet music of the Sidhe.

And when Caoilte saw them there side by side, and elbow by elbow, he made a cast of his spear, and it went through the three women, that they were like a skein of thread drawn together on the spear. And that is the way he made an end of the strange, unknown three. And that place got the name of the Valley of the Shapes of the Wolves.

"Tamlane"

1548, adapted by Sir Walter Scott

The story of cursed fairy prince Tamlane and the brave lass who saves him is possibly the oldest and most complete tale to make vivid use of Hallowe'en (as compared to the Celtic festival of Samhain, which appears throughout earlier literature).

The legend of Tamlane is recorded as early as 1548 (when *The Tayl of the Yong Tamlene* appears in the *Complaynt of Scotland*), although the version presented here was prepared by Sir Walter Scott for publication in his collection *Minstrelsy of the Scottish Border* (1802). The story has been told many times and in many forms (Tamlane's name, for example, has appeared as "Tam Lin," "Thomalin," "Thomas," "Tom-o'-the-Linn," etc.); this version, compiled by Scott from various copies, is the longest telling of the story. "Tamlane" echoes Irish and Scottish folktales of unfortunate folk stolen by fairies (or *sidh*) on Hallowe'en night; however, efforts to save those taken are seldom as successful as the ending of "Tamlane."

Scott's telling of this ancient story is still one of the loveliest depictions of Hallowe'en as a night of magic, terror and wonder.

"O I forbid ye, maidens a',
　　That wear gowd on your hair,
To come or gae by Carterhaugh,[1]
　　For young Tamlane is there.

"There's nane that gaes by Carterhaugh,
　　But maun leave him a wad,[2]
Either gowd rings, or green mantles,[3]
　　Or else their maidenheid.

1. In his notes in *Minstrelsy of the Scottish Border*, Sir Walter Scott provides this description: "Carterhaugh is a plain, at the conflux of the Ettrick and Yarrow, Selkirkshire, about a mile above Selkirk, and two miles above Newark Castle; a romantic ruin, which overhangs the Yarrow, and which is said to have been the habitation of our heroine's father...."

2. "Wad' is a token or an object left as a pledge

3. Fairies were often described as wearing green; see also "Flyting Against Polwart"

"Janet casts the Flaming Sword into the Well"—illustration by John D. Batten (from 1894's *More English Fairy Tales*).

"Now gowd rings ye may buy, maidens,
    Green mantles ye may spin;
But, gin ye lose your maidenheid,
    Ye'll ne'er get that agen."—

But up then spak her, fair Janet,
    The fairest o' a' her kin;
"I'll cum and gang to Carterhaugh,
    And ask nae leave o' him."—

Janet has kilted her green kirtle,
A little abune her knee;
And she has braided her yellow hair,
A little abune her bree.[1]

And when she came to Carterhaugh,
She gaed beside the well;
And there she fand his steed standing,
But away was himsell.

She hadna pu'd a red red rose,
A rose but barely three;
Till up and starts a wee wee man,
At lady Janet's knee.

Says —"Why pu' ye the rose, Janet?
What gars[2] ye break the tree?
Or why come ye to Carterhaugh,
Withouten leave o' me?"—

Says —"Carterhaugh it is mine ain;
My daddie gave it me;
I'll come and gang to Carterhaugh,
And ask nae leave o' thee."

He's ta'en her by the milk-white hand,
Among the leaves sae green;
And what they did, I cannot tell —
The green leaves were between.

He's ta'en her by the milk-white hand,
Among the roses red;
And what they did, I cannot say —
She ne'er return'd a maid.

When she cam to her father's ha',
She looked pale and wan;
They thought she'd dreed some sair sickness,
Or been with some leman.[3]

---

1. "abune her bree" = above her brow
2. "What gars" = why do
3. "leman" = lover

She didna comb her yellow hair,
  Nor make meikle o'er[1] her head;
And ilka[2] thing that lady took,
  Was like to be her deid.[3]

It's four and twenty ladies fair
  Were playing at the ba';
Janet, the wightest of them anes,
  Was faintest o' them a'.

Four and twenty ladies fair
  Were playing at the chess;
And out there came the fair Janet,
  As green as any grass.

Out and spak an auld grey-headed knight,
  Lay o'er the castle wa',—
"And ever, alas! for thee, Janet,
  But we'll be blamed a'!"—

"Now haud your tongue, ye auld grey knight!
  And an ill deid may ye die;
Father my bairn on whom I will,
  I'll father nane on thee."—

Out then spak her father dear,
  And spak meik and mild—
"And ever, alas! my sweet Janet,
  I fear ye gae with child."—

"And if I be with child, father,
  Mysell maun bear the blame;
There's ne'er a knight about your ha'
  Shall hae the bairnie's name.

"And if I be with child, father,
  'Twill prove a wondrous birth;
For weel I swear I'm not wi' bairn
  To any man on earth.

1. "make meikle o'er" = take much care of
2. "ilka" = every
3. "deid" = death

"If my love were an earthly knight,
    As he's an elfin grey,
I wadna gie my ain true love
    For nae lord that ye hae."—

She prink'd[1] hersell and prinn'd hersell,
    By the ae light of the moon,
And she's away to Carterhaugh,
    To speak wi' young Tamlane.

And when she came to Carterhaugh,
    She gaed beside the well;
And there she saw the steed standing,
    But away was himsell.

She hadna pu'd a double rose,
    A rose but only twae,
When up and started young Tamlane,
    Says—"Lady, thou pu's nae mae!

"Why pu' ye the rose, Janet,
    Within this garden grene,
And a' to kill the bonny babe,
    That we got us between?"

"The truth ye'll tell to me, Tamlane;
    A word ye mauna lie;
Gin e'er ye was in haly chapel,
    Or sained[2] in Christentie?"—

"The truth I'll tell to thee, Janet,
    A word I winna lie;
A knight me got, and a lady me bore,
    As well as they did thee.

"Randolph, Earl Murray, was my sire,
    Dunbar, Earl March, is thine;
We loved when we were children small,
    Which yet you well may mind.

1. "prink'd" = adorned
2. "sained" = blessed

"When I was a boy just turn'd of nine,
  My uncle sent for me,
To hunt, and hawk, and ride with him,
  And keep him companie.

"There came a wind out of the north,
  A sharp wind and a snell[1];
And a deep sleep came over me,
  And frae my horse I fell.

"The Queen of Fairies keppit me,
  In yon green hill to dwell;
And I'm a fairy, lyth and limb;
  Fair ladye, view me well.

"Then would I never tire, Janet,
  In Elfish land to dwell;
But aye, at every seven years,
  They pay the teind[2] to hell;
And I am sae fat and fair of flesh,
  I fear 'twill be mysell.

"This night is Hallowe'en, Janet,
  The morn is Hallowday;
And, gin ye dare your true love win,
  Ye hae nae time to stay.

"The night it is good Hallowe'en,
  When fairy folk will ride;
And they that wad their true-love win,
  At Miles Cross they maun bide."

"But how shall I thee ken, Tamlane?
  Or how shall I thee knaw,
Amang so many unearthly knights,
  The like I never saw?"

"The first company that passes by,
  Say na, and let them gae;
The next company that passes by,
  Sae na, and do right sae;
The third company that passes by,
  Then I'll be ane o' thae.

1. "snell" = keen, bitter, sharp
2. "teind" = tax or levy

"First let pass the black, Janet,
    And syne let pass the brown;
But grip ye to the milk-white steed,
    And pu' the rider down.

"For I ride on the milk-white steed,
    And aye nearest the town;
Because I was a christen'd knight,
    They gave me that renown.

"My right hand will be gloved, Janet,
    My left hand will be bare;
And these the tokens I gie thee,
    Nae doubt I will be there.

They'll turn me in your arms, Janet,
    An adder and a snake;
But had me fast, let me not pass,
    Gin ye wad buy me maik.

"They'll turn me in your arms, Janet,
    An adder and an ask[1];
They'll turn me in your arms, Janet,
    A bale[2] that burns fast.

"They'll turn me in your arms, Janet,
    A red-hot gad o' airn[3];
But haud me fast, let me not pass,
    For I'll do you no harm.

"First dip me in a stand o' milk,
    And then in a stand o' water;
But had me fast, let me not pass —
    I'll be your bairn's father.

And next, they'll shape me in your arms,
    A tod, but and an eel;
But had me fast, nor let me gang,
    As you do love me weel.

1. "ask" = newt
2. "bale" = a large fire
3. "gad o' airn" = bar of iron

They'll shape me in your arms, Janet,
   A dove, but and a swan;
And, last, they'll shape me in your arms
   A mother-naked man:
Cast your green mantle over me —
   I'll be myself again." —

Gloomy, gloomy, was the night,
   And eiry was the way,
As fair Janet, in her green mantle,
   To Miles Cross she did gae.

Betwixt the hours of twelve and one,
   A north wind tore the bent[1];
And straight she heard strange elritch sounds
   Upon that wind which went.

About the dead hour o' the night,
   She heard the bridles ring;
And Janet was as glad o' that
   As any earthly thing.

Will o' Wisp before them went,
   Sent forth a twinkling light;
And soon she saw the Fairy bands
   All riding in her sight.

And first gaed by the black black steed,
   And then gaed by the brown;
But fast she gript the milk-white steed,
   And pu'd the rider down.

She pu'd him frae the milk-white steed,
   And loot the bridle fa';
And up there raise an erlish[2] cry —
   "He's won amang us a'!" —

They shaped him in fair Janet's arms,
   An esk, but and an adder;
She held him fast in every shape —
   To be her bairn's father.

---

1. "bent" = a type of grass
2. "erlish" = unearthly

They shaped him in her arms at last,
    A mother-naked man;
She wrapt him in her green mantle,
    And sae her true love wan!

Up then spake the Queen o' Fairies,
    Out o' a bush o' broom —
"She that has borrow'd young Tamlane,
    Has gotten a stately groom." —

Up then spake the Queen o' Fairies,
    Out o' a bush o' rye —
"She's ta'en awa the bonniest knight
    In a' my cumpanie.

"But had I kenn'd, Tamlane," she says,
    "A lady wad borrow'd thee —
I wad ta'en out they twa grey een,
    Put in twa een o' tree.[1]

"Had I but kenn'd, Tamlane," she says,
    "Before ye came frae hame —
I wad ta'en out your heart o' flesh,
    Put in a heart o' stane.

"Had I but had the wit yestreen
    That I hae coft[2] the day —
I'd paid my kane[3] seven times to hell
    Ere you'd been won away!"

1. "twa een o' tree" = two eyes of wood

2. "coft" = acquired

3. "kane" = a payment, often to a lord

"Flyting Against Polwart"

Alexander Montgomerie, 1584

The second stanza of Alexander Montgomerie's poem is one of the most frequently quoted early references to Hallowe'en; its startling depiction of maddened fairies and monsters riding on Allhallow evening remains evocative more than four centuries after its creation.

The traditional title "Flyting Against Polwart" is actually somewhat incorrect; the poem's true title is "Montgomeries Answere to Polwart." The poem is presented as part of a cycle of poems, the overall title of which is "Polwart and Montgomeries Flyting." Alexander Montgomerie was a 16th-century Scottish poet who found favor with the royal court. At the time, poetic "flyting"—or poets warring with words—was much in vogue, and Montgomerie chose to carry on his battle with another royal favorite, probably Sir Patrick Hume of Polwarth. Thus, "Montgomeries Answere to Polwart" is actually a playful comparison of Montgomerie's rival to a monstrous creature birthed on Hallowe'en by witches and fairies.

A fairy—illustration by Henry Coppee from 1859's *A Gallery of Famous English and American Poets.*

The poem is here presented in its original length

19

and dialect, with annotations. I've taken the liberty of replacing the obsolete character ȝ (the "yogh") with its closest modern equivalents, the letters "y" or "z."

Vyle venomous viper, wanthriftiest[1] of things,
Halfe an elfe, halfe ane aipe, of nature deny it,
Thou flait[2] with a countrey, the quhilk[3] was the kings;
Bot that bargan,[4] vnbeast,[5] deare sall thou buy it.
"The cuff is weill waired that twa hame brings."
This prouerb, foule pelt, to thee is applyit :
First, spider, of spyte thou spewes out springs;
Yet, wanshapen woubet,[6] of the weirds invyit,
I can tell thee, how, when, where, and wha gat thee;
    The quhilk was neither man nor wife,
    Nor human creature on life:
    Thou stinkand steirer vp of strife,
        False howlat,[7] have at thee!

In the hinder end of haruest, on Allhallow euen,
When our good nighbours doe ryd, gif I read right,
Some buckled on a bunwand,[8] and some on a been,[9]
Ay trottand in trupes from the twilight;
Some sadleand a shoe aip all graithed[10] into green,
Some hobland on ane hempstalke, hoveand to the hight.
The King of Pharie, and his court, with the Elfe Queen,
With many elrich Incubus, was rydand that night.
There ane elf, on ane aipe, ane vnsell[11] begat,
    Into ane pot, by Pomathorne;
    That bratchart[12] in ane busse was borne;
    They fand ane monster, on the morne,
        War faced nor a cat.

---

1. "wanthrifiest" = unthriftiest
2. "flait with" = scold
3. "quhilk" = which
4. "bargan" = contention
5. "vnbeast" = wild beast, monster
6. "wanshapen woubet " = a malformed, hairy caterpillar
7. "howlat" = general derogatory term for a person
8. "bunwand" = flax or hemp stalk
9. "been" = bone
10. "graithed" = clothed
11. "vnsell" = misery, misfortune
12. "bratchart" = brat

The Weird Sisters wandring, as they were wont then,
Saw reavens rugand at that ratton be a ron ruit.[1]
They mused at the mandrake vnmade lik a man;
A beast bund with a bonevand in ane old buit.
How that gaist[2] had been gotten, to gesse they began,
Well swyld in a swynes skin and smerit ouer with suit;
The bellie that it first bair full bitterly they ban.[3]
Of this mismade mowdewart,[4] mischief they muit.[5]
That cruiked, camschoche croyll,[6] vncristned, they curse;
    They bade that baiche[7] sould not be but
    The glengore, gravell, and the gut,[8]
    And all the plagues that first were put
        Into Pandoraes purse

"The cogh[9] and the connogh, the collicke and the cald,
The cords and the cout-euill, the claisps and the cleiks,
The hunger, the hart-ill, and the hoist still thee hald;
The boch and the barbles, with the Cannigate breikes,
With bockblood and beanshaw, speven sprung in the spald,
The fersie, the falling-euill, that fels manie freikes,
Ouergane all with angleberries, as thou growes ald,
The kinkhost, the charbuckle, and the wormes in the cheiks,
The snuff and the snoire, the chaud-peece, the chanker,
    With the blads and the bellie-thraw,
    The bleiring bates and the beanshaw,
    With the mischiefe of the melt and maw,
        The clape and the canker,

"The frencie, the fluxes, the fyke, and the felt,
The feavers, the fearcie, with the speinzie flees,
The doit and the dismail, indifferentlie delt,
The powlings, the palsay, with pockes like pees,
The swerfe and the sweating, with sounding to swelt,
The weam-eill, the wild-fire, the vomit and the vees,

1. "reavens rugand at that ratton be a ron ruit" = carnivorous animals roaring at that rat by a thicket

2. "gaist" = goblin

3. "ban" = curse

4. "mowdewart" = deformed infant

5. "mischief they muit" = ill will they speak

6. "camschoche croyll" = crooked, dwarfish or stunted person

7. "baiche" = child

8. "glengore, gravell, and the gut" = venereal disease, kidney stones and gout

9. "cogh" etc. = throughout this and the following stanza, virtually all nouns refer to diseases or ailments of some sort

The mair and the migrame, with the meathes in the melt,
The warbles and the wood-worme, whereof dogs dies,
The teasicke, the tooth-aike, the tittes and the tirles,
  The painfull poplesie and pest,
  The rot, the roup, and the auld rest,
  With parles and pleurisies opprest,
    And nipped with nirles.

"Woe worth," quoth the Weirds, "the wights that thee wroght!
Threed-bare bee their thrift[1] as thou art wanthreivin[2]!
Als hard bee their handsell that helps thee to ought!
The rotten rim of thy wombe with rooke shall bee reivin.
All bounds, where thou bides, to baile shall bee brought;
Thy gall and thy guisserne[3] to glaids[4] shall bee given,
Aye short bee thy solace; with shame bee thou sought:
In hell mot thou haunt thee, and hide thee from heauen;
And aye as thou auld growes, swa eikand bee thy anger,
  To liue with limmers[5] and outlawes,
  With hurcheons[6] eatand hips and hawes[7];
  Bot when thou comes where the cocke crawes,
    Tarie there na langer.

"Shame and sorrow on her snout that suffers thee to sowke[8];
Or shoe that cares for thy cradill, cauld bee her cast[9];
Or bringes anie bedding for thy blae bowke[10];
Or louses off thy lingals[11] sa lang as they may last;
Or offers thee anie thing all the lang owke;
Or first refresheth thee with foode, howbeit thou should fast;
Or, when they duddes are bedirtten, that giues them an dowk.[12]
All groomes, when thou greits, at thy ganting[13] bee agast.

1. "thrift" = wealth, property
2. "wanthreivin" = un-thriving, stunted
3. "gall and ... guisserne" = gall bladder and gizzard
4. "glaids" = birds of prey
5. "limmers" = rogues, scoundrels
6. "hurcheon" = slovenly, uncouth persons
7. "eatand hips and hawes" = eating the fruit of the dog-rose and hawthorn berries
8. "sowke" = suck, suckle
9. "cast" = fate
10. "blae bowke" = black bulk
11. "lingals" = thongs or straps
12. "dowk" = ducking, or washing
13. "ganting" = yawning, gaping

Als froward[1] bee thy fortune, as foull is thy forme.
   First, seuen yeires, bee thou dumbe and deiffe;
   And after that, a common thieffe:
   Thus art thou marked for mischieffe,
     Foule vnworthie worme!

"Outrowde bee thy tongue, yet tratling[2] all times.
Aye the langer that thou liues thy lucke be the lesse.
All countries where thou comes accuse thee of crimes;
And false bee thy fingers, bot loath to confesse:
Aye raving and raging in rude rat-rimes.
All ill bee thou vsand, and aye in excesse.
Ilke[3] moone, bee thou mad, fra past bee the prime;
Still plagued with pouertie, thy pride to oppresse.
With warwolfes and wild cates thy weird[4] bee to wander;
   Draiglit throw dirtie dubes[5] and dykes;
   Tousled and tuggled with towne tykes.[6]
   Say, lousie lyar, what thou lykes;
     Thy tongue is na slander."

Fra the sisters had seene the shape of that shit,
"Little lucke bee thy lot, there where thou lyes.
Thy fowmart[7] face," quoith the first, "to flyt sal be fit."
"Nicneuen,"[8] quoith the next, "sall norish thee twyse;
To ride post to Elphin nane abler nor it."
"To driue dogs but to drit,"[9] the third can deuyse:
"All thy day sall thou bee of an bodie bot a bit.[10]
Als such is this sentence as sharpe is thy syse."[11]
Syne duelie they deemde, what death it sould die.
   The first said, "surelie of a shot;"
   The second, "of a running knot;"
   The third, "be throwing of the throate,
     Like a tyke ouer a tree."

1. "froward" = adverse, perverse
2. "tratling" = prattling, gossiping
3. "Ilke" = like, equal to
4. "weird' = fate
5. "dubes" = stagnant pools of water
6. "tykes" = mongrels, curs
7. "fowmart" = contemptuous term for someone
8. "Nicneuen" = a malevolent female Scottish spirit often described as riding at the head of a horde of fairies
9. "drit" = filth
10. "bot a bit" = without food
11. "syse" = jury

When the Weird Sisters had this voted all in an voyce,
The deid[1] of the dablet[2], and syne they with-drew:
To let it lye all alane, they thought it little losse,
In a den[3] bee a dyke, or the day dew.
Then a cleir companie came soone after closse,
Nicneuen with her nymphes, in number anew,
With charmes from Caitness and Chanrie of Rosse,
Whose cunning consists in casting of a clew;
They seeing this sairie thing, said to themselfe,
   "This thriftless is meit for vs,
  And for our craft commodious;
  An vglie ape and incubus,
    Gotten with an elfe."

Thir venerable virgines whom the world call witches,
In the time of their triumph, tirr'd mee the taide:
Some backward raid on brod sows, and some on black bitches;
Some, on steid of a staig, ouer a starke monke straide.
On the how to the hight, some hobbles, some hatches[4];
With their mouthes to the moone, murgeons[5] they maid.
Some, be force, in effect, the four windes fetches;
And, nyne times, withershins,[6] about the thorne[7] raid;
Some glowring to the ground; some grieuouslie gaipe;
  Be craft conjurand fiends perforce.
  Foorth of a cairne[8] beside a croce,[9]
  Thir ladies lighted fra their horse,
    And band them with raipes.

Some bare-foote and bare-leggde, to baptize that bairne,
Still a water they went, be a wood-side;
They fand the shit all beshitten in his awne shearne.[10]
On three headed Hecatus,[11] to heire them, they cryde:

1. "deid" = death
2. "dablet" = devil, imp
3. "den" = hollow between hills
4. "hatches" = move jerkily up and down
5. "murgeons" = grotesque faces
6. "withershins" = counter-clockwise
7. "thorne" = hedge of thorn bushes
8. "cairne" = type of grave or grave marker
9. "croce" = cross
10. "shearne" = dung
11. "Hecatus" = Hecate, a goddess often associated with witchcraft

"As wee have found in the field this findling forfairne,[1]
Lest, his faith hee forsakes, in thee to confide,
By vertue of thir words and this raw yearne[2];
And while this thrise threttie knots on this blue threed byd;
And of thir mens members, well sowd to a shoe,
 Whilke wee haue tane, from top to tae,
 Euen of an hundeth men and mae:
 Now grant vs, goddesse, or wee gae,
  Our dueties to doe.

"Be the hight of the heauens, and be the hownesse of hell,
Be the windes, and the weirds, and the Charlewaine,[3]
Be the hornes, the handstaff, and the king's ell,
Be thunder, be fyreflaughtes, be drouth, and be raine,
Be the poles, and the planets, and the signes all twell,[4]
Be the mirknes of the moone — let mirknes remaine —
Be the elements all, that our crafts can compel,
Be the fiends infernall, and the Furies in paine —
Gar[5] all the gaists of the deid, that dwels there downe,
 In Lethe and Styx that stinkard strands,
 And Pluto, that your court commands,
 Receiue this howlat off our hands,
  In name of Mahowne[6];

"That this worme, in our worke, some wonders may wirk;
And through the poyson of this pod, our pratiques prevaile
To cut off our cumber[7] from comming to the kirk,
For the half of our helpeand hes it heir haill.
Let neuer this vndought[8] of ill doing irk,
Bot ay blyth[9] to begin all barret and baill.[10]
Of all blis let it be als bair as the birk,[11]

1. "forfairne" = destitute, forlorn
2. "raw yearne" = unworked yarn
3. "Charlewaine" = the constellation of the Great Bear
4. "the signes all twell" = the twelve signs of the zodiac
5. "Gar" — to cause, to make
6. "Mahowne" = Mahound, a devil and a variant form of the name Muhammad
7. "cumber" = trouble, disturbance
8. "vndought" = ineffective, worthless person
9. "blyth" = happy
10. "barret and baill" = trouble and misery
11. "birk" = birch tree

That tittest the taidrell[1] may tell ane ill taill:
Let no vice in this warld in this wanthrift be wanted."
    Be they had said, the fire-flaughts flew;
    Baith thunder, raine and windis blew;
    Wherebe there comming commers[2] knew
        Their asking was graunted.

When thae dames deuoutly had done their devore,[3]
In heauing this hurcheon, they hasted them hame.
Of that matter to make remained no more;
Sauing, nixt, how the nunnes that worlin[4] sould name.
They kowd all the kytrall,[5] the face of it before;
And nippd[6] it sa doones neir, to see it was shame:
They calld it peild POLWART: they pulld[7] it so sore.
"Where wee clip," quoth the commers, "there needs na kame[8];
For wee haue heght to Mahoun, for handsell, this hair."
    They made it like ane scraped swyne;
    And as they cowd they made it whryne.[9]
    It shavd the selfe aye on sensyne[10]
        The beard of it sa baire.

Fra the kummers that crab had with Pluto contracted,
They promeist, as parants, syne, for their owne part,
A mouer of mischief, and they might, for to make it;
As an imp of all ill, maist apt for their arte.
Nicneuen, as nurish, to teach it, gart take it
To saill sure in a seiffe,[11] but compass or cart[12];
And milk of an hairne tedder, though wiues sould be wrackit,
And the kow giue a chapin was wont to giue a quart.
Manie babes and bairnes sall bliss they baire banes,
    When they haue neither milke nor meill;

1. "taidrell" = little toad
2. "commers" = female gossips
3. "devore" = duty
4. "worlin" = stunted, deformed person
5. "kowd all the kytrall" = shaved the despicable creature
6. "nippd" = pinched
7. "pulld" = "plucked"
8. "kame" = comb
9. "whryne" = whine
10. "sensyne" = from that time on
11. "seiffe" = sieve; it was a common belief that witches could sail in sieves
12. "cart" = map

Compelde for hunger for to steill:
Then sall they giue thee to the deuill,
   Able ofte nor anes.

Be ane after mid-night, their office was ended:
At that tyd was na time for trumpers to tarie:
Syne backward, on horse-backe, brauely they bended;
That cammosed[1] cocatrice they quite with them carie.
To Kait of Criefe,[2] in an creill,[3] soone they gard send it;
Where, seuin yeir, it sat, baith singed and sairie,
The kin of it, be the cry, incontinent kend it;
Syne fetcht food for to feid it, foorth fra the Pharie.
Ilke elfe of them all brought an almous house oster;
   Indeid it was a daintie dish;
   A foull flegmaticke foulsome fish;
   In steid of sauce, on it they pish.
      Sik foode feed sike a foster!

Syne, fra the fathers side finelie had fed it,
Manie monkes and marmasits came with the mother —
Blacke botch[4] fall the breist and the bellie that bred it!
Ay offered they that vndoght fra ane to another;
Where that smatched[5] had sowked, so sair it was to shed it:
Bot belyue it beganne to buckie the brother.
In the barke of ane bourtree whylome they bed it.
All talking with their tongues the ane to the other,
With flirting and flyring, their physnome they flype;
   Some, luikand[6] lyce, in the crowne of it keeks;
   Some choppes the kiddes[7] into their cheeks;
   Some in their oxster[8] hard it cleeks,[9]
      Like ane old bag-pipe.

With mudyons, and murgeons, and mouing the braine,
They lay it, they lift it, they louse it, they lace it,

1. "cammosed" = pug-nosed
2. "Criefe" = Criefe was an ancient judgment-seat where witches were hung
3. "creill" = wicker basket
4. "botch" = contagious disease
5. "smatched" = scamp, rascal
6. "luikand" = looking at
7. "kiddes" = sheep-lice
8. "oxster" = armpit
9. "cleeks" = snatches, grabs

They graip it, they grip it; it greets and they grane.
They bed it, they baw it, they bind it, they brace it.
It skittered and skarted, they skirled ilk ane;
All the ky[1] in the countrey they skarred and chased,
That roaring they wood-ran, and routed in a reane.
The wild deere fra their den their din has displaced.
The cry was sa ouglie, of elfes, aips, and owles,
   That geise and gaislings cryes and craikes;
   In dubs douks down the duiks and draikes;
   All beasts, for feir, the feilds forsakes;
      And the towne tykes yowles.

Sik a mirthlesse musick their menstralls did make,
While ky kest caprels behind with their heeles;
Litill tent to their time the tone leit them take,
Bot ay rammeist redwood, and raveld in their reeles.
Then the cummers that yee ken came all with a clak,[2]
To conjure tha coidyoch,[3] with clewes in their creeles;
Whill all the bounds them about grew blaikned and blak:
For the din of thir daiblets raisd all the deils.
To concurre in the cause they were come sa far;
   For they their god-bairnes giftes wald give,
   To teach the child to steale and reiue;
   And ay the langer that it liue,
      The warld sould be the war.

Pulling "corn" (oats) from a stack (1913 postcard)

1. "ky" = cows
2. "clak" = shock
3. "coidyoch" = puny creature

"Hallowe'en"

Robert Burns, 1785

If Hallowe'en can be said to have a single exemplary poem the equivalent of Clement Moore's "'Twas the Night Before Christmas," it would undoubtedly be Robert Burns's "Hallowe'en." This piece, dating to 1785, has served as both a source of Hallowe'en history (because of its detailed descriptions of Scottish fortune-telling practices) and a romantic (and bawdy) paean to the evening.

Included here are James Currie's introduction and annotations from the 1850 volume *The Works of Robert Burns: With an Account of His Life, and Criticism on His Writings*. It's interesting to note that, in 1850, Currie felt it more necessary to explain the traditions of kail-pulling and nut-burning than the poem's employment of Scottish dialect, suggesting that, mid–19th-century, Hallowe'en celebrations were still confined largely to rural areas.

"Hallowe'en"[1]

The following Poem will, by many readers, be well enough understood; but for the sake of those who are unacquainted with the manners and traditions of the country where the scene is cast, notes are added, to give some account of the principal charms and spells of that night, so big with prophecy to the peasantry in the west of Scotland. The passion of prying into futurity makes a striking part of the history of human nature in its rude state, in all ages and nations; and it may be some entertainment to a philosophic mind, if any such should honour the author with a perusal, to see the remains of it, among the more unenlightened in our own.

> Yes! let the rich deride, the proud disdain,
> The simple pleasures of the lowly train;
> To me more dear, congenial to my heart,
> One native charm, than all the gloss of art.
> GOLDSMITH.

1. Is thought to be a night when witches, devils, and other mischief-making beings are all abroad on their baneful, midnight errands; particularly those aerial people the Fairies, are said on that night, to hold a grand anniversary.

I.

Upon that night, when fairies light
On *Cassilis Downans*[1] dance,
Or owre the lays, in splendid blaze,
On sprightly coursers prance;
Or for *Colean* the route is ta'en,
Beneath the moon's pale beams;
There, up the cove[2], to stray and rove,
Amang the rocks and streams
To sport that night.

II.

Amang the bonny winding banks,
Where *Doon* rins, wimpling clear,
Where Bruce[3] ance rul'd the martial ranks,
An' shook his *Carrick* spear,
Some merry, friendly, countra folks,
Together did convene,
To *burn* their nits, an' *pou* their stocks,
An' haud their *Halloween*
Fu' blythe that night.

III.

The lasses feat, an' cleanly neat,
Mair braw than when they're fine;
Their faces blythe, fu' sweetly kythe,
Hearts leal, an' warm, an' kin';
The lads sae trig, wi' wooer-babs,
Weel knotted on their garten,
Some unco blate, and some wi' gabs,
Gar lasses' hearts gang startin
Whiles fast at night.

IV.

Then first and foremost, thro' the kail,
Their *stocks*[4] maun a' be sought ance;

1. Certain little, romantic, rocky, green hills, in the neighbourhood of the ancient seat of the Earls of Cassilis.

2. A noted cavern near Colean-house, called The Cove of Colean; which, as Cassilis Downans, is famed in country story for being a favourite haunt of fairies.

3. The famous family of that name, the ancestors of Robert, the great deliverer of his country, were Earls of Carrick.

4. The first ceremony of Halloween is, pulling each a *stock*, or plant of kail. They must go out, hand in hand, with eyes shut, and pull the first they meet with: Its being big or little, straight or crooked, is prophetic of the size and shape of the grand object of all their spells — the husband or wife. If any *yird*, or earth, stick

They steek their een' an' graip an' wale,
    For muckle anes an' straught anes.
Poor hav'rel Will fell aff the drift,
    An' wander'd thro' the *bow-kail*,
An' pow't, for want o' better shift,
    A *runt* was like a sow-tail,
           Sae bow't that night.

V.

Then, staught or crooked, yird or nane,
    They road and cry a' throu'ther;
The vera wee things, todlin, rin
    Wi' stocks out-owre their shouther;
An' gif the *custoc's* sweet or sour,
    Wi' joctelegs they taste them;
Syne coziely, aboon the door,
    Wi' cannie care they place them
           To lie that night.

VI.

The lasses staw frae 'mang them a'
    To pou their *stalks of corn*;[1]
But Rab slips out, an' jinks about,
    Behint the muckle thorn:
He grippet Nelly hard an' fast;
    Loud skirl'd a' the lasses;
But her *tap-pickle* maist was lost,
    When kiuttlin in the fause-house[2]
           Wi' him that night.

VII.

The auld guidwife's weel hoordet *nits*[3]
    Are round an' round divided,

---

4. (*cont.*) to the root, that is *tcher*, or fortune; and the taste of the *custoc*, that is, the heart of the stem, is indicative of the natural temper and disposition. Lastly, the stems, or, to give them their ordinary appellation, the *runts*, are placed somewhere above the head of the door: and the Christian names of the people whom chance brings into the house, are, according to the priority of placing the *runts*, the names in question.

1. They go to the barn-yard and pull each, at three several times, a stalk of oats. If the third stalk wants the *top-pickle*, that is, the grain at the top of the stalk, the party in question will come to the marriage-bed any thing but a maid.

2. When the corn is in a doubtful state, by being too green, or wet, the stack-builder, by means of old timber, &c., makes a large apartment in his stack, with an opening in the side which is fairest exposed to the wind: this he calls a *fause-house*.

3. Burning the nuts is a famous charm. They name the lad and lass to each particular nut, as they lay them in the fire, and accordingly as they burn quietly together, or start from beside one another, the course and issue of the courtship will be.

An' monie lads' and lasses' fates,
   Are there that night decided:
Some kindle, couthie, side by side
   An' burn thegither trimly;
Some start awa wi' saucie pride,
   And jump out-owre the chimlie
                    Fu' high that night.

VIII.

Jean slips in twa, wi' tentie e'e
   Wha 'twas she wadna tell;
But this is *Jock*, an' this is *me*,
   She says in to hersel:
He bleez'd owre her, an' she owre him,
   As they wad never mair part;
Till, fuff! he started up the lum,
   And Jean had e'en a sair heart
                    To see't that night.

IX.

Poor Willie, wi' his *bow-kail runt*,
   Was *brunt* wi' primsie Mallie;
An' Mallie, nae doubt, took the drunt,
   To be compar'd to Willie;
Mall's nit lap out wi' pridefu' fling,
   An' her ain fit it burnt it;
While Willie lap, and swoor by *jing*,
   'Twas just the way he wanted
                    To be that night.

X.

Nell had the fause-house in her min',
   She pits hersel an' Rob in;
In loving bleeze they sweetly join,
   Till white in ase they're sobbin:
Nell's heart was dancin at the view,
   She whisper'd Rob to leuk for't:
Rob, stowlins, prie'd her bonny mou,
   Fu' cozie in the neuk for't,
                    Unseen that night.

XI.

But Merran sat behint their backs,
   Her thoughts on Andrew Bell;
She lea'es them gashin at their cracks,

And slips out by hersel:
She thro' the yard the nearest taks,
    An' to the kiln goes then,
An' darklins grapit for the bauks,
    And in the *blue-clue*[1] throws then,
            Right fear't that night.

XII.

An' ay she win't, an' ay she swat,
    I wat she made nae jaukin;
Till something held within the pat,
    Guid L — d! but she was quakin!
But whether 'twas the deil himsel,
    Or whether 'twas a bauken,
Or whether it was Andrew Bell,
    She didna wait on talkin
            To spier that night.

XIII.

Wee Jenny to her Grannie says,
    "Will ye go wi' me, grannie?
I'll *eat the apple*[2] at the glass
    I gat frae Uncle Johnie:"
She fuff't her pipe wi' sic a lunt,
    In wrath she was sae vap'rin,'
She notic't na, an azle brunt
    Her braw new worset apron
            Out thro' that night.

XIV.

"Ye little skelpie-limmer's face!
    How daur you try sic sportin,
As seek the foul Thief ony place,
    For him to spae your fortune:
Nae doubt but ye may get a *sight*!
    Great cause ye hae to fear it;
For monie a ane has gotten a fright,

1. Whoever would, with success, try this spell, must strictly observe these directions: Steal out, all alone, to the *kiln*, and, darkling, throw into the *pot* a clue of blue yarn; wind it in a new clue off the old one; and, towards the latter end, something will hold the thread; demand *wha hauds*? i.e. who holds? an answer will be returned from the kiln-pot, by naming the Christian and surname of your future spouse.

2. Take a candle, and go alone to a looking glass; eat an apple before it, and some traditions say, you should comb your hair, all the time; the face of your conjugal companion, *to be*, will be seen in the glass, as if peeping over your shoulder.

An' liv'd an' di'd deleeret
           On sic a night.

XV.

"Ae hairst afore the Sherra-moor,
     I mind't as weel' yestreen,
I was a gilpey then, I'm sure
     I was na past fifteen:
The simmer had been cauld an' wat,
     An' stuff was unco green;
An' ay a rantin kirn we gat,
     An' just on *Halloween*
It fell that night.

XVI.

"Our stibble-rig was Rab M'Graen,
     A clever, sturdy fallow;
He's sin gat Eppie Sim wi' wean,
     That liv'd in Achmacalla:
He gat *hemp-seed*,[1] I mind it weel,
     An' he made unco light o't;
But monie a day was *by himsel*,
     He was sae sairly frighted
That vera night."

XVII.

Then up gat fechtin' Jamie Fleck,
     An' he swoor by his conscience,
That he could *saw hemp-seed* a peck;
     For it was a' but nonsense;
The auld guidman raught down the pock,
     An' out a handfu' gied him;
Syne bad him slip frae 'mang the folk
     Sometimes when nae ane see'd him:
           An' try't that night.

XVIII.

He marches thro' amang the stacks,
     Tho' he was something sturtin;
The *graip* he for a *harrow* taks,

---

1. Steal out unperceived, and sow a handful of hemp seed; harrowing it with any thing you can conveniently draw after you. Repeat sow and then, "Hemp seed I saw thee, hemp seed I saw thee; and him (or her) that is to be my true-love, come after me and pou thee." Look over your left shoulder, and you will see the appearance of the person invoked, in the attitude of pulling hemp. Some traditions say, "come after me, and shaw thee," that is, show thyself: in which case it simply appears. Others omit the harrowing, and say, "come after me, and harrow thee."

An' haurls it at his curpin:
An' ev'ry now an' then, he says,
  "Hemp-seed I saw thee,
An' her that is to be my lass,
   Come after me, and draw thee
                As fast this night."

XIX.

He whistl'd up Lord Lenox' march,
   To keep his courage cheerie;
Altho' his hair began to arch,
   He was see fley'd an' eerie:
Till presently he hears a squeak,
   An' then a grane an' gruntle;
He by his shouther gae a keek,
   An' tumbl'd wi' a wintle
                Out-owre that night.

XX.

He roar'd a horrid murder-shout,
   In dreadfu' desperation!
An' young an' auld came rinnin out
   To hear the sad narration;
He swoor 'twas hilchin Jean M'Craw,
   Or crouchie Merran Humphie,
Till stop! she trotted thro' them a';
   An' wha was it but *Grumphie*
                Asteer that night!

XXI.

Meg fain wad to the *barn* gaen
   To *win three wechts o' naething*;[1]
But for to meet the deil her lane,
   She pat but little faith in:
She gies the herd a pickle nits,
   An' twa red cheekit apples,
To watch, while for the *barn* she sets,
   In hopes to see Tam Kipples
                That vera night.

1. This charm must likewise be performed unperceived, and alone. You go to the *barn*, and open both doors, taking them off the hinges, if possible; for there is danger that the *being*, about to appear, may shut the doors, and do you some mischief. Then take that instrument used in winnowing the corn, which, in our country dialect, we call a *wecht*; and go through all the attitudes of letting down corn against the wind. Repeat it three times; and the third time an apparition will pass through the barn, in at the windy door, and out at the other, having both the figure in question, and the appearance or retinue, marking the employment or station in life.

XXII.

She turns the key wi' cannie thraw,
   An' owre the threshold ventures;
But first on Sawnie gies a ca'
   Syne bauldly in she enters:
A ratton rattled up the wa,'
   An' she cry'd L—d preserve her
An' ran thro' midden-hole an' a,'
   An' pray'd wi' zeal an' fervour,
          Fu' fast that night.

XXIII.

They hoy't out Will, wi' sair advice;
   They hecht him some fine braw ane;
It chanc'd the *stack* he *faddom'd thrice*,[1]
   Was timmer propt for thrawin;
He taks a swirlie, auld moss-oak,
   For some black, grousome carlin;
An' loot a winze, an' drew a stroke,
   Till skin in blypes came haurlin
          Aff's nieves that night.

XXIV.

A wanton widow Leezie was,
   As canty as a kittlen;
But Och! that night, amang the shaws,
   She got a fearfu' settlin!
She thro' the whins, an' by the cairn,
   An' owre the hill gaed scrievin,
Whare *three lairds' lands met at a burn*[2]
   To dip her left sark-sleeve in,
          Was bent that night.

XXV.

Whyles owre a linn the burnie plays,
   As thro' the glen it wimpl't;
Whyles round a rocky scar it strays;
   Whyles in a wiel it dimpl't;
Whyles glitter'd to the nightly rays,

1. Take an opportunity of going, unnoticed, to a *Bear stack*, and fathom it three times round. The last fathom of the last time, you will catch in your arms the appearance of your future conjugal yoke fellow.

2. You go out, one or more, for this is a social spell, to a south running spring or rivulet, where "three lairds' lands meet," and dip your left shirt sleeve. Go to bed in sight of a fire, and hang your wet sleeve before it to dry. Lie awake; and sometime near midnight, an apparition, having the exact figure of the grand object in question, will come and turn the sleeve, as if to dry the other side of it.

Wi' bickering, dancing dazzle;
Whyles cookit underneath the braes,
Below the spreading hazel,
                Unseen that night.

XXVI.

Among the brachens, on the brae,
   Between her an' the moon,
The deil, or else an outler quey,
   Gat up an' gae a croon:
Poor Leezie's heart maist lap the hool;
   Neer lav'rock height she jumpit,
But mist a fit, an' in the *pool*
   Out-owre the lugs she plumpit,
             Wi' a plunge that night.

XXVII.

In order, on the clean hearth-stane,
   The *luggies* three[1] are ranged,
And ev'ry time great care is ta'en',
   To see them duly changed:
Auld uncle John, wha wedlock's joys
   Sin' *Mar's year* did desire,
Because he gat the toom-dish thrice,
   He heav'd them on the fire
             In wrath that night.

XXVIII.

Wi' merry sangs, an' friendly cracks,
   I wat they dinna weary;
An' unco tales, an' funnie jokes,
   Their sports were cheap an' cheery,
Till *butter'd so'ns*,[2] wi' fragrant lunt,
   Set a' their gabs a-steerin';
Syne, wi' a social glass o' strunt,
   They parted aff careerin
             Fu' blythe that night.

---

1. Take three dishes; put clean water in one, foul water in another, leave the third empty: blindfold a person, and lead him to the hearth where the dishes are ranged; he (or she) dips the left hand: if by chance in the clean water, the future husband or wife will come to the bar of matrimony a maid; if in the foul, a widow; if the empty dish, it foretells, with equal certainty, no marriage at all. It is repeated three times, and every time the arrangement of the dishes is altered.

2. Sowens, with butter instead of milk to them is always the *Halloween Supper*.

"Of Allhallow Even"

From *Observations on Popular Antiquities*
John Brand, 1810

Brand's *Popular Antiquities* appeared in numerous editions throughout the 19th century, and although later editions featured longer entries on Hallowe'en, the holiday's entry from this earlier edition is interesting for what it reveals about Hallowe'en's importance (or relative lack thereof) in the early 1800s. In the 1810 edition, Brand assigns the holiday four pages in the Appendix, and spends much of that length discussing the historical importance of nuts in other rituals; it's also interesting that he makes no mention of the Burns poem, which had been published twenty-five years earlier. Contrast this to the 1895 edition of Brand's book, in which Hallowe'en receives its own chapter, running nearly 20 pages (likewise, Guy Fawkes Day — which receives no mention whatsoever in the 1810 edition — also receives its own chapter in 1895). The differences between these editions released at the beginning and at the end of the century demonstrate how Hallowe'en's popularity exploded in that time.

OF ALLHALLOW EVEN:

Vulgo Halle E'en, *as also* Nut-crack Night.

Da nuces *pueris,* —
CATULLUS.

In the antient Calendar of the Church of Rome so often cited, I find the following Observation on the 1st of November.[1]

"The Feast of *old Fools* is removed to this Day."

Hallow Even is the Vigil of All Saints' Day.

It is customary on this Night with young People in the North to *dive* for Apples, catch at them when stuck on at one End of a Kind of hanging Beam, at the other Extremity of which is fixed a lighted Candle, and that with their Mouths only, having their Hands tied behind their Backs; with many other Fooleries.

1. "Festum Stultorum veterum hue translatum est." Perhaps it has been afterwards removed to the *First* of *April.*

Nuts[1] and Apples chiefly compose the Entertainment, and from the Custom of *flinging the former into the Fire*, it has doubtless had its vulgar Name of Nutcrack-Night. The catching at the *Apple* and *Candle* at least puts one in mind of the antient English Game of the Quintain, which is now almost forgotten, and of which a Description may be found in Stow's Survey of London.

Mr. Pennant tells us in his Tour of Scotland, that the young Women there deter-mine the Figure and Size of their Husbands by drawing Cabbages blindfold on Allhallow Even, and like the English *fling Nuts into the Fire*.

The last Custom is beautifully described by Gay in his *Spell*:

> Two hazel Nuts I threw into the Flame,
> And to each Nut I gave a Sweetheart's Name:
> This with the *loudest Bounce* me sore amaz'd,
> That in a *Flame of brightest Colour blaz'd*[2];
> And *blaz'd* the *Nut* so *may thy Passion grow*, &c.

1. In the Marriage Ceremonies amongst the antient Romans, the Bride-groom threw *Nuts* about the Room for the Boys to scramble; The Epithalamiums in the Classics prove this. They were supposed to do this in Token of leaving childish Diversions. "Quanquam Plinius, lib. 15. cap. 22, causas alias adfert, quam ob rem Nuces in nuptialibus ceremoniis consueverint antiquitus adhiberi; sed præstat ipsius referre Verga; *Nuces*, inquit, *juglandes*, quanquam et ipsæ nuptialium Fescenniorum comites, multum pineis minores universitate, eædemque portione ampliores nucleo. Nec non et honor his Naturæ peculiaris, gemino pro-tectis operimento, pulvinati primum calyces, mox lignei putaminis. Quæ causa eas nuptiis fecit religiosas, tot modis fœtu munito: quod est verisimilius, &c.

Vide Erasmus on the Proverb: "Nuces relinquere." The Roman Boys had some Sport or other with *Nuts*, to which Horace refers in these Words:

— Te talos Aule *nucesque*.

Nuts have not been excluded from the Catalogue of Superstitions under *papal* Rome. Thus on the 10th of August in the Romish antient Calendar, I find it observed that some religious Use was made of them, and they were in great Estimation.

"*Nuces* in pretio et *religiosæ*."

2. Mr. Gay describes some other rustic Methods of Divination on this head: Thus with *Peascods*:

> As Peascods once I pluck'd, I chanc'd to see
> One that was closely *fill'd with three Times three*;
> Which when I cropt, I safely home convey'd,
> And o'er the Door the Spell in secret laid;
> The latch mov'd up, when who should first come in,
> But in his proper Person, Lubberkin.

> Thus also with the Insect called *Lady Fly*:
> This *Lady Fly* I take from off the Grass,
> Whose spotted Back might Scarlet red surpass.
> *Fly, Lady-Bird, North, South,* or *East* or *West*,
> Fly where the *Man* is *found* that *I love best*.

> Thus also with *Apple-parings*:
> I pare this Pippin round and round again,
> My Shepherds' Name to flourish on the Plain,
> I fling th' *unbroken Paring* o'er my Head,
> Upon the Grass a perfect L is read.

They made Trial also of the Fidelity of their Swains by sticking an *Apple Kernel* on *each Cheek*: that which *fell first* indicated that the Love of him whose Name it bore, was *unsound*. *Snails*, set to *crawl* on the *Hearth*, were thought too to *mark in the Ashes* the *Initial* of the *Lover's Name*.

This 1835 engraving shows nuts burning on the hearth on Hallowe'en night.

The Rev. Mr. Shaw, in his History of the Province of Moray, seems to consider the Festivity of this Night as a Kind of *Harvest home Rejoicing*; "A Solemnity was kept, says he, on the Eve of the first of November as a Thanksgiving for the safe Ingathering of the Produce of the Fields. This I am told, but have not seen it, is observed in Buchan, and other Countries, by having Hallow-Eve-Fires kindled on some rising Ground."

He tells us also in that little Fore-taste of his Work, with which he favoured the Public in an Appendix to Mr. Pennant's Tour, that "on Hallow-Even, they have several superstitious Customs." I wish he had given us *particular* Descriptions of them, for *general* Accounts are exceedingly unsatisfactory. — Curiosity is indeed *tantalized*, not relieved or gratified by them.

"Hallowe'en at Balmoral Castle"

1869

The middle and upper class Victorians were extraordinarily fond of parties and even larger scale celebrations; if we owe our modern celebrations of Christmas to the Victorians (on both sides of the Atlantic), our contemporary Hallowe'en festivities are also in debt to them. On Hallowe'en in 1869, Queen Victoria visited Balmoral Castle (which she had purchased in 1848, and which has served as the Scottish Home of the British Royal Family ever since), and the story was repeated in nearly every Hallowe'en article published for the remainder of the century. It's entirely possible that this single event sparked the holiday's move from rural to sophisticated upper-class Victorian celebration, and so may have led to Hallowe'en as we know it today.

Balmoral Castle in 1905.

41

From the *Dundee Advertiser*, November 1869:

This time-honoured festival was duly celebrated at Balmoral Castle on Saturday evening, in a manner not soon to be forgotten by those who took part in the enjoyments of the evening. As the shades of evening were closing in upon the Strath, numbers of torch-lights were observed approaching the Castle, both from the cottages on the eastern portion of the estate and also those on the west. The torches from the western side were probably the more numerous, and as the different groups gathered together the effect was very fine. Both parties met in front of the Castle, the torch-bearers numbering nearly one hundred. Along with those bearing the torches were a great many people belonging to the neighbourhood. Dancing was commenced by the torch-bearers dancing a "Huachan" in fine style, to the lilting strains of Mr. Ross, the Queen's piper. The effect was greatly heightened by the display of bright lights of various colours from the top of the staircase of the Tower. After dancing for some time, the torch-bearers proceeded round the Castle in martial order, and as they were proceeding down the granite staircase at the northwest corner of the Castle, the procession presented a singularly beautiful and romantic appearance. Having made the circuit of the Castle, the remainder of the torches were thrown in a pile at the south-west corner, thus forming a large bonfire, which was speedily augmented with other combustibles until it formed a burning mass of huge proportions, round which dancing was spiritedly carried on. Her Majesty witnessed the proceedings with apparent interest for some time, and the company enjoyed themselves none the less heartily on that account. Mr. Begg, distiller, Lochnagar, had also a splendid bonfire on Cairnbeg, round which merry groups danced torch in hand.

"October 31"

From *Chambers's Book of Days*
R. Chambers, 1869

Like Brand's *Popular Antiquities, Chambers's Book of Days* was popular throughout virtually the entire 19th century, with numerous printings. Although Chambers also includes fascinating entries on All Saints Day (as differentiated from Halloween), All Souls Day, and Guy Fawkes's Day, the Halloween entry is especially noteworthy not only for its detailed description of bobbing for apples, but also for its retelling of a supposedly-true story involving a Halloween "fetch," or the apparition of someone who is still alive.

This excerpt has been edited only to exclude extensive reference to and quotes from Burns's "Hallowe'en."

OCTOBER 31

Halloween

There is perhaps no night in the year which the popular imagination has stamped with a more peculiar character than the evening of the 31st of October, known as All Hallow's Eve, or Halloween. It is clearly a relic of pagan times, for there is nothing in the church-observance of the ensuing day of All Saints to have originated such extraordinary notions as are connected with this celebrated festival, or such remarkable practices as those by which it is distinguished.

The leading idea respecting Halloween is that it is the time, of all others, when supernatural influences prevail. It is the night set apart for a universal walking abroad of spirits, both of the visible and invisible world; for, as will be afterwards seen, one of the special characteristics attributed to this mystic evening, is the faculty conferred on the immaterial principle in humanity to detach itself from its corporeal tenement and wander abroad through the realms of space. Divination is then believed to attain its highest power, and the gift asserted by Glendower of calling spirits 'from the vasty deep,' becomes available to all who choose to avail themselves of the privileges of the occasion.

There is a remarkable uniformity in the fireside-customs of this night all over the United Kingdom. Nuts and apples are everywhere in requisition, and consumed in immense numbers. Indeed the name of Nutcrack Night, by which Halloween is known

Walnuts are burned as a romantic divination in this 1913 postcard.

in the north of England, indicates the predominance of the former of these articles in making up the entertainments of the evening. They are not only cracked and eaten, but made the means of vatication in love-affairs....

... As to apples, there is an old custom, perhaps still observed in some localities on this merry night, of hanging up a stick horizontally by a string from the ceiling, and putting a candle on the one end, and an apple on the other. The stick being made to twirl rapidly, the merry makers in succession leap up and snatch at the apple with their teeth (no use of the hands being allowed), but it very frequently happens that the candle comes round before they are aware, and scorches them in the face, or anoints them with grease. The disappointments and misadventures occasion, of course, abundance of laughter. But the grand sport with apples on Halloween, is to set them afloat in a tub of water, into which the juveniles, by turns, duck their heads with the view of catching an apple. Great fun goes on in watching the attempts of the youngster in the pursuit of the swimming fruit, which wriggles from side to side of the tub, and evades all attempts to capture it; whilst the disappointed aspirant is obliged to abandon the chase in favour of another whose turn has now arrived. The apples provided with stalks are generally caught first, and then comes the tug of war to win those which possess no such appendages. Some competitors will deftly suck up the apple, if a small one, into their mouths. Others plunge manfully overhead in pursuit of a particular apple, and having forced it to the bottom of the tub, seize it firmly with their teeth, and emerge, dripping and triumphant, with their prize. This venturous procedure is generally rewarded with a hurrah! by the lookers-on, and is recommended, by those versed in Halloween-aquatics, as the only sure method of attaining success. In recent years, a practice has been introduced, probably by some tender mammas, timorous on the subject of their offspring catching cold, of dropping a fork from a height into the tub among the apples, and thus turning the sport into a display of marksmanship. It forms, however, but a very indifferent substitute for the joyous merriment of ducking and diving.

It is somewhat remarkable, that the sport of ducking for apples is not mentioned by Burns, whose celebrated poem of Halloween presents so graphic a picture of the ceremonies practised on that evening in the west of Scotland, in the poet's day. Many of the rites there described are now obsolete or nearly so, but two or three still retain place in various parts of the country. Among these is the custom still prevalent in Scotland, as the initiatory Halloween ceremony, of pulling kailstocks or stalks of colewort....

... It may here be remarked, that popular belief ascribes to children born on Halloween, the possession of certain mysterious faculties, such as that of perceiving and holding converse with supernatural beings. Sir Walter Scott, it will be recollected, makes use of this circumstance in his romance of The Monastery.

In conclusion, we shall introduce an interesting story, with which we have been favoured by a lady. The leading incidents of the narrative may be relied on as correct, and the whole affair forms matter of curious thought on the subject of Halloween divination:

Mr. and Mrs. M- were a happy young couple, who, in the middle of the last century, resided on their own estate in a pleasant part of the province of Leinster, in Ireland. Enjoying a handsome competence, they spent their time in various rural occupations; and the birth of a little girl promised to crown their felicity, and provide them with an object of perpetual interest. On the Halloween following this last event, the parents retired to rest at their usual hour, Mrs. M- having her infant on her arm, so that she might be roused by the slightest uneasiness it might exhibit. From teething or some other ailment, the child, about midnight, became very restless, and not receiving the accustomed attention from its mother, cried so violently as to waken Mr. M-. He at once called his wife, and told her the baby was uneasy, but received no answer. He called again more loudly, but still to no purpose; she seemed to be in a heavy uneasy slumber, and when all her husband's attempts to rouse her by calling and shaking proved ineffectual, he was obliged to take the child himself, and try to appease its wailings. After many vain attempts of this sort on his part, the little creature at last sobbed itself to rest, and the mother slept on till a much later hour than her usual time of rising in the morning. When Mr. M- saw that she was awake, he told her of the restlessness of the baby during the night, and how, after having tried in vain every means to rouse her, he had at last been obliged to make an awkward attempt to take her place, and lost thereby some hours of his night's rest. 'I, too,' she replied, 'have passed the most miserable night that I ever experienced; I now see that sleep and rest are two different things, for I never felt so unrefreshed in my life. How I wish you had been able to awake me — it would have spared me some of my fatigue and anxiety! I thought I was dragged against my will into a strange part of the country, where I had never been before, and, after what appeared to me a long and weary journey on foot, I arrived at a comfortable looking house. I went in longing to rest, but had no power to sit down, although there was a nice supper laid out before a good fire, and every appearance of preparations for an expected visitor. Exhausted as I felt, I was only allowed to stand for a minute or two, and then hurried away by the same road back again; but now it is over, and after all it was only a dream.' Her husband listened with interest to her story, and then sighing deeply, said: 'My dear Sarah, you will not long have me beside you; whoever is to be your second husband played last night some evil trick of which you have been the victim.' Shocked as she felt at this announcement, she endeavoured to suppress her own feelings and rally her husband's spirits, hoping that it would pass from his mind as soon as he had become engrossed by the active business of the day.

Some months passed tranquilly away after this occurrence, and the dream on Halloween night had well nigh been forgotten by both husband and wife, when Mr. M-'s health began to fail. He had never been a robust man, and he now declined so rapidly, that in a short time, notwithstanding all the remedies and attentions that skill could suggest, or affection bestow, his wife was left a mourning widow. Her energetic mind and active habits, however, prevented her from abandoning herself to the desolation of grief. She continued, as her husband had done during his life, to farm the estate, and in this employment, and the education of her little girl, she found ample and salutary occupation. Alike admired and beloved for the judicious management of her worldly affairs, and her true Christian benevolence and kindliness of heart, she might easily, had she been so inclined, have established herself respectably for a second time in life, but such a thought seemed never to cross her mind. She had an uncle, a wise, kind old man, who, living at a distance, often paid a visit to the widow, looked over her farm, and gave her useful advice and assistance. This old gentleman had a neighbour named C-, a prudent young man, who stood very high in his favour. Whenever they met, Mrs. M-'s uncle was in the habit of rallying him on the subject of matrimony. On one occasion of this kind, C-

excused himself by saying that it really was not his fault that he was still a bachelor, as he was anxious to settle in life, but had never met with any woman whom he should like to call his wife. 'Well, C-,' replied his old friend, 'you are, I am afraid, a saucy fellow, but if you put yourself into my hands, I do not despair of suiting you.' Some bantering then ensued, and the colloquy terminated by Mrs. M-'s uncle inviting the young man to ride over with him next day and visit his niece, whom C- had never yet seen. The proffer was readily accepted; the two friends started early on the following morning, and after a pleasant ride, were approaching their destination. Here they descried, at a little distance, Mrs. M- retreating towards her house, after making her usual matutinal inspection of her farm. The first glance which Mr. C- obtained of her made him start violently, and the more he looked his agitation increased. Then laying his hand on the arm of his friend, and pointing his finger in the direction of Mrs. M-, he said: 'Mr -, we need not go any further, for if ever I am to be married, there is my wife!' 'Well, C-,' was the reply, 'that is my niece, to whom I am about to introduce you; but tell me,' he added, 'is this what you call love at first sight, or what do you mean by your sudden decision in favour of a person with whom you have never exchanged a word?' 'Why, sir,' replied the young man, 'I find I have betrayed myself, and must now make my confession. A year or two ago, I tried a Halloween spell, and sat up all night to watch the result. I declare to you most solemnly, that the figure of that lady, as I now see her, entered my room and looked at me. She stood a minute or two by the fire and then disappeared as suddenly as she came. I was wide awake, and felt considerable remorse at having thus ventured to tamper with the powers of the unseen world; but I assure you, that every particular of her features, dress, and figure, have been so present to my mind ever since, that I could not possibly make a mistake, and the moment I saw your niece, I was convinced that she was indeed the woman whose image I beheld on that never-to-be-forgotten Halloween.' The old gentleman, as may be anticipated, was not a little astonished at his friend's statement, but all comments on it were for the time put a stop to by their arrival at Mrs. M'-s house. She was glad to see her uncle, and made his friend welcome, performing the duties of hospitality with a simplicity and heartiness that were very attractive to her stranger guest. After her visitors had refreshed themselves, her uncle walked out with her to look over the farm, and took opportunity, in the absence of Mr. C-, to recommend him to the favourable consideration of his niece. To make a long story short, the impression was mutually agreeable. Mr. C-, before leaving the house, obtained permission from Mrs. M- to visit her, and after a brief courtship, they were married. They lived long and happily together, and it was from their daughter that our informant derived that remarkable episode in the history of her parents which we have above narrated.

"Hallowe'en"

From *Godey's Lady's Book and Magazine,*
Helen Elliott, 1870

This charming short story, from the November 1870 issue of *Godey's Lady's Book and Magazine,* is not only one of the earliest pieces of fiction to use Hallowe'en as a central device, it's also interesting for its historical data.

Elliott seems to suggest here that in America of 1870, Hallowe'en was largely thought of as an "English" custom; note, for example, that Ned knows the backwards-stairs charm only because he and the British daughter Nell "have often talked of it." Also, the details that Elliott applies to describing the events at the Hallowe'en party take up half the story's length, and would imply that she thought American readers might be unfamiliar with the various fortune-telling rituals.

It's also worth noting that this story appeared exactly one year after Queen Victoria's famed Hallowe'en celebration at Balmoral Castle, suggesting that that particular event had increased public interest (both English and American) in Hallowe'en. The Barlowes were English, and wherever they moved, kept up their English habits and customs. Mr. Barlowe was addicted to roast beef, plum pudding, and pale ale. I heard him say once, when he was in a speculative mood, that "he supposed he *could* live without plum pudding, but, as for enduring existence without roast beef, that was out of the question." And I believe him. I think he would have insisted upon having it, even in a community of vegetarians, where such a thing would be looked upon as an enormity.

The Barlowes moved from England, first to India, which place Mr. Barlowe pronounced too hot; next to Halifax, Nova Scotia, where a residence of two years inclined him to think was too cold. My story now finds them settled in a large town on the banks of the beautiful Ohio River.

The family consisted of five persons; the father, mother, and three daughters. The oldest, Nell, was twenty-one, fair-haired, blue-eyed, and with a cordial, joyous manner. Everybody admired and loved Nell Barlowe. The children in the neighborhood thought her an angel, and so did Ned Graham. Poor Ned! He and Nell had been engaged for two bright months, when they managed to quarrel about a photograph, which Nell had given to a friend. Ned said "she ought not to give her photograph to any gentleman friend,

Fortune-telling by cards is suggested on this 1913 postcard.

young or old." Nell said she "would do as she liked." So Master Ned marches down town the same evening, gets a commission as lieutenant, and leaves the place, without bidding Nell goodby. My lady cried incessantly for two days. Ned's sister, Anna, called on Nell to scold her for sending Ned into the army, found how disheartened she was, soothed her, and promised to arrange matters.

The second daughter, Lou, was the opposite of Nell in every respect. She had black hair and eyes, her manners were stately, and her disposition so reticent that persons on first acquaintance were apt to call her haughty.

Last of all, Miss Maud, aged ten.

One holiday in particular the Barlowes loved to keep, as it seemed to bring them nearer to their far-off English home, and that was Hallowe'en. Their custom was to give a children's party on that night, ostensibly for Maud; but, as Nell planned it, saw that it was carried through, and entered into the enjoyment of the children with as much heart and spirit as if she were a child herself, I am of the opinion that the party was for Nell, and no one else.

This Hallowe'en I speak of finds Nell at the front door, the entrance barred by a broom to keep the witches out, and encouraging a group of little girls to step over it, which they do in great glee, raising their feet unnecessarily high. Except one, Lulu Beck, who sits on the top step disconsolately, refusing to enter, and more afraid of the broom than she is of the witches. After some coaxing, and finding it useless, Nell carries the broom away, and allows the child entrance in the usual manner.

Then they proceed with the business of the evening. The first duty to be performed is to pull molasses candy. Nell waits on a dozen little ones at once, and pulls a piece of candy for half as many more. Lulu, always in trouble, winds a piece of hers in a half-hardened state around her neck, where it seems inclined affectionately to remain, in spite of all Nell's efforts to remove it. The candy at last is done; braided, twisted, and put into innumerable shapes. Most of the girls wrapping theirs up with many coverings of paper, and undoing it every two minutes to take a bite.

Now for "Snap-dragon." Nell brings in a platter heaped up with raisins. She pours some alcohol on them, and sets it on fire. As soon as it burns well, the girls snatch at the raisins, whirling the little fire-balls through the air; and, when they fall, scrambling for them, not caring in the least for their having been on the floor. Nell watches this game anxiously, and is rather glad when it is concluded.

"What shall we do next?" the children cry.

"We will tell fortunes now," says Nell. She puts nuts on the fire to burn, in order to find out who loves them best. She tells their fortunes by pouring hot lead in a tumbler of water, and by cards. But the best way of all is this: She brings a basin of water into the room, a pan of ashes, and the wing of a goose, and sets them on the floor. A little girl has her eyes bandaged, the rest looking on joyously. The position of the basin, etc., is changed, and the child is to grope her way to one of them. If she puts her hand into the ashes, she will die an old maid; if she touches the wing of the goose, she will marry an old man; if it is the water, she will marry for love. Molly Guild, after making a prodigious flourish in the air, just tips the ashes with the ends of her fingers, without resting in them, and plunges them boldly, almost up to her elbow, in the water.

"What does that mean?" the girls ask of Nell.

"That means," says Nell, oracularly, "that she won't get married until late in life, but she will marry for love at last."

Lulu, when it comes her turn, grasps a whole handful of ashes.

"Ah! ha!" sing out the children, "Lulu is to be an old maid."

"I won't!" says Lulu, defiantly.

One girl oversets the basin of water, which puts an end to the fortune-telling.

"Now," Molly Guild proposes, "Nelly, go down the cellar stairs backwards, and try if you can see your sweetheart over your shoulder."

Nell demurs at first, but to please the children at last consents. There are no cellar stairs in the house, but those descending into the basement will do as well. In the entry below there are three doors. The one on the right hand belongs to the kitchen, that on the left to the coal-cellar, and the one opposite the stairs, having its upper part of glass, leads into the garden. They turn off the gas for the two entries, and Nell begins to go down stairs backwards in solemn silence, the children crowding round the banisters at the top, giggling and pushing each other. She reaches the last step, and turns her head, when a pair of warm lips are pressed to hers. With a loud scream, Nell rushes up stairs and into the parlor, the children flying, too, like leaves before the wind. Nell is as much scared as they.

"Nelly! Nelly!" calls a familiar voice, and Lieutentant Ned Graham puts his handsome head in at the door.

What a joyful surprise! Nell is so surprised, in fact, that she kisses him before all the little girls, and immediately feels immensely ashamed of having done it. "How did you come there, Ned?" she asks him.

"I heard from mother that you were having a Hallowe'en party," he answered, "and thought I would steal round by the glass door, and see what you were doing. When I saw you going down stairs backwards, Nell, I knew what you were at; you know we have often talked of it. But don't let me spoil the sport. We will have time enough to talk over everything; I have come home on a furlough."

"Nell is going to make a fate cake," here interrupted Molly Guild, "and I wish she would begin now."

"Yes, do, Nelly," says Ned, "and I will help you eat it. "How is it made?"

"You mix an egg-shell full of butter, and one of sugar, and one of flour together," explains Molly, "and bake it over the fire. Nobody must laugh or say a word while it is doing, and then you dream over a piece of it."

She looks so serious about it that Ned laughs. Nelly sets to work; and, after various failures on the part of the children to keep silence, owing to Ned's mischievousness, manages to bake a cake in the griddle over the fire. It is then cut up; all the girls take a piece, and make a wish over it. Ned takes his along with the rest, with such an awe-struck expression that it is beyond the power of a human being not to laugh.

Supper is just over when some one rings the bell, and all simultaneously glance at the clock. Half-past ten! Who would have thought it so late? The servants arrive for the children, and the bustle of departure takes place. The girls crowd around Nelly to kiss her good-night, every one but Lulu, who is discovered, after a search, in the next room, sitting in a corner, her face in her hands, and crying in a business-like manner truly heart-rending.

"What is the matter, dear Lulu?" asks Nelly, caressingly.

"Why," sobs Lulu, "Molly Guild says I am to be an old maid sure now, and wear spectacles, and have red hair like Miss Simpson."

"Nonsense!" exclaims Nelly. "How is your hair ever going to turn red when it is dark brown now? And, besides, you have not dreamed on your fate cake, yet; perhaps that will tell you differently."

Lulu listens comforted, and concludes, after a second's deliberation, to defer her lamentations until she has further revealings from fate.

"Come and take breakfast with us to-morrow, Lulu, and tell us your dream," says Nelly, kindly, with the parting kiss. "And you come too," nodding to Ned, who is standing near.

Now, I will not follow all this young couple have to say to each other, else my story will be as long as Ned was getting to the garden gate.

Next morning at breakfast, after the chatter had somewhat subsided, Nelly turned to Lulu, who was seated at her right hand according to promise. "What did you dream, Lulu?"

"I dreamed I married a princess," answered Lulu, radiantly, whereat they all laughed.

"And I dreamed," said Ned, "that I came home on a furlough, and married a certain young lady before my stay was out. What do you think of that for a dream, Mr. Barlowe?"

"Rubbish!" growled Mr. Barlowe, under his breath, and, I am sorry to say, with his mouth full.

"Not rubbish, is it, Mrs. Barlowe? I think my dream ought to come true."

Mrs. Barlowe smiled assent. She regarded this young man, the son of her husband's old friend, with motherly affection, and the match was the darling wish of her heart. So, between the two, by dint of laughing appeal and cogent reasoning, they soon induced Mr. Barlowe to give his consent to Ned's plan. Nell's approval was not asked, but she did not appear much aggrieved thereby.

Only five days for preparation! Fancy the bustle and confusion! For Nell declared that everything must be done for her that could be done in so short a time. How the girls and their mother flew round, worrying over the sewing-girls, dress-makers, confectioners, etc.!

At last all was finished, and the eventful evening had arrived. With it the guests, bridesmaids, flowers, clergyman, and last, but not least, the bridal dress reached home in time. In which Nelly descended to the parlor, in a glory of lace, orange flowers, and white veil, looking her loveliest, and knew she did, too, the little witch! As of how Ned looked, that is a matter of no consequence, the bride is always the chief attraction.

The wedding vows were uttered, the ring safe and secure on Nell's finger, and she received, half-smiling, half-tearful, the congratulations of parents and friends. The supper next received due attention from the guests, for the hour of the evening train had approached unaccountably fast; and Nelly, hardly more than glancing at the table, hastily changed her dress for a gray travelling suit, and bade goodby to all, returning once again to give that dear mother, whose loving care had watched over through infancy and youth, another and last kiss.

How shall I describe the parting of the married lovers, when, Ned's furlough at an end, he was obliged to return to the army? My pen fails me. Nelly sat on the sofa in the parlor, declaring, between sobs, "that she knew Ned would be killed, and she would never see him again!"

Ned wore much the same expression on his face that he would have had, if he had been attending his own funeral.

Last strapping of trunks! Soothing Nelly! Hand-shaking and kisses all round. "God bless you, my boy!" "Good-by, my darling, darling little wife!!"

Oh! dismal! I leave you to imagine the rest. When the last hand-shake was over, and the carriage had disappeared down the street, no one daring to watch it for fear of ill luck, Nell went up stairs. Mother Barlowe sat at the window, staring at the houses opposite, and Father Barlowe marched up and down the room in solemn silence for half an hour. Mother Barlowe then ascended the stairs, with the intention of comforting Nelly, if possible, knocked unavailingly at her door, and returned to assume the same position as before. Another silence, and Lou went on the same errand.

"Why is she gone so long, I wonder?" said Mr. Barlowe, moving restlessly about, feeling much, but as incapable of affording consolation as a big brown bear. Another march, and then Father Barlowe walked with resolute steps into the dining-room, and up to the sideboard, where he unfastened a bottle of pale ale, and, after some demonstration on the part of cork and foam, he managed to fill a goblet brimming full. This he carried to Nelly, and commanded her with a grim air, slightly tinctured with pity, to drink, which Nelly did, appreciating the intention.

From this date Nelly lived, the long winter through, chiefly on letters. Good, long letters they were, truly, of twelve, sixteen, and eighteen pages; arriving irregularly, sometimes three or four in a week, at others six together, and in interval without any. The closing week of May came, and Nelly had had no letter for ten day, but as that had happened several before, she did not feel uneasy. Six weeks had passed, and still no letters, neither had his family received word from him. Nelly doubled the number of her own, and sent messages by friends to Ned. At the end of two months she became seriously alarmed. The family read the papers diligently, gleaning up every item concerning *the* regiment.

One morning a gentleman called, whom Nelly remembered as a friend of Ned's. She hurried to the parlor with the card in her hand, inquiring, almost before they had exchanged the usual civilities, whether he was direct from the army, and if he had brought a letter from Ned.

Mr. Holcombe regarded her so compassionately, and hesitated so long in his answer, that Nelly said, with blanched face, "If you have any ill news to tell me, pray tell it quickly."

Thus pressed, Mr. Holcombe told his tale, with much circumlocution, and sundry breaks. He said that Ned had been sent with a company as guard to a wagon train some miles from Battle Creek, Tennessee, and while resting with the men under the trees of a farmyard, a dash had been made upon them by the enemy. A fight had ensued, and the enemy proving victorious, our men fled. Ned had never turned up, and whether wounded or dead no one knew.

Nelly listened to this story much relieved, and turning to her mother, who was just entering, calmly repeated it, evidently determined to believe that no harm had happened to her husband. Now, Mrs. Barlowe settled immediately to the fact that the worst had come to pass.

Mr. Holcombe took his leave, glad that he had not been obliged to witness a trying scene.

Nell, on her father's return home, besought him to take her to Tennessee to find Ned, who was wounded, she was sure, and needed her care.

Mr. Barlowe endeavored to dissuade her from the journey, told her he would go himself, and do all that was necessary, but to no purpose. Nelly declared her place was by her suffering husband's side. Therefore, they made ready what little they needed, and the morning found them on the train bound for Tennessee. No food passed Nelly's lips, no sleep came to her eyes. The train, although moving swiftly, seemed to her to creep. Hurry! hurry! Was the sole thought of her mind.

The locality reached at last, they tried to find the house themselves from Mr. Holcombe's description, travelled miles in the wrong direction, listened to a story about an entirely different man, and were obliged to retrace their steps.

The regiment Ned had belonged to was encamped, with others, at Battle Creek. They sought the captain of his company there, and he went back with them to the house where he had last been seen.

The woman who owned the house was very kind. She told the group that an officer, answering the description Nelly gave, had been wounded on the day of the skirmish, two months previous, and had died there. That he had been buried with some dead in a trench. Nelly gave a groan of anguish. The woman further said she would show them where, if they liked; had supposed that the gentleman, despite his Northern uniform, belonged to the Southern army. Nelly made a move towards the door, and the rest of the party followed.

Their hostess led them across the yard in front, and to the edge of a cornfield separated from the dusty road by a crooked rail-fence. In a corner of this fence Nell's quick eye descried a wide mound, on top of which a couple of purple thistles flaunted, half-concealing a forlorn little board, on whose sides were painted in black letters the names of the dead. The blazing noon-day sun was pouring his blinding rays on this dreary scene.

Ah me! this was the last resting-place of gallant, brown-eyed, laughter-loving Ned. The wretched little widow laid her head down among the parched grass and wept bitter tears, tears like drops of blood. The eyes of the lookers-on grew dim, and Mr. Barlowe abstractedly gathered a handful of thistles and feathery white flowers, kept afterwards by his daughter all her life.

Useless to try and take the body up out of a grave of fifteen, to bury in the cemetery at home, as had been Mrs. Barlowe's tearful suggestion. The Southern woman cared for Nelly as a mother might have done. "Poor lamb!" she called her. Ned's uniform, penknife, revolver and leather belt had been left in her possession. These she returned to Nelly, refusing aught in pay, good soul. A pocket of the coat contained two old letters of Nelly's, and one of Ned's to her, begun in pencil.

The two, father and daughter, turned their faces homeward, there to be received by the sympathizing mother, upon whose bosom Nelly poured out all her sorrow. Grief, fatigue, and fasting combined, made her ill, and she hoped in her despair that she would die. But this was only the momentary wish of a sick mind and heart. For Nelly was a Christian, anxious to perform her duty for the love of God, and knowing that there was much for her to do in the world, even though her bright hopes were laid in the dust, and she should never have another happy hour. Neither was she of a selfish disposition, inclined, because of her own despondency, to throw a gloom over the family circle. No, she took her place among them as soon as she was able, trying to pursue her usual occupations with as much interest as she could master. Thanking with wan smiles the unwearied efforts of parents and sisters to turn her thoughts from the one subject, and raise her spirits.

With such pale cheeks and dressed in the deepest mourning, she looked like a fading lily. Mr. Barlowe watched his favorite daughter with wistful eyes, doing for her kind things in various odd ways. For the drooping of his fair-haired Nelly saddened him.

Lulu Beck spent a great deal of her time with Nelly, consoling and petting her in her childish fashion, saying sometimes in a sage little whisper, "I know that Ned is not dead; I am sure he will come back again." Sending with the words such a thrill through Nelly's heart, that it was almost more than she could bear.

The summer months wore on, oppressive days of heat and languor. Nelly grew more and more fragile, and with failing health her courage was fast waning away, despite her brave endeavors to bear with fortitude the trial God had sent her.

On the 31st of October a severe headache obliged her to remain in bed, sorely against her will. Through her mind revolved continually the events of the past year, that miserable grave in the South holding its place as the predominant image. Compelling herself to rise, although still far from well, she joined the family, seeking relief by companionship from distracting thought.

At dusk she seated herself near the door in the parlor, which opened immediately upon the garden. With her hand covering her face, absorbed in thought, time passed unheeded, until, feeling a gentle touch on her shoulder, she looked up with a start. The gas had been lit, and Lulu was standing before her, with a huge ball of yarn hugged up to her breast. A ball that Lulu had been working at the livelong day, winding three together, belonging to her grandmother, to produce this one. She fancied, child-like, that much of the charm lay in the largeness of the ball.

"What are you going to do with that, dearie?" inquired Nelly.

"Why, don't you remember, Nelly?" answered Lulu. "It is Hallowe'en. You take the end of this worsted in your hand, and roll the ball into the dark, and your true love will lift it."

Nelly put her hand before her eyes, and the tears trickled down her cheeks. Lulu did not notice her emotion. She placed the yarn in Nelly's hand, and shut the fingers upon it one by one; then gave the ball a slight push, which sent it rolling off of Nelly's lap, and, giving a whirl or two, disappeared out of the door.

Lulu heard it thump softly on each step as it fell on it, and also heard a step upon the gravel. The child was standing with her little neck leaned forward, listening eagerly; and, at this sound, Nelly straightened herself, and, putting her hand on Lulu's head, watched the door breathlessly. The yarn slackened, and then drew taut, as the sailors say, as though some one had lifted the ball, and drawn it to him. Nearer and nearer advanced the well-known step; and, when the dear old face of Ned, haggard and pale as a ghost, appeared at the door, Nelly stretched her arms towards him, gasped "Ned!" and fainted.

The ghost, if ghost it were, walked into the room, and raised the insensible form in his arms, retreating with it to the sofa, where he sat down with her head upon his shoulder.

Lulu, at this, fled affrighted into the other parlor, uttering, as she went, piercing little screams.

The alarmed household rushed to the rescue, to find Ned bending anxiously over Nelly, and half-fearing that his sudden return had caused her death. But happiness never kills any one, and Nelly soon recovered.

Oh! the scene that ensued, and the joy of that family! Mr. Barlowe shook Ned's hand with such a hearty pressure that his friendly digits left black and blue marks on the unfortunate member for weeks after. A tear actually hopped to that good man's eye, traversed the broad expanse of his cheek, and lodged on the toe of his boot. His next movement was to leave the house for a few moments, returning ere long, hatless and panting, with Ned's widowed mother and two young sisters to add their affectionate welcome and delight to the general happiness.

And now I must tell how Ned happened to come back at all. It seems that he really was wounded on the day of the skirmish, though not severely, and was immediately sent to prison. But, before his departure, a soldier, who had fancied Ned's clothes and effects, made him exchange them for his old rags.

This soldier had a slight attack of hemorrhage of the lungs in the morning, brought on by the excitement of the fight. Ned supposed it must have increased, and that he died that very afternoon, and no doubt was buried in the trench. The woman who had charge of the house that eventful noon was not the same one who was so kind to Nelly. Hence the cause of the mistake. Ned, with others, had made his escape from prison, and, with the aid of a friend that he had found in a Southern village, had been enabled to proceed straight home. Another kiss ended the narrative.

"O Nelly!" said Lulu, giving her a smothering embrace, "I brought Ned back again. If I were you, I would keep Hallowe'en every year as long as I lived."

"Indeed, I will," said Nelly, smiling. And so she did.

The Return of the Native

Excerpt, Thomas Hardy, 1878

Early on in his 1878 novel *The Return of the Native*, Thomas Hardy writes of a provincial Guy Fawkes celebration by describing the construction and enjoyment of a traditional hilltop bonfire. Hardy wanted to establish a pagan character for the novel's setting, the isolated Egdon Heath, and he perfectly captures the universal, wild joy of a large fire, noting that the celebrants' enjoyment of the spectacle really has very little to do with the Gunpowder Plot they're supposedly remembering. Hardy makes no mention of Hallowe'en in the book, however, which does suggest that the holiday was little celebrated in rural England in the mid 19th-century (although, like the 5th of November, it was celebrated in other provinces with bonfires — see *The Golden Bough*'s chapter on "The Hallowe'en Fires"). The excerpt chosen here ends with an aged spectator reciting a traditional ballad called "Queen Eleanor's Confession," a somewhat curious choice on Hardy's part, since the ballad was actually connected to neither Guy Fawkes nor this area of England.

---

3 — The Custom of the Country

Had a looker-on been posted in the immediate vicinity of the barrow, he would have learned that these persons were boys and men of the neighbouring hamlets. Each, as he ascended the barrow, had been heavily laden with furze faggots, carried upon the shoulder by means of a long stake sharpened at each end for impaling them easily — two in front and two behind. They came from a part of the heath a quarter of a mile to the rear, where furze almost exclusively prevailed as a product.

Every individual was so involved in furze by his method of carrying the faggots that he appeared like a bush on legs till he had thrown them down. The party had marched in trail, like a travelling flock of sheep; that is to say, the strongest first, the weak and young behind.

The loads were all laid together, and a pyramid of furze thirty feet in circumference now occupied the crown of the tumulus, which was known as Rainbarrow for many miles round. Some made themselves busy with matches, and in selecting the driest tufts of furze, others in loosening the bramble bonds which held the faggots together. Others, again, while this was in progress, lifted their eyes and swept the vast expanse of country

Building up a bonfire — photograph by Sir Benjamin Stone (1910).

commanded by their position, now lying nearly obliterated by shade. In the valleys of the heath nothing save its own wild face was visible at any time of day; but this spot commanded a horizon enclosing a tract of far extent, and in many cases lying beyond the heath country. None of its features could be seen now, but the whole made itself felt as a vague stretch of remoteness.

While the men and lads were building the pile, a change took place in the mass of shade which denoted the distant landscape. Red suns and tufts of fire one by one began to arise, flecking the whole country round. They were the bonfires of other parishes and hamlets that were engaged in the same sort of commemoration. Some were distant, and stood in a dense atmosphere, so that bundles of pale straw-like beams radiated around them in the shape of a fan. Some were large and near, glowing scarlet-red from the shade, like wounds in a black hide. Some were Maenades, with winy faces and blown hair. These tinctured the silent bosom of the clouds above them and lit up their ephemeral caves, which seemed thenceforth to become scalding caldrons. Perhaps as many as thirty bonfires could be counted within the whole bounds of the district; and as the hour may be told on a clock-face when the figures themselves are invisible, so did the men recognize the locality of each fire by its angle and direction, though nothing of the scenery could be viewed.

The first tall flame from Rainbarrow sprang into the sky, attracting all eyes that had been fixed on the distant conflagrations back to their own attempt in the same kind. The cheerful blaze streaked the inner surface of the human circle — now increased by other stragglers, male and female — with its own gold livery, and even overlaid the dark turf around with a lively luminousness, which softened off into obscurity where the barrow rounded downwards out of sight. It showed the barrow to be the segment of a globe, as perfect as on the day when it was thrown up, even the little ditch remaining from which the earth was dug. Not a plough had ever disturbed a grain of that stubborn soil. In the heath's barrenness to the farmer lay its fertility to the historian. There had been no obliteration, because there had been no tending.

It seemed as if the bonfire-makers were standing in some radiant upper story of the world, detached from and independent of the dark stretches below. The heath down there was now a vast abyss, and no longer a continuation of what they stood on; for their eyes, adapted to the blaze, could see nothing of the deeps beyond its influence. Occasionally, it is true, a more vigorous flare than usual from their faggots sent darting lights like aides-de-camp down the inclines to some distant bush, pool, or patch of white sand, kindling these to replies of the same colour, till all was lost in darkness again. Then the whole black phenomenon beneath represented Limbo as viewed from the brink by the sublime Florentine in his vision, and the muttered articulations of the wind in the hollows were as complaints and petitions from the "souls of mighty worth" suspended therein.

It was as if these men and boys had suddenly dived into past ages, and fetched therefrom an hour and deed which had before been familiar with this spot. The ashes of the original British pyre which blazed from that summit lay fresh and undisturbed in the barrow beneath their tread. The flames from funeral piles long ago kindled there had shone down upon the lowlands as these were shining now. Festival fires to Thor and Woden had followed on the same ground and duly had their day. Indeed, it is pretty well known that such blazes as this the heathmen were now enjoying are rather the lineal descendants from jumbled Druidical rites and Saxon ceremonies than the invention of popular feeling about Gunpowder Plot.

Moreover to light a fire is the instinctive and resistant act of man when, at the winter ingress, the curfew is sounded throughout Nature. It indicates a spontaneous, Promethean rebelliousness against that fiat that this recurrent season shall bring foul times, cold darkness, misery and death. Black chaos comes, and the fettered gods of the earth say, Let there be light.

The brilliant lights and sooty shades which struggled upon the skin and clothes of the persons standing round caused their lineaments and general contours to be drawn with Düreresque vigour and dash. Yet the permanent moral expression of each face it was impossible to discover, for as the nimble flames towered, nodded, and swooped through the surrounding air, the blots of shade and flakes of light upon the countenances of the group changed shape and position endlessly. All was unstable; quivering as leaves, evanescent as lightning. Shadowy eye-sockets, deep as those of a death's head, suddenly turned into pits of lustre: a lantern-jaw was cavernous, then it was shining; wrinkles were emphasized to ravines, or obliterated entirely by a changed ray. Nostrils were dark wells; sinews in old necks were gilt mouldings; things with no particular polish on them were glazed; bright objects, such as the tip of a furze-hook one of the men carried, were as glass; eyeballs glowed like little lanterns. Those whom Nature had depicted as merely quaint became grotesque, the grotesque became preternatural; for all was in extremity.

Hence it may be that the face of an old man, who had like others been called to the heights by the rising flames, was not really the mere nose and chin that it appeared to be, but an appreciable quantity of human countenance. He stood complacently sunning himself in the heat. With a speaker, or stake, he tossed the outlying scraps of fuel into the conflagration, looking at the midst of the pile, occasionally lifting his eyes to measure the height of the flame, or to follow the great sparks which rose with it and sailed away into darkness. The beaming sight, and the penetrating warmth, seemed to breed in him a cumulative cheerfulness, which soon amounted to delight. With his stick in his hand he began to jig a private minuet, a bunch of copper seals shining and swinging like a pendulum from under his waistcoat: he also began to sing, in the voice of a bee up a flue —

> "The king' call'd down' his no-bles all,'
> 　By one,' by two,' by three';
> Earl Mar'-shal, I'll' go shrive'-the queen,'
> 　And thou' shalt wend' with me.'
>
> "A boon,' a boon,' quoth Earl' Mar-shal,'
> 　And fell' on his bend'-ded knee,'
> That what'-so-e'er' the queen' shall say,'
> 　No harm' there-of' may be.'"

"Halloween:
A Threefold Chronicle"

From *Harper's Monthly Magazine*
William Sharp, 1886

The length and detail of this article, which appeared in the popular American maga-zine *Harper's*, suggest that by 1886 Halloween was a topic of great interest to middle- and upper-class Americans. Sharp not only provides some history (with the requisite references to Burns's "Hallowe'en"), but also several eerie or humorous anecdotes; especially notewor-thy is his account of a sea voyage during which the Scottish sailors were so determined to keep their Halloween celebrations that they endured roiling waves to bob for apples.

Sharp, who begins his article questioning the holiday's ability to endure, would no doubt be pleased to know that Halloween survived past the 20th century and into the 21st, albeit in somewhat different form from the holiday he knew and cherished.

Old superstitions die hard, and it will certainly be long before the festival of Hal-loween becomes as much a thing of the past as has practically become the Guy Fawkes cele-bration on the 5th of November. Long before the Christian faith made way among the untutored peoples of ancient Britain, the Druids had performed special rites on what is now known as Hallowmas Eve: fires were lit deep in remote forests, upon outlying spurs of hills, even upon the great plains that stretched between dense forests and partially cleared woodlands; mystic rites were performed, the help of the true God was implored, the machinations of evil powers were protested against. The earliest records bear witness to a universal belief that on this night the powers of darkness muster in great force, that all supernatural beings hold revel within the sphere of humanity, and that therefore it behooved all persons to be careful on this night of all nights, for any sin committed ren-dered the perpetrator liable to be brought under the influence of some evil spirit through-out a whole year thereafter. To this day any child born in Scotland on the eve of the 31st of October is supposed to be in possession of certain mysterious faculties, to hold — if not consciously, at least unconsciously in the midnight hours when the senses are obscured by sleep — communion with the supernatural world, and to be at all times a person whose actions, however eccentric, must be regarded charitably. Those who have read Sir Walter

Illustration by W. Small and T. Heard of "Red Mike's Rest."

Scott's *Monastery* will remember that he has made use of this circumstance. "She's as flytie as a Halloween wean" is a phrase that may even yet be occasionally heard north of the Tweed, and in most of the popular accounts of wizards and all uncanny folk the date of their births is generally set down as on the last day of October. When, later on, All-hallow Eve became a Christian observance, the old customs pertinent to its celebration did not pass into disuse; on the contrary, they became more and more deeply established, every here and there accumulating some new superstition, or annexing some old belief that had long lingered without direct association with any special day, season, or locality. Bonfires are still lit on Hallowmas Eve, though perhaps only one or two here and there among the members of the innumerable village communities who thus celebrate the great event know that the practice is a remnant of paganism; indeed, it is surprising, in the use of this as of many other popular customs, to find how few know anything whatever of the significance of their celebrations. "We do as our fathers did before us," is sufficient to account for everything. In Protestant countries the vigil of All-souls is no longer a religious observance, or, at any rate, is not so in Scotland, England, or Germany. It may be said that Halloween, as we understand it, is only celebrated by the Teutonic and Celtic races; with the Latins it is merely a religious vigil, round its observance clinging few if any of those wild legends or superstitions that are so plentiful in Scandinavia, Scotland, and Ireland. The nearest approach to the Northern solemnity, and even weirdness, is the Venetian *notte delle morti*, or night of all the dead; but the religious ceremonies attendant thereon take place not on the 31st of October, but on the eve of All-souls Day, that is, the day following. It is in Scotland and Ireland that Halloween is kept in its entirety; in the former, curiously enough, more in the east, mid-country, and Lowlands than in the remoter Highland districts; in other words, more among the Scots proper than among the pure Celts. The best chronicle of Hallowmas Eve that exists is the well-known poem of Burns, containing as it does some record of the most generally practised customs in connection with this really ancient vigil, but, considering the popularity of the subject, there is a wonderfully limited "Halloween" literature. The succeeding threefold chronicle may possibly, then, contain something novel as well as of interest to many readers. It may be that the time is not far distant when All-hallows Eve will lose its hold upon rural as completely as it has upon urban populations, when bonfires will be lit only by a few youngsters, when apples will cease to be ducked for, and when nuts will no longer be set ablaze amid the red-hot coals; but the writer, for one, believes that such a time is not yet at hand, and disbelieves that Halloween will disappear altogether as a festival.

It is not only that there would be a revolution in the child-world if such sacrilegious disuse were to become the fashion, but that there are too many older children interested in the famous eve to allow its celebration to drop altogether yet awhile. At sea, in Canada, the States, Australia, even in India, wherever a true Scottish or Irish family is located, there is sure to be at least one voice raised in favor of the genial old custom. Its superstitious observances must undoubtedly pass away—have, indeed, to a great extent already become obsolete—but the good-fellowship, the laughter, the nut-roasting, the apple-ducking, the candle-singeing, ought long to be specially associated with the 31st of October.

Of some of these weirder observances, and of some strange stories connected with them, the writer will now give a short account, in great part a record of what he has himself witnessed.

I.— Halloween in Ireland.

One wild, blustering afternoon—the afternoon of the last day of October—I made my way as best I could across a stretch of hilly moorland, vainly hoping that I might meet with some one able to direct me to my destination. I was on a visit to an old college friend, the vicar of a place I shall call Derree, in the western county of Clare, and at his hospitable table had met with a Mr. Connolly, who, hearing that my friend had to go south to Limerick on the last day of the month on important business, pressed me so hard to join his family circle on Hallowmas Eve that I could not with courtesy have refused his genial invitation, even had I wished to do so. As a matter of fact, I was only too glad to agree to his kind proposals, and listened attentively to his instructions as to the route I was to take. I was to go along the Derree road till I came to the base of the high hill called Creachan Knoc, which I was to skirt to the left, and then to cross the moor as if making for the central height of the Caisteall Abhaill, or Peaks of the Castles, and when I came to the stream I was to look for the ford, and having crossed this, to branch off abruptly to the left, and walk onward for about a mile, till I should see the farm-house nestling at the base of the strangely shaped, apparently insecurely poised hill locally known as Drunken Tim. These were Mr. Connolly's directions, in the event of the 31st proving a fine day, and of my continuing in my determination to reach his farm on foot; otherwise I was to drive along the Derree road for some ten miles to the village of Clac-mha-reagh, and thence north ward by the Castle road. The forenoon turned out to be bright and fine, to my great satisfaction, and I started in good hope, not only of enjoying the walk, but also of reaching the farm of my new acquaintance early in the afternoon. But by the time I had skirted the Creachan Knoc a white autumnal mist had shrouded the Caisteall Abhaill from view, so I had only to make a guess as to the right direction. Plunging suddenly into the edge of a bog made me realize that I had diverged from the route I was told to keep. The wind was rising with boisterous gusts, and I was beginning to wish that I had taken Mr. Connolly's advice and started by the more circuitous but safer way *via* Clac-mha-reagh, when I heard a loud hail far away to the right. Looking round, I perceived a man waving his arm to me, and as I approached him I noticed that he was a piper — a fact of which he soon informed me himself, adding that he was on the way to Mr. Connolly's farm to provide the music for the dancing that was sure to follow the regular Halloween festivities. It was well he descried me on the moor, for if I had proceeded further in the direction I had been following I would have probably found myself floundering in the huge and treacherous bog called in the neighborhood Red Mike's Rest. On the way Larry O'Hara — for so I learned was the piper's name — gave me much curious information about the customs of Hallowmas Eve in that part of Ireland, and as his account of how the great bog from which I had narrowly escaped got its name is germane to my subject, I will give it here.

"Red Mike, your honor, was the only son of Widow O'Flaherty. He was a queer one from his birth, an' no wonder, for he first saw the light atween dusk an' dark o' a Hallowmas Eve. Hereabouts the people say that if a babby be born on this night, it rins a moighty good chance o' bein' possessed by some sproite or other; it may or may not be true, oi'm sure it's beyont the likes o' me to say whether soch things are possible or not, but oi *will* say that Mike O'Flaherty was different to other men from the first. He wor always up to some game, he wor, an' nivver for good — leastways I nivver heard o' anny good he iver did. He lied and broke his troth to man an' woman, an' got into bad odor with priest an' magistrate, for nigh upon twelve years arter he came to manhood, until the judgment o' God came upon him. One Hallow Eve he was at the house o' the Flannigans, up by Glen Creachan. He was courtin' Mary Flannigan, though ivery one on us knew she didn't care two straws for Red Mike, but was all aglow wi' love for Larry O'Rourke, the Limerick carrier. It's the custom in these parts for the childer to run into the cabbage yard afore the evenin' fun begins, an' to pick out a number o' cabbage stalks, an' name them arter any seven o' the folk they have annything to do with; then, having finished wi' this choosin',' they dance round the place, shouting out,

> 'One, two, three, an' up to seven;
> If all are white, all go to heaven;
> If one is black as Murtagh's evil,
> He'll soon be screechin' wi' the devil.'

No, your honor," responded O'Hara to my question, "I don't know what's the maning of Murtagh's evil, nor, for that matter, which Murtagh is meant; no one in our time, any-way — for I sang the same loines meself whan I wor a spalpeen. Well, as I wor about to tell ye, Flannigan's childer, havin' finished their song, ran into the house an' asked all the folk to come out an' see *their sowls*. Ould Flannigan pulled *his* cabbage stalk, an' Mrs. Flannigan hers, an' young Tim Flannigan his, an' Mrs. Tim hers, an' purty Mary Flannigan hers, an' Larry O'Rourke his, until it came to Mike O'Flaherty's turn. The stalks of all the others had been quite clean an' white, but when Red Mike pulled up his, it was all black and foul wi' worms an' slugs, an' wi' a real bad smell ahint it. Larry O'Rourke laughed, an' Mary Flannigan giggled, an' the others all looked moighty consarned. Mike glared ahout him for a moment, more like a mad bull or a haythin Turk nor a Christian. Then he up an' says: 'Ye may laugh, Larry O'Rourke, but ye'll no be laughin' long; ay, ye may snigger, Mary, but ye'll be cryin' for manny a day, whan yer lover's below the sod, as he will be before the year's out. As for you, ould Flannigan, you an' your son an' all that belong to ye will have cause to curse the day when ye mocked Red Mike, as ye call me. Ye forget I was born on Hallow Eve! I've the gift o' the sight, I have, and on this day my curse can blast whatever I choose.' What more Red Mike would have said I don't know, but at that moment Father O'Connor came up to where all were standin'. 'Curses come home to roost,' says he to O'Flaherty, in a starn voice 'an' it's you that'll suffer, Mike O'Flaherty, an' no one here. Get ye gone at once, or I'll put the word on ye.'[1] 'I'll go whan I choose, Father O'Connor,' says Red Mike, surlily. The next moment the priest drew a crucifix from his breast, saying to O'Flaherty that even if he wor in league wi' the devil, he could not withstand *that*. Mike gave a howl jist loike a wild baste, an' thin turned an' ran down the glen as fast as he could. Ould Thady King, the piper (now dead, God rest his sowl!), wor crossing this moor that night, an' who should he see but Red Mike dancin' an' shoutin' like mad, an' screamin' in mortal fear. 'Mike! Mike!' ould Thady cried; but O'Flaherty paid no attintion to him, but kept on screamin' an' sometimes shoutin' out, 'My time is up! my time is up!' Suddenly he bent forrard an' ran like the wind, took one great leap, an' disappeared in the ground as if he had jumped into the sea. Nothin' more wor ever seen o' Red Mike, *leastwise as a man*. An' that's why the great bog yonder is called Red Mike's Rest."

O'Hara's narrative made me feel all the more thankful that I had not been left to

---

1. An expression often heard in some parts of western Ireland, to denote a priestly anathema.

blunder on as best I could, especially with a stormy night fast closing round. Even the fact that I was not born on All-hallows Eve would have stood me in little stead if I had once floundered into the actual quagmire of Red Mike's Rest. I thought the piper's "leastwise as a man" a finely suggestive way of hinting at something weirdly supernatural, but before I could draw anything further out of him we came in sight of The Three Larches, as Mr. Connolly's farm was called. As we arrived at the low doorway of the large, old-fashioned house there was quite a noisy chorus of hospitable greetings, mainly, of course, addressed to my evidently eagerly anticipated companion.

"Cead-mille-a-faltha — a hundred thousand welcomes," cried my host himself, and erelong I found myself at a table literally covered with good things, but none so pleasant to look upon as the fresh faces of a troop of children and some eight or ten young men and girls around its sides. The dinner was a great success; and if hunger is the best sauce, every one present seemed amply supplied with that condiment.

After the dinner was over, and after each one had taken at least a sip of the fragrant punch that had been brought in in a great bowl, there was a general break up. One ceremony that had been held, Mr. Connolly was going to have omitted, but a smiling assurance from his wife caused him to change his mind. This was the "livelong" ceremony. "Livelong" is the local name of certain green plants that are hung up in a loft or barn or disused room as early as midsummer; in fact, they must be hung up on Midsummer Eve; and if on Halloween they are still green, all will be well throughout the year with the children who had hung them up. If one should be sickly or dead, so will it be with the child. One of the little Connolly girls was a delicate child, and her father feared that if perchance any decay were visible in the "livelong" she had hung up, it would have a bad effect on her susceptible nature. Mrs. Connolly, however, had privately paid a visit to the tool shed where they had been hung, and seeing that all the plants were undecayed, she thought the observance of the old custom would do the children more good than harm. What a shout of joy there was when all the "livelongs" were seen to be in good preservation! and this, the first ceremony of the evening, being so successful, was taken as a good augury for all to follow.

When we entered the house again, and passed into the great kitchen, wherein the shadows and the fire-light gleams held revel in a fashion that would have delighted Rembrandt himself, we caught a glimpse of some half-dozen dairy-maids and farm servants sitting dumbly in one corner of the room, and apparently engaged in moulding something with their hands.

"They're going through the dumb-cake ceremony," whispered Mrs. Connolly, "which consists in their kneading with their left thumbs a piece of cake without uttering a single word. If one of them intentionally or accidentally should breathe a single syllable, the charm would be broken, and not one of them would have her burning hopes of seeing her future husband in her dreams fulfilled."

The sturdy damsels certainly seemed in dead earnest, clinching their lips so that not a sound should escape them, one stout dairy-maid actually panting in her excitement or under the unwonted restraint. Meanwhile the children had fairly started the game of "snap-apple." Neither the dipping for apples nor the degenerate fork-dropping had any fascination for these young "spalpeens o' Clare" in comparison with this older and much more exciting form of the game. High up among the dusky rafters — wherefrom hung flitches of bacon, ox tongues, onions and other articles of strange hue and shape — one of the boys had fastened a piece of strong cord; suspended at the lower end of this, within a few feet from the ground, was a short skewer gripped about midway by the knot of the string, and at either end of the skewer was respectively a tempting ruddy apple and a lighted tallow candle. As soon as the cord was set in motion, the game began. Little Harry Connolly was the first to essay for the luscious prize; but in his eager spring he missed both apple and candle, springing past the novel pendulum, and landing with a loud whack on the feet of gouty old Peter McMullen, the chemist and village doctor from Clac-mha-reagh, whose agonized "Oh, mother of Moses!" caused a roar of laughter from every one. Young Jack Hennessy, a cousin of the first youngster, and as fiery-haired a young Celt as ever revelled in mischief, tried next. Carefully watching his opportunity as the cord swung back from right to left, he sprang like an arrow, but was just a moment too soon, for he hit the candle with his face, and sent it spinning to the floor. His red locks were well singed, and a goodly splotch of tallow lay on his perky nose; but he laughed as heartily as the others, and seemed in no wise put out at his discomfiture. With varying adventures the different children all had their chances, no one, however, to the general merriment, proving successful — till at last young Hennessy's turn came round again. This time his sharp white teeth grabbed the coveted prize, and he retired from the game, another equally tempting apple being put in the last one's place. Much amusement was caused by little Johnnie Stevens, a pale-faced, apathetic-looking youngster. When his turn came he quietly slid under the swinging cord, waited for its backward motion from left to right, and then, meeting the apple full face, secured it with ease. "He's a cautious yin, he is," chuckled old Macfarlane, Lord Donaghadee's Scotch bailiff; "an' it's weel seen he comes o' guid Scottish bluid: he war determeened that if he didna grab the aipple, he wud at enny rate mak sicker o' no bein' singed wi' the cawnle."

Leaving the children still enjoying this their favorite sport, we passed by the servant-maids again. Their dumb-cake ceremony was long over, and they were now busily engaged in finding out the state of life to which their respective future lovers belonged. To gain this interesting information it was necessary that molten lead should be poured into cold spring-water. According to the fanciful shapes the lead took as each small quantity was poured out, so each girl framed her fancy: now something like a horse would cause the jubilant maiden to call out, "A dragoon!" now some dim resemblance to a helmet would suggest a handsome member of the mounted police; or a round object with a spike would seem a ship, and this of course meant a sailor; or a cow would suggest a cattle dealer, or a plough a farmer, and so forth. Anyhow, great amusement seemed to be got from the rite, and in one or two cases, to judge by the laughter and blushing denials, the guesses seemed to be based on something more substantial than mere fancy.

At last came the crowning delight of the evening, the Halloween jig. This was a reel in which every one joined, and there was nothing short of ecstasy in the tumult of stamping feet, snapping fingers, happy laughter, mingling with the wild music of Larry O'Hara's pipes, and the frantic screams — for they were nothing else — from the fiddle of the great musician, One-eyed Murtagh.

It was late that night before even the youngest went to bed, and certainly enough noise was made to scare away any evil spirits that might be hoping to gain some advantage on this night of all nights. The music came to an end at last, and the latest words that One-eyed Murtagh sighed out to his friend O'Hara, before both succumbed under their last glass of whiskey punch, were, "Larry, me boy, in hiven 'twill always be Halloween."

II.—In Scotland.

In the last week of a certain October I got an invitation from a connection in whose genial household I had spent many a happy Halloween. An answer in the affirmative was at once sent to The Shaws, as my friend Campbell's place was called. Linlithgow was little more than an hour's railway drive from Glasgow, but though I reached the old town shortly after four o'clock, it was quite dark, partly owing to the dense mass of dull gray snow-clouds that obscured the sky. When, after a drive of half an hour, the dog-cart stopped before the old manor-house, the first of the winter's storms had fairly set in, and the great flakes of snow were whirling wildly under the branches of the beeches, oaks, and elms that lined the avenue, seeming, indeed, as if they had straggled out of the adjacent forest of Polmont for that very purpose.

After dinner we went forth in a party—a small one, and well protected with wraps, owing to the steady snow-storm outside—to witness the pulling of the kale stalks. Some of the house servants, and of course all the dairy-maids and farm girls, as well as all the young men in the neighborhood, had come together in the great kitchen of the home-farm; some of them, and the older and younger folk, were busy with preparations for all the customary festivities. No engaged and of course no married persons can participate in the "kaling." The right way is for two young people (in some parts of the country it must be two of one sex, in others each pair must consist of youth and lass) to go hand in hand, blindfolded, out into the kale or cabbage yard, and there pull the first stalks they meet with, returning at once to the fire-side, when they are unbandaged, and left to read their matrimonial fortunes as fore-told in the kale stalks. In the notes to his poem, Burns has explained the method of prediction. According as the stalk is big or little, straight or crooked, so shall the future wife or husband be of the party by whom it is pulled; the quantity of *yird*, or earth, sticking to the root denotes the amount of *tocher* (*i.e.,* fortune, or dowry); and the taste of the pith, or *custoc*, indicates the temper. Finally, the stalks, or runts, are placed, one after another over the door, and the Christian names of the persons who chance thereafter to enter the house are held in the same succession to indicate those of the individuals whom the parties are to marry.

With much amusement all watched the fortune-seekers of the night. A huge carter named Jock Meiklejohn, a man about six feet two, stolidly allowed himself to be coupled with a bouncing partner, and without the slightest apparent interest, pulled the first cabbage stalk he came across; great laughter, however, came from every one at the rueful expression which stole over his honest face when he saw what augury of the future had been vouchsafed to him—a dumpy, crooked little kale stalk, devoid of a particle of *yird*. "Taste the *custoc*, Jock," "Taste the pith, mon," came from many of his tormentors; but while he mournfully shook his head, a pretty girl undertook the experiment on his behalf, and when her wry face showed what the real or pretended taste of the *custoc* was, every one laughed louder than before, and Jock's cup of misery was full. "D'ye think I'm a gowk tae believe a' this tamfoolery?" I heard him muttering to a sympathetic friend, though I noticed that the gloom of his predicted fate oppressed him throughout the whole evening. While others were trying their fortune I spoke to Mr. Macdonald, the bailiff, asking him if the superstition had any real hold upon the people in the neighborhood.

"Weel, sir, it's dying oot. Schoolin' an' railways an' a' the rest o't's bad for auld cus-

"Tasting the custoc."

toms like these. In some airts the pu'in' o' the kale stalks is no' to be seen at a'; in ithers it's lingerin' on amang the farm folk; but every here and there it's believed in as firmly as it was in the day o' oor grandfaithers."

Meanwhile two washing-tubs had been placed in the centre of the great kitchen, and round them was gathered an eager company intensely enjoying the fun of the apple-dipping. In the cold water bobbed about a few rosy-cheeked apples, so round and red and tempting, and yet so slippery, so apparently aggravatingly coy, that the excitement of the participators in the "dipping" grew almost into frenzy. Now and again some youngster grew desperate, and thrusting head and neck below the icy water, pursued an apple till he had pinned it against the bottom, and then grabbed it with his teeth. One young fellow, whose carroty locks had been plentifully bear's-greased in honor of the festivity, and perhaps of some fair farm girl, caused great laughter. With utmost caution he advanced his protruding lips toward a large pippin as it bobbed toward him, and it seemed as if the next moment his teeth would be firmly fixed in it; a slight wobble, however, sent it bumping against his nose, and then away it swam, with quite a coquettish little hitch, just as if it knew what was going on, and relished the fun as much as any one. Red-hair finally grew desperate, as the same thing occurred again and again. Reckless of all consequences to his carefully brushed and richly greased locks, he plunged his head deep into the water, and grubbed about frantically for the aggravating pippin. A roar of laughter came from all around as the latter was seen to bob up close behind Red-hair's head, the latter all unconscious of the fact, and with closed eyes still struggling with adverse fate.

Further away, around the huge fire-place, sat and stood a number of laughing lads and lasses, finding their existent or expected courtship imaged forth for them in the way the nuts on the red-hot bars or among the coals blazed or sputtered. No better description could be given than Burns's well-known lines:

"The auld guidwife's weel-hoardet nits
    Are round an' round divided,
An' monie lads' an' lasses' fates
    Are there that night decided:
Some kindle, couthie, side by side,
    An' burn thegither trimly;
Some start awa wi' saucie pride,
    An' jump out owre the chimlie
                Fu' high that night.

"Jean slips in twa, wi' tentie e'e;
    Wha 'twas she wadna tell;
But this is Jock and this is me,
    She says in to hersel.'
He bleez'd owre her, an' she owre him,
    As they wad never mair part;
Till, fuff! he started up the lum,
    An' Jean had e'en a sair heart
                To see't that night.

"Nell had the fause-house in her min'
    She pits hersel' an' Rob in :
In loving bleeze they sweetly join,
    Till white in ase[1] they're sobbin.'
Nell's heart was dancin' at the view;
    She whisper'd Rob to leuk for't;
Rob, stowlins, pried her bonnie mon,'
    Fa' cozie in the neuk for't,
                Unseen that night."

    The still lingering superstitious practices of the sark sleeve, the stalks o' corn, the kiln pot, the sowing of hemp-seed, the Halloween winnowing, the bean stack, the three dishes, and the looking-glass are to all intents customs of a by-gone day. The writer has only personally met with the "hemp-seed" and "the three luggies." All deal with the same matter of interest, namely, the state of one's future husband or wife. In the winnowing ceremony it is necessary for the experimentalist to go alone to the barn, and to be unperceived by any one; he should then, if he can manage it, unhinge the doors, for, as Burns says, there is danger that the *being* who is about to appear may shut the doors and work his summoner some mischief. The next thing is to take the flail, or *wecht*, "and go through all the attitudes of letting down corn against the wind." The action must be thrice repeated, "and the third time an apparition will pass through the barn, in at the windy door and out at the other," having the features and figure and marks of the station in life of the seer's future partner. The "sark sleeve" is another weird ceremony. The eager prier into futurity must go out after dark to a south-running streamlet where "three lairds' lands meet," and in the flowing water thereof dip his left shirt sleeve. On returning to the house he must go to bed

1. Ash.

in sight of a fire, having first hung his shirt before it to dry. About midnight an apparition, exactly resembling the future partner in life, will glide up to the shirt, and turn the wet sleeve as if to dry the other side of it. Needless to say, there are many stories extant of sark-sleeve apparitions, mostly accounted for in each case by the fact that the swain did not go to bed without freely screwing up his courage with strong "barley brie." In "sowing the hemp-seed" the same imaginary performance must be gone through as in the case of the "winnowing the corn"; that is, "one must steal out unperceived, and sow a handful of hemp-seed," harrowing it with anything that can conveniently be drawn after one. On repeating now and then, "Hemp-seed, I sow thee; hemp-seed, I sow thee; and him [or her] that is to be my true love, come after me and pou thee," and on looking over the left shoulder, the apparition of the person invoked will be seen in the attitude of pulling hemp. The "kiln trial" is perhaps even more eerie. Burns again is responsible for the following explanation: Steal out all alone to the kiln, and, darkling, throw into the pot a clew of blue yarn; wind it in a new clew off the old one; and toward the latter end something will hold the thread. Demand, "Wha hauds?" (*i.e.*, who holds?) An answer will be returned from the kiln pot, naming the Christian and surname of your future spouse.

The "bean stack" ceremony is calculated to try the nerves of an excitable person more than any other Halloween rite, except perhaps the "looking-glass" spell. The first stipulation characterizes each of these rites, viz., the necessity of proceeding alone and unnoticed. One must then go to a bean stack, fathom it round three times, and, just as this is accomplished, "you will catch in your arms the apparition of your future conjugal yoke-fellow."

A much more social and less dubious experiment is that of the "three luggies," or dishes. On the hearth-stone the three chosen vessels are placed, one of them containing clean water, another turbid, and the last being empty. Blindfolded, the person about to essay his or her fortune is led up to where the dishes stand. If she (supposing the questioner to be a woman) chances to dip her hand—which, by-the-bye, must be the left one—into the clean water, then her future spouse will come to the marriage altar a bachelor; if in the turbid water, then he will be a widower; and if by ill luck she dips her finger into the *toom* or empty dish, then it is a sure sign that she will never be married at all. It is *vice versa*, of course, in the case of a man being the inquirer; in either case, however, the ceremony must be gone through three times, and correctly each time, otherwise the predictions have no value. Many may remember the humorous stanza in Burns's poem:

> "In order, on the clean hearth-stane,
>   The luggies three are ranged,
> And ev'ry time great care is ta'en
>   To see them duly changed
> Auld Uncle John, wha wedlock's joys
>   Sin' Mar's year did desire,
> Because he gat the toom dish thrice,
>   He heav'd them on the fire
>   In wrath that night."

A strange story connected with the looking-glass rite came under my notice thousands of miles away from Scotland, which, as it is short, I shall be able to narrate in the space at my command. But first I must say that still another quotation from Burns's poem should be made in connection with that delightful evening at The Shaws, now, alas! gone out of the possession of the family who had owned it for ten generations. "Fu' blythe that night" we were indeed, and of all there it might verily be said:

> "Wi' merry sangs, an' friendly cracks,
>   I wat they didna weary;
> Wi' unco tales, an' funnie jokes,
>   Their sports were cheap an' cheery."

III.—At Sea.

For three days we had been driving along before a fierce westerly gale. The *Glenlyon*, as our stout ship was called, had left the west of Scotland more than two months before, and now we were rather more than half-way between the Cape of Good Hope and that Cape Otway which would be the first glimpse of Australia we would have. The captain had informed us at breakfast that toward the late afternoon we should probably sight St. Paul's, that loneliest and most desolate of islands in the track of any great trade route; but our pleasure was a little damped by the additional information that unless the wind fell rapidly he might not only have to give the barren isle a wide berth, but also that our projected Halloween sports would not be feasible. For we were as Scotch all round as could well be the case: the *Glenlyon* bad been built on the Clyde, and belonged to a famous Glasgow shipping company; the officers all hailed from the land o' cakes, as did the crew, with the exception of the English steward and a couple of Swedish seamen; and of the thirty cabin and second-cabin passengers there was only one who had the misfortune (as he was often jokingly reminded) to belong to another nationality. Thus it was quite natural that we should wish to keep Halloween as best we could under the circumstances; but the only custom it was in our power to observe was that of dipping for apples; this, however, would prove impossible unless the sea greatly moderated, for it was all the steadiest of us could do to keep our feet at all.

About half an hour after noon, however, the wind died away completely — or rather it seemed to do so, for, as a matter of fact, there was still enough pressure to prevent the main-sail from idly flapping to and fro. Nevertheless, so threatening was the aspect of the sea that none of us expected there would be any material change before night, if then. The writer has sailed on many seas, but not even off the iron coast of Tierra del Fuego has he seen such enormous billows as those that followed the *Glenlyon* that 31st of October far down in the Southern Ocean. Huge masses of lustrous emerald, with an enormous crown of white foam on their summits, they rolled their vast volume of water after and alongside our vessel much in the way that a herd of wild horses might career round a flying pony, which any moment they might overwhelm and crush to death. Nor has he ever seen any turbulent sea subside with such extraordinary rapidity. In the early morning, with the gale passed away but the wind still fresh, these gigantic billows had been so terrible that if they had not been avoided by the most skilful steering it would have gone badly with our vessel, A1 1400-tonner though she was; by noon they were still phenomenally large and magnificent, but by four o'clock there was a marked subsidence, and two hours later the sea was, comparatively speaking, quite moderate.

Twilight arrived without our catching any glimpse of St. Paul's — much to our disappointment, as for two months we had sighted no land whatever — but this was partly owing to a slight mist that hung away to starboard, for we were really in close proximity to the island.

In tin wash cans, potato tins, and other vessels were soon bobbing about a number of apples, turned out by the steward in liberal quantity by the command of Captain Bennett. Every now and again a sudden lurch of the ship would send one or more of these flying over, and great was the agility displayed in the efforts to escape wetting, and loud the laughter that greeted every mishap. The passengers of both cabins and most of the crew indulged in the amusement as heartily as if they had all been school-boys, and of course the few children were in a perfect frenzy of delight. At length the last apple was disposed of, and nearly every one turned his or her attention to the music and dancing that immediately began. On the foredeck some of the sailors had dressed themselves in fantastic costumes, and as they sprung to and fro to the shrill sounds of the cook's fiddle, while the red gleam of the galley fire or the foremast lantern flashed across them, the scene was at once wild and picturesque. Life, movement, loud laughter, brilliant light, and shifting shadow within these planks; without, the dark, shoreless sea, the long waves heavily rising and falling; and above, the vague whiteness of the sails stretching cloud-like up toward the mysterious depths of heaven.

A little later, leaning over the taffrail on the poop, I was joined by a fellow-passenger. After some conversation anent our varied experiences of Halloween, he confided to me a strange story of an event which had happened in his own family, of which the following is a condensed account. As I have already hinted, this story deals with the looking-glass superstition.

Some ten or twelve years ago a family named Falconer had an estate in western Perthshire, the family consisting, besides husband and wife, of three daughters. A short distance away lived some neighbors of the name of Morgan. The only son of John Morgan — Ralph — was only seventeen years old, and Madge, the youngest daughter of the Falconers, only fourteen, yet they managed to fall in love with each other. Of course their boy-and-girl passion was not as deep as that of lovers of maturer age, but at the same time it was ardent and sincere enough to exercise a strong influence on their lives. At last came news of young Ralph's appointment to a good position on a coffee plantation in Ceylon, and before leaving home he determined to speak to Mr. Falconer concerning his love for Madge; but though, after the confession was duly made, the young girl's father did not absolutely prohibit her entertaining the idea of ultimate marriage with Ralph Morgan, he insisted that there should be no engagement, explicit or tacit, until she was of age, and in a better position to be sure of her sentiments. So the matter had to remain. Years passed, not without occasional correspondence, but slowly the love of the girl for her absent lover faded, though it did not quite pass away. A November was almost at hand — a November wherein Madge's twenty-first birthday would arrive; but before this family festival came round there was the still greater annual one of Halloween. In the midst of the fun of the evening a sudden fancy seized the youngest Miss Falconer. She had often heard of and laughed at the superstition of the Halloween mirror, as a looking-glass in a moonlit room on this night is called. As soon as she reached her bedroom she saw that one circumstance, at any rate, was favorable — a long moonbeam streamed in at a side window, and fell so near the looking-glass that in a minute or two it would shine right into it. Madge had brought the apple with her to munch before the glass, but she forgot all about this part of the ceremony as her thoughts brought back to her the memory of Ralph Morgan. She remembered, too, that her twenty-first birthday was almost at hand, and a sudden emotion of tenderness came over her as she thought of her absent lover and his long patience. She felt certain that he still hoped she would be his wife, but as for herself, she doubted much if she any longer loved him in return. As a matter of fact, a certain tender affection was all she experienced toward Ralph, the girlish passion having completely died away.

A burst of laughter from down-stairs brought Madge out of her reverie. She felt inclined to laugh at her own foolishness, and was just about to rejoin her friends without looking into the glass, when she suddenly yielded to an irresistible influence and passed rapidly toward it. She looked eagerly into it, but saw nothing save her own pale face and startled eyes. Suddenly she grew chill with horror as she distinctly saw another face close to her own — a face that she did not know, and of a type altogether different from that of Ralph Morgan; even in her sickening dread she noticed a peculiar scar over the right eyebrow, such as she had never seen in any one she had ever met. The next moment she fainted, and a little later her alarmed friends found her lying insensible on the floor. When she came round again she managed to pass the whole thing off as a stupid fright she had given herself when in an overexcited state, and in a short time every one except herself forgot all about the incident.

A few days after her birthday Madge received two letters from India — one from Ralph Morgan, who was now a partner in the Bombay branch of the firm, and one from an aunt, a Mrs. Martin, who resided in the same city. The former letter she fancied strangely cold, and she could not help feeling that Ralph was writing more out of duty than from affectionate impulse: the latter was an invitation to Madge to go and live with Mrs. Martin and her husband for a year, or for as long as she felt inclined. To make my friend's narrative as short as possible, I may briefly state that after much consideration Madge Falconer decided to accept her aunt's invitation, while she explained to Ralph Morgan that nothing could be decided until after they had met again. In due time she reached Bombay, but at the very first interview the two former lovers perceived that some radical change had taken place in each other. Before a month had elapsed Madge frankly told the young man that she could not marry him, and it was with real pleasure she learned that to Ralph also their mutual agreement was welcome. A few months later the latter married — Madge shrewdly suspecting that the young lady had been the main factor in Ralph's readiness to break off his long engagement.

But, before this marriage took place, Madge met at the house of her aunt a certain Major Colville. On their first meeting his face puzzled her greatly. She knew she had seen it before, but could not recollect where. Suddenly a memory flashed through her mind. On only one face had she ever seen such a scar as that over the right eyebrow of Major Colville — a scar which in the latter's case had been caused by a bullet in one of the battles during the Sikh war. It was with a strange and uncomfortable sense of something eerie that she remembered the face in the looking-glass last Hallowmas Eve: that face and the face of Major Colville were absolutely identical. Perhaps this strange fact predisposed the girl in the young major's favor. In any case, the result was that, not long after Ralph Morgan's marriage, Madge Falconer became Mrs. Colville.

This was the strange story told me by my friend; the names are altered, but the personages signified are all living. Madge was the narrator's own sister, and he informed me that even yet Mrs. Colville felt troubled at times at the mysterious event of that memorable Halloween.

Three Stories from
Ancient Legends, Mystic Charms, and Superstitions of Ireland

Lady Wilde, 1887

Lady Wilde (née Jane Francesca Elgee) was not only the mother of Oscar Wilde and the niece of the great Gothic novelist Charles Maturin (*Melmoth the Wanderer*), she was also an active supporter of Irish independence who wrote under the pen name "Speranza" and stirred considerable controversy when she called for armed revolution by the Irish.

In 1887 and 1890, respectively, she published the books *Ancient Legends, Mystic Charms, and Superstitions of Ireland*, and *Ancient Cures, Charms, and Usages in Ireland*. Later folk-lorists (including Douglas Hyde, whose collection *Beside the Fire* includes the Hallowe'en story "Guleesh na Guss dhu") have suggested that some of the content of the books may have been considerably supplemented by the author (since no sources are provided for any of the tales collected therein); however, even those experts who question the authenticity of the stories couldn't deny their charm.

Note how two of the three stories included here — "The Stolen Bride" and "November Eve" — refer to the holiday as "November Eve," while the third story, "The Dance of the Dead," implies that the fairies and the spirits of the dead dance for the entire month of November, and that it's the final day of that month that is most dangerous to mortals.

"The Stolen Bride"

About the year 1670 there was a fine young fellow living at a place called Querin, in the County Clare. He was brave and strong and rich, for he had his own land and his own house, and not one to lord it over him. He was called the Kern of Querin. And many a time he would go out alone to shoot the wild fowl at night along the lonely strand and sometimes cross over northward to the broad east strand, about two miles away, to find the wild geese.

One cold frosty November Eve he was watching for them, crouched down behind the ruins of an old hut, when a loud splashing noise attracted his attention. "It is the

75

A wild Hallowe'en dance is shown on an early postcard.

wild geese," he thought, and raising his gun, waited in death-like silence the approach of his victim.

But presently he saw a dark mass moving along the edge of the strand. And he knew there were no wild geese near him. So he watched and waited till the black mass came closer, and then he distinctly perceived four stout men carrying a bier on their shoulders, on which lay a corpse covered with a white cloth. For a few moments they laid it down, apparently to rest themselves, and the Kern instantly fired; on which the four men ran away shrieking, and the corpse was left alone on the bier. Kern of Querin immediately sprang to the place, and lifting the cloth from the face of the corpse, beheld by the freezing starlight, the form of a beautiful young girl, apparently not dead but in a deep sleep.

Gently he passed his hand over her face and raised her up, when she opened her eyes and looked around with wild wonder, but spake never a word, though he tried to soothe and encourage her. Then, thinking it was dangerous for them to remain in that place, he raised her from the bier, and taking her hand led her away to his own house. They arrived safely, but in silence. And for twelve months did she remain with the Kern, never tasting food or speaking word for all that time.

When the next November Eve came round, he resolved to visit the east strand again, and watch from the same place, in the hope of meeting with some adventure that might throw light on the history of the beautiful girl. His way lay beside the old ruined fort called *Lios-na-fallainge* (the Fort of the Mantle), and as he passed, the sound of music and mirth fell on his ear. He stopped to catch the words of the voices, and had not waited long when he heard a man say in a low whisper —

"Where shall we go to-night to carry off a bride?"

And a second voice answered —

"Wherever we go I hope better luck will be ours than we had this day twelve-months."

"Yes," said a third; "on that night we carried off a rich prize, the fair daughter of O'Connor; but that clown, the Kern of Querin, broke our spell and took her from us. Yet little pleasure has he had of his bride, for she has neither eaten nor drank nor uttered a word since she entered his house."

"And so she will remain," said a fourth, "until he makes her eat off her father's table-cloth, which covered her as she lay on the bier, and which is now thrown up over the top of her bed."

On hearing all this, the Kern rushed home, and without waiting even for the morning, entered the young girl's room, took down the table-cloth, spread it on the table, laid meat and drink thereon, and led her to it. "Drink," he said, "that speech may come to you." And she drank, and ate of the food, and then speech came. And she told the Kern her story—how she was to have been married to a young lord of her own country, and the wedding guests had all assembled, when she felt herself suddenly ill and swooned away, and never knew more of what had happened to her until the Kern had passed his hand over her face, by which she recovered consciousness, but could neither eat nor speak, for a spell was on her, and she was helpless.

Then the Kern prepared a chariot, and carried home the young girl to her father, who was like to die for joy when he beheld her. And the Kern grew mightily in O'Connor's favour, so that at last he gave him his fair young daughter to wife; and the wedded pair lived together happily for many long years after, and no evil befell them, but good followed all the work of their hands.

This story of Kern of Querin still lingers in the faithful, vivid Irish memory, and is often told by the peasants of Clare when they gather round the fire on the awful festival of *Samhain*, or November Eve, when the dead walk, and the spirits of earth and air have power over mortals, whether for good or evil.

"November Eve"

It is esteemed a very wrong thing amongst the islanders to be about on November Eve, minding any business, for the fairies have their flitting then, and do not like to be seen, or watched; and all the spirits come to meet them and help them. But mortal people should keep at home, or they will suffer for it; for the souls of the dead have power over all things on that one night of the year; and they hold a festival with the fairies, and drink red wine from the fairy cups, and dance to fairy music till the moon goes down.

There was a man of the village who stayed out late one November Eve fishing, and never thought of the fairies until he saw a great number of dancing lights, and a crowd of people hurrying past with baskets and bags, and all laughing and singing and making merry as they went along.

"You are a merry set," he said, "where are ye all going to?"

"We are going to the fair," said a little old man with a cocked hat and a gold band round it. "Come with us, Hugh King, and you will have the finest food and the finest drink you ever set eyes upon."

"And just carry this basket for me," said a little red-haired woman.

So Hugh took it, and went with them till they came to the fair, which was filled with a crowd of people he had never seen on the island in all his days. And they danced and laughed and drank red wine from little cups. And there were pipers, and harpers, and little cobblers mending shoes, and all the most beautiful things in the world to eat and drink, just as if they were in a king's palace. But the basket was very heavy, and Hugh longed to drop it, that he might go and dance with a little beauty with long yellow hair, that was laughing up close to his face.

"Well, here put down the basket," said the red-haired woman, "for you are quite tired, I see;" and she took it and opened the cover, and out came a little old man, the ugliest, most misshapen little imp that could be imagined.

"Ah, thank you, Hugh," said the imp, quite politely; "you have carried me nicely; for I am weak on the limbs — indeed I have nothing to speak of in the way of legs: but I'll pay you well, my fine fellow; hold out your two hands," and the little imp poured down gold and gold and gold into them, bright golden guineas. "Now go," said he, "and drink my health, and make yourself quite pleasant, and don't be afraid of anything you see and hear."

So they all left him, except the man with the cocked hat and the red sash round his waist.

"Wait here now a bit," says he, "for Finvarra, the king, is coming, and his wife, to see the fair."

As he spoke, the sound of a horn was heard, and up drove a coach and four white horses, and out of it stepped a grand, grave gentleman all in black and a beautiful lady with a silver veil over her face.

"Here is Finvarra himself and the queen," said the little old man; but Hugh was ready to die of fright when Finvarra asked —

"What brought this man here?"

And the king frowned and looked so black that Hugh nearly fell to the ground with fear. Then they all laughed, and laughed so loud that everything seemed shaking and tumbling down from the laughter. And the dancers came up, and they all danced round Hugh, and tried to take his hands to make him dance with them.

"Do you know who these people are; and the men and women who are dancing round you?" asked the old man. "Look well, have you ever seen them before?"

And when Hugh looked he saw a girl that had died the year before, then another and another of his friends that he knew had died long ago; and then he saw that all the dancers, men, women, and girls, were the dead in their long, white shrouds. And he tried to escape from them, but could not, for they coiled round him, and danced and laughed and seized his arms, and tried to draw him into the dance, and their laugh seemed to pierce through his brain and kill him. And he fell down before them there, like one faint from sleep, and knew no more till he found himself next morning lying within the old stone circle by the fairy rath on the hill. Still it was all true that he had been with the fairies; no one could deny it, for his arms were all black with the touch of the hands of the dead, the time they had tried to draw him into the dance; but not one bit of all the red gold, which the little imp had given him, could he find in his pocket. Not one single golden piece; it was all gone for evermore.

And Hugh went sadly to his home, for now he knew that the spirits had mocked him and punished him, because he troubled their revels on November Eve — that one night of all the year when the dead can leave their graves and dance in the moonlight on the hill, and mortals should stay at home and never dare to look on them.

"The Dance of the Dead"

It is especially dangerous to be out late on the last night of November, for it is the closing scene of the revels — the last night when the dead have leave to dance on the hill with the fairies, and after that they must all go back to their graves and lie in the chill, cold earth, without music or wine till the next November comes round, when they all spring up again in their shrouds and rush out into the moonlight with mad laughter.

One November night, a woman of Shark Island, coming home late at the hour of the dead, grew tired and sat down to rest, when presently a young man came up and talked to her.

"Wait a bit," he said, "and you will see the most beautiful dancing you ever looked on there by the side of the hill."

And she looked at him steadily. He was very pale, and seemed sad.

"Why are you so sad?" she asked, "and as pale as if you were dead?"

"Look well at me," he answered. "Do you not know me?"

"Yes, I know you now," she said. "You are young Brien that was drowned last year when out fishing. What are you here for?"

"Look," he said, "at the side of the hill and you will see why I am here."

And she looked, and saw a great company dancing to sweet music; and amongst them were all the dead who had died as long as she could remember — men, women, and children, all in white, and their faces were pale as the moonlight.

"Now," said the young man, "run for your life; for if once the fairies bring you into the dance you will never be able to leave them any more."

But while they were talking, the fairies came up and danced round her in a circle, joining their hands. And she fell to the ground in a faint, and knew no more till she woke up in the morning in her own bed at home. And they all saw that her face was pale as the dead, and they knew that she had got the fairy-stroke. So the herb doctor was sent for, and every measure tried to save her, but without avail, for just as the moon rose that night, soft, low music was heard round the house, and when they looked at the woman she was dead.

"Elsie's Hallowe'en Experience"

Mary D. Brine, 1888

"Elsie's Hallowe'en Experience" is both the title of a long short story and the 1888 book it appears in. The collection, by children's author Mary D. Brine, centers around stories involving various times of year, and it probably says something about Halloween's popularity by 1888 that this title was used to represent the entire book (sadly the cover doesn't tie into Halloween, with the possible exception of surrounding a girl's portrait with notably orange tulips!). This little tale is also one of the earliest examples of a children's story centering on Halloween; just over fifty years after "Elsie's," Halloween stories for children would become an entire cottage industry.

"Elsie's Hallowe'en Experience" is presented here in its entirety, despite a lengthy middle section in which three children recite poems that have little to do with the holiday.

Elsie stood beside her mother one afternoon — restlessly twining and untwining her small fingers, as she watched with earnest, imploring eyes her mother's smiling face. And what was mamma smiling about, do you think? Let us read with her the note which had just come to Elsie, and which the little girl had joyfully, and yet so anxiously, placed in mamma's hand.

It was written by a little schoolmate who, having moved a short distance out of the city, now lived in a large old-fashioned country house. Here is the note:

"DEAR ELSIE: We're going to have such fun! Mamma says Mamie and I may have lots of nuts and apples and candy and things on Hallowe'en night, and play games, and we have asked Johnny and Willie Green, our cousins, you know, to come and stay a few days with us, and mamma says we may ask *you* to come and stay all night, for papa says he'll take you safely home next day. Do *coax* your mother to let you come; mamma says she'll take good care of you. You *must, must*, MUST come. We'll go to the depot to meet you by the noon train, so don't stay away and disappoint us.

"Your loving
"BESS."

Now how could Elsie's mamma help smiling over such an earnest, eager little note of invitation as that! Of course she knew what a good time Elsie would have. She didn't forget that she had been a "little girlie" herself once on a time (it didn't seem so very long ago, either), and had attended Hallowe'en frolics too.

May you have good luck on Hallow e'en.

Children play a Hallowe'en fortune-telling game by seeing how many candles they can blow out in one breath (1912 postcard).

But oh dear! there were so many things to be considered before she said "yes" to Elsie's coaxing.

Would Elsie be a *good* girl? Would she get lonely and homesick, after all, in a strange house so far away from her own mamma? Would she fall into any danger apart from mother's watchful care? And so on ran mamma's thoughts even while she read the note a second time, and Elsie's eyes grew more eager and wistful.

"Do, *do* let me go, mamma darling!" plead Elsie. "I'll be so good, and so happy! Do *please* say yes, dear sweet mamma?"

Well, maybe mamma thought it would be a good time to obey the "Golden Rule," and do as she would be done by were she in Elsie's place, you see. At any rate, she finally said "yes," and Elsie's little heart was in a tumult of joyous anticipation until the answer to her note was really written and mailed, and she felt sure mamma would not change her mind.

But at last the day came, and Elsie was, for the first time in her life, to travel quite alone, "like a real grown-up lady," as she proudly said; and prepared to be very dignified and *au fait* in her manners for the sake of the occasion.

Her little friend had been told the exact hour in which she would start, and had promised to be on hand promptly at the station in M-. So mamma put all anxious thoughts away as she prepared her little girl for the short journey.

"What is Hallowe'en, anyway, mamma?" questioned Elsie, as her mother brushed out the curls on the restless little head.

"It is the vigil of Hallowmas, or 'All Saints' Day,' dear," replied her mother, "and is a relic of pagan times, when people were given to superstitious, heathenish ideas and notions, and were great believers in mysterious rites and ceremonies. The Scotch people of old times kept to the custom of celebrating Hallowe'en, and fancied it to be a night when fairies were unusually active, and spirits walked about. In the North of England it is called 'nut-crack night.' There's really nothing in it at all, but like many of those queer ancient customs it hangs on as years go by, and has become a sort of institution now, as they call it,—a night devoted to fun and all sorts of frolic, as your little friends will probably show you."

Elsie had listened to this so attentively that she had never once jerked her head, or wriggled about as mamma was getting rid of the tangles, and so that part of her toilet was quickly finished.

"I ain't afraid of ghosts," declared Elsie stoutly. "There ain't such things anyway. Ghosteses don't have feet and so they can't walk, and if they can't walk, they can't *run*, and if they can't *run*, they can't catch folks, and who's going to be 'fraid of things that can't catch you."

"No doubt you'll be very brave," laughed mamma; "but come, we must hurry now; it is almost time to go to the depot."

Well, we needn't describe Elsie's ride to the depot, nor linger over the sudden lonely feeling which possessed her when finally mamma kissed her good-by, and stepped out upon the platform, waving her handkerchief as the train began to move, until presently Elsie found herself whizzing rapidly past the fences and buildings, speeding on and on towards the little friends who were expecting her. In one little hour and half of another she would reach M-station; but Elsie considered it a very dreadful length of time to be journeying along, and in spite of her dignified intentions she felt much inclined to cry.

Nevertheless the train sped on, and before Elsie had fully decided whether she should cry or not, lo and behold! the conductor called out "M-," and there were Bess and Mamie and Johnny and Willie, all on the platform awaiting her, and shouting her name at the top of their lungs. Oh, how happy she was then! and what a merry time she had going in the pretty wagonette to the house of her friends. Johnny and Willie were not a bit bashful, so they made friends with her right off, and Mrs. Brown, Bessie's mamma, was on the piazza waiting to welcome her.

The rest of the day was delightful for Elsie.

Mrs. Brown let the children do as they pleased, and by and by when twilight came they gathered about her for a story.

"Ah, no!" she said, laughing, "it is only fair that you should take your turn in amusing *me*, now. I've played with you youngsters all the afternoon, and now I'm tired out, and must be amused myself a little. Come, Johnny, tell me a story; don't you know something nice?"

Johnny blushed. "I don't know a story, ma'am," he said finally, blushing still more at feeling himself to be the main point of interest just at that moment, "but I guess I can recite a poem that's got Elsie's name in it. I recited it at school once, an' it's real jolly; shall I say it?"

"By all means," said Mrs. Brown, leaning comfortably back in her chair, and stroking Elsie's hand in both hers, for she feared the little girl would be getting homesick.

So Johnny pulled his jacket down smooth, tossed his hair from his forehead, stood up, coughed a little from embarrassment, and began.

THE FAIRY STORY

She carried her book to the river bank,
And there 'neath a spreading tree,

She thought, "I will read a fairy tale,
   And no one may hinder me."
She sat her down amid fern and brake,
   And tangled grasses wild growing,
Where down from the hills the autumn winds
   Were ever merrily blowing.
She opened her book, and the pages glowed
   With a tale all weird and new,
And many a picture lay therein
   In colors of every hue.
But Elsie had caught the song of birds
   And she lifted her soft blue eyes
To follow the flash of skimming wings
   Far up to the azure skies.
The breezes flustered and rustled past,
   And the sunbeams downward glancing,
Bathed themselves in the river's breast,
   And over the field went dancing.
The slender brown wasps came wandering by,
   The fat bees hid in the clover,
And the world — so far as Elsie could see —
   Seemed fair, as she looked it over.
The distant mountains, how blue they were!
   And down by the steep hillside
How wonderfully the shadows played,
   And the sunshine loved to glide;
And down beneath the ripples so bright
   Lay shadows cool and green,
While over them all the river flowed
   All bright in its silver sheen.
Adown the tide the white-winged ships
   Sailed slowly one by one,
And — Elsie started! The western sky
   Gleamed gold with the setting sun.
While all unread was the fairy tale
   In the book upon her knees,
And all unnoticed, how long had stretched
   The shadows beneath the trees.
"And how did you like your story, dear?"
   I asked, when after awhile,
My girlie came and stood by me.
   She answered me with a smile
And a long-drawn breath, — "It was not in my *book*
   That the fairy story lay,
But oh! mamma! it was *all around*,

And written in all the day.
For everything that my eyes could see
    Seemed wonderful, strange, and new,
And tho' 'twas all *like* a fairy tale,
    I liked it *because it was true.*
And I quite forgot in my *book* to read,
    As I watched *God's* story, you know,
And I never guessed how easy it is
    To read stories in things that grow.
There wasn't a picture in all my book
    So beautiful, gay and bright
As the *red-gold leaves on the trees* around
    All bathed in the glad sunlight.
There wasn't a story in all my book
    Could have been so sweet to me
As the story that God was telling me,
    As I sat there under the tree,"
Thus Elsie, down by the river bank —
    Her story-book all unheeding —
While *watching the landscape*, the *best of all*
    Sweet fairy stories was reading.

When Johnny had finished his recitation, he bowed and sat down amidst clapping of hands, and much pleasure expressed by his small audience.

"Now, Willie, it's your turn," said mamma; "come, think up something nice for us."

Willie declared he couldn't think of anything, and looked so shy that Elsie quite pitied him.

"Oh, yes, you do know something, Will," cried Johnny. "Say that thing gran'pa gave you a quarter for learning one day."

"Ho, that's only 'bout tangles," replied Willie; "no one wants to hear 'bout tangles!"

"Oh, yes, Willie dear," urged Bessie, "do please tell us about it. I hate tangles 'cause they pull in your hair so, an' don't they hurt!"

"That's why gran'pa made me learn 'bout 'em," said Willie, looking up with interest as Bessie spoke. "So I'll say it if you really want me to."

Then he straightened his jacket just as Johnny had done, and stood up to recite.

THOSE TANGLES.

Oh! those tangles, don't they pull!
    Never mind! who cares?
There are other tangles, boy,
    Worse than tangled hairs.
Now when *I* was young, you know,
    Grandma used to say —
Life was like a youngster's head,

Getting snarled each day.
I've grown old, and yet that truth
   To my mind still clings.
For indeed this world's a place
   Full of tangled things:
Tangled notions, tangled ways,
   Tangled habits, too,
And oh, what patience does it need
   To *comb those tangles through!*

Pull? Well, yes, and hurt as well.
   They set the world to crying,
For mother Nature's comb is fine,
   That fact there's no denying —
But *patience*, boys, as you will see,
   In time, must smooth away
The worst of tangles wheresoe'er
   They cluster day by day.
So now my sermon's finished, and
   I've worked away so fast,
That here's this curly head of yours
   All smoothed from snarl at last.
And just remember there are things
   Far worse than *tangled hairs*,
So when they pull, why never mind,
   But bravely say, "Who cares?"

"Well," said Mrs. Brown, when Willie had finished and seated himself, "I think there's a good deal of sound sense in that rhyme, but seems to me the writer of the poem might have mentioned some of the best kinds of combs for smoothing away those tangles. There are other kinds of combs save that of 'Patience,' but we won't have a sermon now. Come, Elsie, let us hear from you. Why, I'm having a splendid time, and being amused beautifully. You shall have some fun this evening to pay for all this. Elsie, dear, what have *you* for us?"

Elsie took *her* turn at blushing, and felt as though she could never stand up and be looked at and be listened to. But mamma had taught her little girl to be willing and obliging, and when she was *able* to do a thing asked of her, always to try her best in the doing. So she said timidly, "I only know a little poem mamma read me once that belonged to a lovely picture of a little bit of a girl with curly hair, and a white dress on, standing in the corner with tears in her eyes, and her little sweet face all sorrowful. And she had one little arm up by her head, and she looked so unhappy, and all alone by herself leaning against the wall in the corner. She had been naughty, and the picture was called 'Confession.' Mamma said it had big words in it — in the poem, I mean — for a little girl to learn, but, oh, I just *loved* the picture, and I coaxed mamma to teach me the verses, and — when I'd learned 'em, what do you think! papa was so proud of me he gave me a big shining silver dollar!"

"Quite right of papa, too," laughed Mrs. Brown, as she watched the shining stars that served as eyes in Elsie's head; "and now let us hear the poem, dearie, maybe it will have a little lesson in it for all of us, who get so naughty sometimes," looking around her with a twinkle in her eyes, and laughing again to see Bessie blush up all of a sudden. Bessie, her troublesome little daughter, who was always getting into scrapes, and repenting faults so often.

So Elsie mustered courage and stood up beside Mrs. Brown, and swallowing a few timid little lumps in her throat, she began.

THE CONFESSION.

She had been naughty; the dear little heart
    Was timid and tired with pain
And begged for the mother-love tender and true,
    To comfort and cheer it again.
Slowly the hours of the daylight had passed,
Down fell the shadows of twilight at last,
And tears in her young eyes were gathering fast,
    While friends offered comfort in vain.

She had been naughty; mamma's little girl
    Had grieved the dear love that was best,
And over the shine of the beautiful day
    Had fallen the cloud of unrest.
What though her playmates were merry, since she
At peace with her own wilful heart could not be?
No wonder the sobs came pitifully,
    While sorrow was still unconfessed.

But presently slipped little Edna away
    In search of the heart ever true,
Whose love and whose tenderness waited for her
    All full of forgiveness, she knew.
"I'm sorry, mamma! love me! love me again!
My heart's full of lumps an' it's got *such a pain*!"
And over her cheeks fell the tear-drops like rain,
    From the sorrowful eyes so blue.

Oh! the sweet peace of forgiveness conferred;
    The infinite peace and rest!
Oh, bountiful love that endureth through all!
    Oh, hearts so tenderly blest!
We may strive as we will when a wrong we have done,
Forgetting our error, contrition to shun;
But the peace and the comfort never are won
    Till we turn to the Saviour's breast,

And telling our sorrow with many a tear
    Cry "Love me, dear Father, again,"

And close to His heart, as we trustingly lean,
  Lose all the regret and the pain.
For dearer than mother-love, strong though it be,
Is the love of "the Father," for you and for me,
And the sweetest of comforters always is He,
  Whose children ne'er seek Him in vain.

Mrs. Brown drew Elsie to her and kissed her fondly.

"Very well recited, dear," she said, "and a nice little poem, though rather old for little tongues to trip through. And now it is tea time or I should expect Bess and Mamie to do their share. There's the bell now." So she arose and the children followed her down to the dining-room.

After the meal was finished, "Now, nurse," said mamma, "papa and I are going to a neighbor's for a little while, and I want you to help these little folks have as merry a time as possible, bobbing apples, cracking nuts, and listening to your wonderful stories. But at half-past nine, I want them all snug in bed, remember, for we expect to return with a party of friends, and take *our* turn at a good time."

Nurse Janet, who was also the faithful old housekeeper, and who loved "her lady's bairns," with all her honest old heart, promised to fulfil all commands, and as soon as her mistress had departed, she placed the tub half full of water in the middle of the kitchen floor, emptied some rosy-cheeked apples into it, and bade the children "bob" for them while she attended to some few duties before joining them again.

Alas! when all bade fair to be so pleasant and happy, why need a quarrel have stepped in to mar the Hallowe'en night so sadly?

But so it was, and this is how it came about: Johnny had bobbed for his apple and succeeded in bringing the biggest one out after all. Then came Willie's turn, and the mischievous Johnny could not resist the sly shove which sent his unsuspecting brother over head and shoulders in the large and well-filled tub of water, from which Willie immediately lifted himself, a dripping, spluttering, boy, vowing revenge on Johnny, and shaking the drops off of him in all directions.

"I shan't speak a word more to you tonight," cried he, and Johnny replied:

"Nor I to you! such a mean boy to get mad over a little trick!"

"'*Twasn't* a little trick! it was a great big trick and I'm all over wet and horrid! an' you're the meanest I ever saw, so now!"

"Ain't half so mean as you, an' you're a silly! so now!" retorted Johnny, angrily enough, while the little girls stood by with distressed faces, and troubled hearts, and wished nurse Janet would come.

So the two little brothers, usually so loyal and so devoted to each other, turned apart with sullen looks and angry feelings, and when nurse Janet came, she found everything wrong side up, and gloomy enough in her bright cheery kitchen. She hastily emptied the tub, and suggested a new game. But while the spirits of anger walked about so freely in the hearts of Willie and Johnny, no games seemed very pleasant, and Elsie began to wish she had not come.

"Come on, noo, an' I'll tell ye stories," said Janet, at last, hoping to dispel the cloud of discord that had settled down upon the group.

HALLOWE'EN GREETINGS

Bobbing for apples (from an early postcard).

So she led them all into the large nursery room, where the shadows of the October night were lightened only by the fitful flames of the wood-fire on the broad old-fashioned hearth.

"Ain't we going to have any lamps?" asked Johnny.

"I just *hate* dark rooms."

"Hoot, laddie! do ye call this dark, with the beautiful firelight on your faces?" reproved Janet, and Willie, whose conscience was not very clear, as we know, whispered to Elsie that "he hated dark places, too."

"Noo, me bairns," said nurse, "sit ye here in a row," placing chairs before the fire, and seating herself near.

Willie and Johnny, still bitter foes, refused to sit next each other (though they were known as "the boy lovers" amongst their friends, so devoted and fond of each other they always had been, sharing alike, and refusing to be separated at any time, either for pain or pleasure. But this was a serious thing which had come between the little brothers, and no doubt it was because Johnny had played his naughty, yet playful trick *before the girls*, that Willie felt so resentful about a matter which at another time he would have laughed about), and so Elsie was seated between them, like "a rose between two thorns," quoted Janet grimly, and with good sense, for oh! how very prickly and thorny were the little boys then!

Then the stories began. Ghostly weird stories which the old Scotch Janet delighted to tell. Funny stories, sad stories, all kinds of stories in fact, which we haven't time to read about here, and the children peered about the shadowy room with awe-struck faces, and clasped each other's hands, while the woman's low, thrilling voice set afloat in their imagination all kinds of odd shapes and fancies.

"An' it's weel known, too," she continued, "that there's always good fairies hoverin' aboot on this night, ready to grant any favor we may want to ask, an' make us feel good when things are vexin' us, an' wearyin' the spirits of us. An' I'll tell ye how to make the charm work," she said, a twinkle in her eyes which the children didn't happen to notice, or they might have suspected that she was making fun of them.

"You must gang along to a dark room, where only the light o' the moon comes in, an' that light must shine on a lookin' glass. Ye must stand before the glass an' make a wish for somethin' ye'll be wantin' very much, an' it'll surely come to pass."

"Oh, I'd be afraid to do that," cried Mamie, and Bess laughed at her.

"I wouldn't, would you, Elsie?" she asked.

Elsie shivered a little, and shook her head.

"We're only girls," she said, "and girls ought to be 'fraider than boys. I guess Johnny ain't afraid, a bit, nor Willie either," with a look at the boys and the secret desire that one of them would prove her words to be true. She did so want to see it done.

Bessie's nose went up high. "Pooh! Willie an' Johnny are the cowardest boys you ever saw! They're dreadful scared in the dark. I'm a girl, but I'm braver than they are!"

Johnny's face reddened.

"You ain't either, Bess Brown,' he cried. "I ain't 'fraid of a thing!"

"Weel, then, laddie, s'pose ye try the charm. Sure there's some wish in your heart ye'll be wantin' the fairies to grant for ye?"

That was all true. There was a wish in Johnny's heart, and also in Willie's, that each wanted should be granted. But both were timid, and Janet's hobgoblin stories had made them more so just now. But when Bessie finally declared "she was going to shame the boys an' do it herself," Johnny sprang from his seat, and nerved himself to courage.

"I'll just show you, Bess Brown, you can't say *I'm* a coward, if Will is. I'll go, but —" turning to Janet, "where'll I go to?"

"Gang along wi' ye to the big front spare room, where the moon'll be sure to be shinin' on the glass by the bureau. An' be sure your wish'll be a *good* one, bairn, or it won't be comin' true."

So Johnny reluctantly shuffled along the hall, and found himself presently within the "spare room," through the windows of which the big round moon was peeping with a great light from her eyes. Johnny shuddered and turned back as if he meant to fly back to the protection of his friends, but afraid of Bessie's laughter, he nerved himself and went bravely through the shadows towards the large mirror upon which the moonbeams were lying in broad patches.

Meanwhile Willie, not to be outdone, had volunteered to go alone to a room also, and nurse bade him take the room next to where Johnny had gone. So he started as bold as a lion till he reached the dark hall through which Johnny had passed.

Tremblingly he turned the knob of the door and entered the room to which as he supposed he had been directed. As he crept in and looked towards the glass, he heard a voice which was saying, "Good fairy, I wish to be friends with my brother, but he won't speak to me. Make him want to be friends with me again."

Willie stood amazed. Why that was what *he* had come to say, and by some mistake he had entered the wrong room, and had caught Johnny making his wish. And then suddenly Johnny turned and saw him, and with a sudden impulse born of timidity, and joy at being alone together, the little fellows ran into each other's arms, and with, "Hello, Johnny," "Hello, Will!" the quarrel was ended.

"You were wishin' jus' what *I* came to wish," said Will, as they ran together through the dark hall back to the other children.

"I'm glad we tried the fairies," was John's reply, and then they burst in before the children together with a loud whoop!

Janet looked up and laughed. "Ay, lads, I can see noo that the spell has worked, an' the fairies have been good to ye."

"H'm, I guess the thing would have worked all right in the light room, without any fairies, if we fellers had had any chance," said Will. "I don't much believe in fairies. Girls do — but boys only *fun*, when they say they do, don't they, Johnny?"

"Yes, of course they do," was the latter's reply, and Janet was content to twinkle her eyes and laugh secretly on the success of her ruse. Well, after that there were nuts and apples, and games, and then, all too soon, came the bed hour. Janet, mindful of her mistress's orders, had her little flock safe in the fold of each snug bed before the mother, father, and friends came in to fill the parlor, and have a share of the Hallowe'en.

Mamie and Bessie in their own little room were presently fast asleep. Willie and Johnny in the room above, slumbered also, as boys do. But Elsie, alone in a strange bed, and strange room, which, though it adjoined the smaller room where Bess and Mamie were lying asleep — still seemed so lonely and far off from everybody — could not sleep, try though she did, to keep her eyes shut tight, and let herself slide into dreamland.

She turned from side to side, and saw in the darkness which only the faint starlight coming in at the window dispelled, all kinds of goblins and forms floating about near the ceiling. She grew frightened, as any little girl under those circumstances would, and sleep was further and further away from her, though the clock on the mantel had just chimed the hour of twelve.

Suddenly Elsie heard a noise, only a slight one, but yet a decided noise which proceeded from the closet at the far end of the room. She strained her poor little tired eyes in that direction, and finally sat up in bed, trembling from head to foot.

Yes, there was no doubt about it. The closet door moved ajar a very little. Then a scratching sound followed, and the door opened still a little more. Elsie's eyes were riveted upon it with terrible fascination. She tried to call Bessie, but had no power to make a sound. Wider and wider the door seemed to open, and yet no form appeared. The scratching was heard plainly, but the presence of the cause was invisible. "Oh it is, it *is* a ghost!" thought our poor little Elsie, quite forgetful of her former assertion that because "ghosts hadn't legs and couldn't catch folks, there was no need to be afraid of 'em."

But Elsie's assertion had been made in broad daylight, and here in a dark room, away from mamma, and in a strange bed, it was all a very different matter, you see, and Elsie was just at this minute a very firm believer in ghosts, with or without feet. With one strong effort she found her voice, and used it in a loud scream of terror, as bounding from the bed she flew down the staircase and darted, little white-robed figure as she was, right into the parlor where Mrs. Brown was entertaining her guests. How everybody started as she rushed in amongst them, clinging to Bessie's mother, and begging to be taken to her own mamma! How quickly Bessie and Mamie, in their little night-robes also, followed Elsie to the parlor!

There was a great time, you may be sure, and when Elsie realized that she had made her appearance before so many strangers in such negligé, she was overcome with dismay, though Bess and Mamie whispered that as *they* didn't care, she needn't. Mrs. Brown led the children from the parlor and up the stairs, and how they all laughed when they met the "ghost" walking down to meet them. Only the big black cat which had in some way been shut in the closet of Elsie's room, and little by little had worked her way out.

But all the same poor little Elsie had been wofully frightened, and for the rest of the night her big bed was shared by Bessie and Mamie, and when the morning sunbeams awakened the trio, Elsie gave a laugh of delight because she knew she was going home very soon to her own dear mother, where black cats and ghost stories were not allowed to frighten and make little girls of her age nervous.

That night while sitting on papa's knee, by her "ain fireside," she told him all about her Hallowe'en visit and experience, and slipped her hand into mamma's with a sense of solid comfort and safety.

She owns a little black kitten now which was sent her one day, not long after, by Bessie, and which is the son of the black pussie that frightened her so on that Hallowe'en night.

She named her kitten "Ghostie,"—not a pretty name, but then the kitten is a "souvenir," you know.

"Guleesh na Guss dhu"

From *Beside the Fire: A Collection of Irish Gaelic Folk Stories,* adapted by Douglas Hyde, 1890

Douglas Hyde was a folklorist and language professor who also served as Ireland's first president. His 1890 classic *Beside the Fire* is a collection of orally-transmitted Irish Gaelic folk-tales, about half of which had appeared in his earlier volume *Leabhar Sgeuluigheachta.* "Guleesh na Guss dhu" ("Guleesh Black-foot") was told to Hyde by two different Irish gentlemen (Shamus O'Hart and Martin Brennan); however, in his notes to the book he states that this tale was somewhat unusual. "The story of Guleesh appears to be a very rare one. I have never been able to find a trace of it outside the locality (near where the counties of Sligo, Mayo, and Roscommon meet) in which I first heard it."

"Guleesh na Guss dhu" is a lengthy and playful tale that begins and ends on November Night, and, like another traditional Hallowe'en tale, "The Stolen Bride," features a leading lady who is speechless until the hero listens to the fairies and learns how to break their curse. It's also worth noting that Guleesh himself was born on Hallowe'en, which ties in with legends that suggest special abilities or powers (such as second sight) for those children born on this day.

There was once a boy in the County Mayo, and he never washed a foot from the day he was born. Guleesh was his name; but as nobody could ever prevail on him to wash his feet, they used to call him Guleesh na guss dhu, or Guleesh Black-foot. It's often the father said to him: "Get up, you *strone-sha* (lubber), and wash yourself," but the devil a foot would he get up, and the devil a foot would he wash. There was no use in talking to him. Every one used to be humbugging him on account of his dirty feet, but he paid them no heed nor attention. You might say anything at all to him, but in spite of it all he would have his own way afterwards.

One night the whole family were gathered in by the fire, telling stories and making fun for themselves, and he amongst them. The father said to him: "Guleesh, you are one and twenty years old to-night, and I believe you never washed a foot from the day you were born till to-day."

"You lie," said Guleesh, "didn't I go a' swimming on May day last? and I couldn't keep my feet out of the water."

Young girl apparently about to fall under a malevolent Hallowe'en spell (1911 postcard).

"Well, they were as dirty as ever they were when you came to the shore," said the father.

"They were that, surely," said Guleesh.

"That's the thing I'm saying," says the father, "that it wasn't in you to wash your feet ever."

"And I never will wash them till the day of my death," said Guleesh.

"You miserable *behoonugh*! you clown! you tinker! you good-for-nothing lubber! what kind of answer is that?" says the father; and with that he drew the hand and struck him a hard fist on the jaw. "Be off with yourself;" says he, "I can't stand you any longer."

Guleesh got up and put a hand to his jaw, where he got the fist. "Only that it's yourself that's in it, who gave me that blow," said he, "another blow you'd never strike till the day of your death." He went out of the house then and great anger on him.

There was the finest *lis*, or rath, in Ireland, a little way off from the gable of the house, and he was often in the habit of seating himself on the fine grass bank that was running round it. He stood, and he half leaning against the gable of the house, and looking up into the sky, and watching the beautiful white moon over his head. After him to be standing that way for a couple of hours, he said to himself: "My bitter grief that I am not gone away out of this place altogether. I'd sooner be any place in the world than here. Och, it's well for you, white moon," says he, "that's turning round, turning round, as you please yourself, and no man can put you back. I wish I was the same as you."

Hardly was the word out of his mouth when he heard a great noise coming like the sound of many people running together, and talking, and laughing, and making sport, and the sound went by him like a whirl of wind, and he was listening to it going into the rath. "Musha, by my soul," says he, "but ye're merry enough, and I'll follow ye."

What was in it but the fairy host, though he did not know at first that it was they who were in it, but he followed them into the rath. It's there he heard *the fulparnee, and the folpornee, the rap-lay-hoota, and the roolya-boolya*,[1] that they had there, and every man of them crying out as loud as he could: "My horse, and bridle and saddle! My horse, and bridle, and saddle!"

"By my hand," said Guleesh, "my boy, that's not bad. I'll imitate ye," and he cried out as well as they: "My horse, and bridle, and saddle! My horse, and bridle, and saddle!" And on the moment there was a fine horse with a bridle of gold, and a saddle of silver, standing before him. He leaped up on it, and the moment he was on its back he saw clearly that the rath was full of horses, and of little people going riding on them.

Said a man of them to him: "Are you coming with us to-night, Guleesh?"

"I am, surely," said Guleesh.

"If you are, come along," said the little man, and out with them altogether, riding like the wind, faster than the fastest horse ever you saw a' hunting, and faster than the fox and the hounds at his tail.

The cold winter's wind that was before them, they overtook her, and the cold winter's wind that was behind them, she did not overtake them. And stop nor stay of that full race, did they make none, until they came to the brink of the sea.

Then every one of them said: "Hie over cap! Hie over cap!" and that moment they

1. Untranslatable onomatopaeic words expressive of noises.

were up in the air, and before Guleesh had time to remember where he was, they were down on dry land again, and were going like the wind. At last they stood, and a man of them said to Guleesh: "Guleesh, do you know where you are now?"

"Not a know," says Guleesh.

"You're in Rome, Guleesh," said he; "but we're going further than that. The daughter of the king of France is to be married to-night, the handsomest woman that the sun ever saw, and we must do our best to bring her with us, if we're only able to carry her off; and you must come with us that we may be able to put the young girl up behind you on the horse, when we'll be bringing her away, for it's not lawful for us to put her sitting behind ourselves. But you're flesh and blood, and she can take a good grip of you, so that she won't fall off the horse. Are you satisfied, Guleesh, and will you do what we're telling you?"

"Why shouldn't I be satisfied?" said Guleesh. "I'm satisfied, surely, and anything that ye will tell me to do I'll do it without doubt; but where are we now?"

"You're in Rome now, Guleesh," said the sheehogue (fairy).

"In Rome, is it?" said Guleesh. "Indeed, and no lie, I'm glad of that. The parish priest that we had he was broken (suspended) and lost his parish some time ago; I must go to the Pope till I get a bull from him that will put him back in his own place again."

"Oh, Guleesh," said the sheehogue, "you can't do that. You won't be let into the palace; and, anyhow, we can't wait for you, for we're in a hurry."

"As much as a foot, I won't go with ye," says Guleesh, "till I go to the Pope; but ye can go forward without me, if ye wish. I won't stir till I go and get the pardon of my parish priest."

"Guleesh, is it out of your senses you are? You can't go; and there's your answer for you now. I tell you, you can't go."

"Can't ye go on, and to leave me here after ye," said Guleesh, "and when ye come back can't ye hoist the girl up behind me?"

"But we want you at the palace of the king of France," said the sheehogue, "and you must come with us now."

"The devil a foot," said Guleesh, "till I get the priest's pardon; the honestest and the pleasantest man that's in Ireland."

Another sheehogue spoke then, and said:

"Don't be so hard on Guleesh. The boy's a kind boy, and he has a good heart; and as he doesn't wish to come without the Pope's bull, we must do our best to get it for him. He and I will go in to the Pope, and ye can wait here."

"A thousand thanks to you," said Guleesh. "I'm ready to go with you; for this priest, he was the sportingest and the pleasantest man in the world."

"You have too much talk, Guleesh," said the sheehogue, "but come along now. Get off your horse and take my hand."

Guleesh dismounted, and took his hand; and then the little man said a couple of words he did not understand, and before he knew where he was he found himself in the room with the Pope.

The Pope was sitting up late that night reading a book that he liked. He was sitting on a big soft chair, and his two feet on the chimney-board. There was a fine fire in the grate, and a little table standing at his elbow, and a drop of ishka-baha (eau-de-vie) and sugar on the little table*een*; and he never felt till Guleesh came up behind him.

"Now Guleesh," said the sheehogue, "tell him that unless he gives you the bull you'll set the room on fire; and if he refuses it to you, I'll spurt fire round about out of my mouth, till he thinks the place is really in a blaze, and I'll go bail he'll be ready enough then to give you the pardon."

Guleesh went up to him and put his hand on his shoulder. The Pope turned round, and when he saw Guleesh standing behind him he frightened up.

"Don't be afraid," said Guleesh, "we have a parish priest at home, and some thief told your honour a lie about him, and he was broken; but he's the decentest man ever your honour saw, and there's not a man, woman, or child in Ballynatoothach but's in love with him."

"Hold your tongue, you *bodach*," said the Pope. "Where are you from, or what brought you here? Haven't I a lock on the door?"

"I came in on the keyhole," says Guleesh, "and I'd be very much obliged to your honour if you'd do what I'm asking."

The Pope cried out: "Where are all my people? Where are my servants? Shamus! Shawn! I'm killed; I'm robbed."

Guleesh put his back to the door, the way he could not get out, and he was afraid to go near Guleesh, so he had no help for it, but had to listen to Guleesh's story; and Guleesh could not tell it to him shortly and plainly, for he was slow and coarse in his speaking, and that angered the Pope; and when Guleesh finished his story, he vowed that he never would give the priest his pardon; and he threatened Guleesh himself that he would put him to death for his shamelessness in coming in upon him in the night; and he began again crying out for his servants. Whether the servants heard him or no, there was a lock on the inside of the door, so that they could not come in to him.

"Unless you give me a bull under your hand and seal, and the priest's pardon in it," said Guleesh; "I'll burn your house with fire."

The sheehogue, whom the Pope did not see, began to cast fire and flame out of his mouth, and the Pope thought that the room was all in a blaze. He cried out: "Oh, eternal destruction! I'll give you the pardon; I'll give you anything at all, only stop your fire, and don't burn me in my own house."

The sheehogue stopped the fire, and the Pope had to sit down and write a full pardon for the priest, and give him back his old place again, and when he had it ready written, he put his name under it on the paper, and put it into Guleesh's hand.

"Thank your honour," said Guleesh; "I never will come here again to you, and *bannacht lath* (goodbye)."

"Do not," said the Pope; "if you do I'll be ready before you, and you won't go from me so easily again. You will be shut up in a prison, and you won't get out for ever."

"Don't be afraid, I won't come again," said Guleesh. And before he could say any more the sheehogue spoke a couple of words, and caught Guleesh's hand again, and out with them. Guleesh found himself amongst the other sheehogues, and his horse waiting for him.

"Now, Guleesh," said they, "it's greatly you stopped us, and we in such a hurry; but come on now, and don't think of playing such a trick again, for we won't wait for you."

"I'm satisfied," said Guleesh, "and I'm thankful to ye; but tell me where are we going."

"We're going to the palace of the king of France," said they; "and if we can at all, we're to carry off his daughter with us."

Every man of them then said, "Rise up, horse;" and the horses began leaping, and running, and prancing. The cold wind of winter that was before them they overtook her, and the cold wind of winter that was behind them, she did not overtake them, and they never stopped of that race, till they came as far as the palace of the king of France.

They got off their horses there, and a man of them said a word that Guleesh did not understand, and on the moment they were lifted up, and Guleesh found himself and his companions in the palace. There was a great feast going on there, and there was not a nobleman or a gentleman in the kingdom but was gathered there, dressed in silk and satin, and gold and silver, and the night was as bright as the day with all the lamps and candles that were lit, and Guleesh had to shut his two eyes at the brightness. When he opened them again and looked from him, he thought he never saw anything as fine as all he saw there. There were a hundred tables spread out, and their full of meat and drink on each table of them, flesh-meat, and cakes and sweet-meats, and wine and ale, and every drink that ever a man saw. The musicians were at the two ends of the hall, and they playing the sweetest music that ever a man's ear heard, and there were young women and fine youths in the middle of the hall, dancing and turning, and going round so quickly and so lightly, that it put a *soorawn* in Guleesh's head to be looking at them. There were more there playing tricks, and more making fun and laughing, for such a feast as there was that day had not been in France for twenty years, because the old king had no children alive but only the one daughter, and she was to be married to the son of another king that night. Three days the feast was going on, and the third night she was to be married, and that was the night that Guleesh and the sheehogues came, hoping if they could, to carry off with them the king's young daughter.

Guleesh and his companions were standing together at the head of the hall, where there was a fine altar dressed up, and two bishops behind it waiting to marry the girl, as soon as the right time should come. Nobody could see the sheehogues, for they said a word as they came in, that made them all invisible, as if they had not been in it at all.

"Tell me which of them is the king's daughter," said Guleesh, when he was becoming a little used to the noise and the light.

"Don't you see her there from you?" said the little man that he was talking to.

Guleesh looked where the little man was pointing with his finger, and there he saw the loveliest woman that was, he thought, upon the ridge of the world. The rose and the lily were fighting together in her face, and one could not tell which of them got the victory. Her arms and hands were like the lime, her mouth as red as a strawberry, when it is ripe, her foot was as small and as light as another one's hand, her form was smooth and slender, and her hair was falling down from her head in buckles of gold. Her garments and dress were woven with gold and silver, and the bright stone that was in the ring on her hand was as shining as the sun.

Guleesh was nearly blinded with all the loveliness and beauty that was in her; but when he looked again, he saw that she was crying, and that there was the trace of tears in her eyes. "It can't be," said Guleesh, "that there's grief on her, when everybody round her is so full of sport and merriment."

"Musha, then, she is grieved," said the little man; "for it's against her own will she's marrying, and she has no love for the husband she is to marry. The king was going to give her to him three years ago, when she was only fifteen, but she said she was too young, and requested him to leave her as she was yet. The king gave her a year's grace, and when that year was up he gave her another year's grace, and then another; but a week or a day he would not give her longer, and she is eighteen years old to-night, and it's time for her to marry; but, indeed," says he, and he crooked his mouth in an ugly way; "indeed, it's no king's son she'll marry, if I can help it."

Guleesh pitied the handsome young lady greatly when he heard that, and he was heart-broken to think that it would be necessary for her to marry a man she did not like, or what was worse, to take a nasty Sheehogue for a husband. However, he did not say a word, though he could not help giving many a curse to the ill-luck that was laid out for himself, and he helping the people that were to snatch her away from her home and from her father.

He began thinking, then, what it was he ought to do to save her, but he could think of nothing. "Oh, if I could only give her some help and relief;" said he, "I wouldn't care whether I were alive or dead; but I see nothing that I can do for her."

He was looking on when the king's son came up to her and asked her for a kiss, but she turned her head away from him. Guleesh had double pity for her then, when he saw the lad taking her by the soft white hand, and drawing her out to dance. They went round in the dance near where Guleesh was, and he could plainly see that there were tears in her eyes.

When the dancing was over, the old king, her father, and her mother, the queen, came up and said that this was the right time to marry her, that the bishop was ready and the couch prepared, and it was time to put the wedding-ring on her and give her to her husband.

The old king put a laugh out of him: "Upon my honour," he said, "the night is nearly spent, but my son will make a night for himself. I'll go bail he won't rise early to-morrow."

"Musha, and maybe he would," said the Sheehogue in Guleesh's ear, "or not go to bed, perhaps, at all. Ha, ha, ha!"

Guleesh gave him no answer, for his two eyes were going out on his head watching to see what they would do then.

The king took the youth by the hand, and the queen took her daughter, and they went up together to the altar, with the lords and great people following them.

When they came near the altar, and were no more than about four yards from it, the little sheehogue stretched out his foot before the girl, and she fell. Before she was able to rise again he threw something that was in his hand upon her, said a couple of words, and upon the moment the maiden was gone from amongst them. Nobody could see her, for that word made her invisible. The little man*een* seized her and raised her up behind Guleesh, and the king nor no one else saw them, but out with them through the hall till they came to the door.

Oro! dear Mary! it's there the pity was, and the trouble, and the crying, and the wonder, and the searching, and the *rookawn*, when that lady disappeared from their eyes, and without their seeing what did it. Out on the door of the palace with them, without being stopped or hindered, for nobody saw them, and, "My horse, my bridle, and saddle!" says every man of them. "My horse, my bridle, and saddle!" says Guleesh; and on the moment the horse was standing ready caparisoned before him. "Now, jump up, Guleesh," said the little man, "and put the lady behind you, and we will be going; the morning is not far off from us now."

Guleesh raised her up on the horse's back, and leaped up himself before her, and, "Rise horse," said he; and his horse, and the other horses with him, went in a full race until they came to the sea.

"Highover, cap!" said every man of them.

"Highover, cap!" said Guleesh; and on the moment the horse rose under him, and cut a leap in the clouds, and came down in Erin.

They did not stop there, but went of a race to the place where was Guleesh's house and the rath. And when they came as far as that, Guleesh turned and caught the young girl in his two arms, and leaped off the horse.

"I call and cross you to myself; in the name of God!" said he; and on the spot, before the word was out of his mouth, the horse fell down, and what was in it but the beam of a plough, of which they had made a horse; and every other horse they had, it was that way they made it. Some of them were riding on an old besom, and some on a broken stick, and more on a *bohalawn* (rag weed), or a hemlock-stalk.

The good people called out together when they heard what Guleesh said:

"Oh, Guleesh, you clown, you thief; that no good may happen you, why did you play that trick on us?"

But they had no power at all to carry off the girl, after Guleesh had consecrated her to himself.

"Oh, Guleesh, isn't that a nice turn you did us, and we so kind to you? What good have we now out of our journey to Rome and to France? Never mind yet, you clown, but you'll pay us another time for this. Believe us you'll repent it."

"He'll have no good to get out of the young girl," said the little man that was talking to him in the palace before that, and as he said the word he moved over to her and struck her a slap on the side of the head. "Now," says he, "she'll be without talk any more; now, Guleesh, what good will she be to you when she'll be dumb? It's time for us to go — but you'll remember us, Guleesh na Guss Dhu!"

When he said that he stretched out his two hands, and before Guleesh was able to give an answer, he and the rest of them were gone into the rath out of his sight, and he saw them no more.

He turned to the young woman and said to her: "Thanks be to God, they're gone. Would you not sooner stay with me than with them?" She gave him no answer. "There's trouble and grief on her yet," said Guleesh in his own mind, and he spoke to her again: "I am afraid that you must spend this night in my father's house, lady, and if there is anything that I can do for you, tell me, and I'll be your servant."

The beautiful girl remained silent, but there were tears in her eyes, and her face was white and red after each other.

"Lady," said Guleesh, "tell me what you would like me to do now. I never belonged at all to that lot of sheehogues who carried you away with them. I am the son of an honest farmer, and I went with them without knowing it. If I'll be able to send you back to your father I'll do it, and I pray you make any use of me now that you may wish."

He looked into her face, and he saw the mouth moving as if she was going to speak, but there came no word from it.

"It cannot be," said Guleesh, "that you are dumb. Did I not hear you speaking to the king's son in the palace to-night? Or has that devil made you really dumb, when he struck his nasty hand on your jaw?"

The girl raised her white smooth hand, and laid her finger on her tongue, to show him that she had lost her voice and power of speech, and the tears ran out of her two eyes like streams, and Guleesh's own eyes were not dry, for as rough as he was on the outside he had a soft heart, and could not stand the sight of the young girl, and she in that unhappy plight.

He began thinking with himself what he ought to do, and he did not like to bring her home with himself to his father's house, for he knew well that they would not believe him, that he had been in France and brought back with him the king of France's daughter, and he was afraid they might make a mock of the young lady or insult her.

As he was doubting what he ought to do, and hesitating, he chanced to put his hand in his pocket, and he found a paper in it. He pulled it up, and the moment he looked at it he remembered it was the Pope's bull. "Glory be to God," said he, "I know now what I'll do; I'll bring her to the priest's house, and as soon as he sees the pardon I have here, he won't refuse me to keep the lady and care her." He turned to the lady again and told her that he was loath to take her to his father's house, but that there was an excellent priest very friendly to himself, who would take good care of her, if she wished to remain in his house; but that if there was any other place she would rather go, he said he would bring her to it.

She bent her head, to show him she was obliged, and gave him to understand that she was ready to follow him any place he was going. "We will go to the priest's house, then," said he; "he is under an obligation to me, and will do anything I ask him."

They went together accordingly to the priest's house, and the sun was just rising when they came to the door. Guleesh beat it hard, and as early as it was the priest was up, and opened the door himself. He wondered when he saw Guleesh and the girl, for he was certain that it was coming wanting to be married they were.

"Guleesh na Guss Dhu, isn't it the nice boy you are that you can't wait till ten o'clock or till twelve, but that you must be coming to me at this hour, looking for marriage, you and your *girshuch*. You ought to know that I'm broken, and that I can't marry you, or at all events, can't marry you lawfully. But ubbubboo!" said he, suddenly, as he looked again at the young girl, "in the name of God, who have you here? Who is she, or how did you get her?"

"Father," said Guleesh, "you can marry me, or anybody else, any more, if you wish; but it's not looking for marriage I came to you now, but to ask you, if you please, to give a lodging in your house to this young lady." And with that he drew out the Pope's bull, and gave it to the priest to read.

The priest took it, and read it, and looked sharply at the writing and seal, and he had no doubt but it was a right bull, from the hand of the Pope.

"Where did you get this?" said he to Guleesh, and the hand he held the paper in, was trembling with wonder and joy.

"Oh, musha!" said Guleesh, airily enough, "I got it last night in Rome; I remained a couple of hours in the city there, when I was on my way to bring this young lady, daughter of the king of France, back with me."

The priest looked at him as though he had ten heads on him; but without putting any other question to him, he desired him to come in, himself and the maiden, and when they came in, he shut the door, brought them into the parlour, and put them sitting.

"Now, Guleesh," said he, "tell me truly where did you get this bull, and who is this young lady, and whether you're out of your senses really, or are only making a joke of me?"

"I'm not telling a word of lie, nor making a joke of you," said Guleesh; "but it was from the Pope himself I got the paper, and it was from the palace of the king of France I carried off this lady, and she is the daughter of the king of France."

He began his story then, and told the whole to the priest, and the priest was so much surprised that he could not help calling out at times, or clapping his hands together.

When Guleesh said from what he saw he thought the girl was not satisfied with the marriage that was going to take place in the palace before he and the sheehogues broke it up, there came a red blush into the girl's cheek, and he was more certain than ever that she had sooner be as she was — badly as she was — than be the married wife of the man she hated. When Guleesh said that he would be very thankful to the priest if he would keep her in his own house, the kind man said he would do that as long as Guleesh pleased, but that he did not know what they ought to do with her, because they had no means of sending her back to her father again.

Guleesh answered that he was uneasy about the same thing, and that he saw nothing to do but to keep quiet until they should find some opportunity of doing something better. They made it up then between themselves that the priest should let on that it was his brother's daughter he had, who was come on a visit to him from another county, and that he should tell everybody that she was dumb, and do his best to keep everyone away from her. They told the young girl what it was they intended to do, and she showed by her eyes that she was obliged to them.

Guleesh went home then, and when his people asked him where he was, he said that he was asleep at the foot of the ditch, and passed the night there.

There was great wonderment on the neighbours when the honest priest showed them the Pope's bull, and got his old place again, and everyone was rejoiced, for, indeed, there was no fault at all in that honest man, except that now and again he would have too much liking for a drop of the bottle; but no one could say that he ever saw him in a way that he could not utter "here's to your health," as well as ever a man in the kingdom. But if they wondered to see the priest back again in his old place, much more did they wonder at the girl who came so suddenly to his house without anyone knowing where she was from, or what business she had there. Some of the people said that everything was not as it ought to be, and others that it was not possible that the Pope gave back his place to the priest after taking it from him before, on account of the complaints about his drinking. And there were more of them, too, who said that Guleesh na Guss Dhu was not like the same man that was in it before, and that it was a great story (*i.e.*, a thing to wonder at) how he was drawing every day to the priest's house, and that the priest had a wish and a respect for him, a thing they could not clear up at all.

That was true for them, indeed, for it was seldom the day went by but Guleesh would go to the priest's house, and have a talk with him, and as often as he would come he used to hope to find the young lady well again, and with leave to speak; but, alas! she remained dumb and silent, without relief or cure. Since she had no other means of talking she carried on a sort of conversation between herself and himself, by moving her hand and fingers, winking her eyes, opening and shutting her mouth, laughing or smiling, and a thousand other signs, so that it was not long until they understood each other very well. Guleesh was always thinking how he should send her back to her father; but there was no one to go with her, and he himself did not know what road to go, for he had never been out of his own country before the night he brought her away with him. Nor had the priest any better knowledge than he; but when Guleesh asked him, he wrote three or four letters to the king of France, and gave them to buyers and sellers of wares, who used to be going from place to place across the sea; but they all went astray, and never one came to the king's hand.

This was the way they were for many months, and Guleesh was falling deeper and deeper in love with her every day, and it was plain to himself and the priest that she liked him. The boy feared greatly at last, lest the king should really hear where his daughter was, and take her back from himself, and he besought the priest to write no more, but to leave the matter to God.

So they passed the time for a year, until there came a day when Guleesh was lying by himself on the grass, on the last day of the last month in autumn (*i.e.*, October), and he thinking over again in his own mind of everything that happened to him from the day that he went with the sheehogues across the sea. He remembered then, suddenly, that it was one November night that he was standing at the gable of the house, when the whirlwind came, and the sheehogues in it, and he said to himself: "We have November night again to-day, and I'll stand in the same place I was last year, until I see will the good people come again. Perhaps I might see or hear something that would be useful to me, and might bring back her talk again to Mary"— that was the name himself and the priest called the king's daughter, for neither of them knew her right name. He told his intention to the priest, and the priest gave him his blessing.

Guleesh accordingly went to the old rath when the night was darkening, and he stood with his bent elbow leaning on a gray old flag, waiting till the middle of the night should come. The moon rose slowly, and it was like a knob of fire behind him; and there was a white fog which was raised up over the fields of grass and all damp places, through the coolness of the night after a great heat in the day. The night was calm as is a lake when there is not a breath of wind to move a wave on it, and there was no sound to be heard but the *cronawn* (hum) of the insects that would go by from time to time, or the hoarse sudden scream of the wild-geese, as they passed from lake to lake, half a mile up in the air over his head; or the sharp whistle of the fadogues and flibeens (golden and green plover), rising and lying, lying and rising, as they do on a calm night. There were a thousand thousand bright stars shining over his head, and there was a little frost out, which left the grass under his foot white and crisp.

He stood there for an hour, for two hours, for three hours, and the frost increased greatly, so that he heard the breaking of the *traneens* under his foot as often as he moved. He was thinking, in his own mind, at last, that the sheehogues would not come that night, and that it was as good for him to return back again, when he heard a sound far away from him, coming towards him, and he recognised what it was at the first moment. The sound increased, and at first it was like the beating of waves on a stony shore, and then it was like the falling of a great waterfall, and at last it was like a loud storm in the tops of the trees, and then the whirlwind burst into the rath of one rout, and the shee-hogues were in it.

It all went by him so suddenly that he lost his breath with it, but he came to himself on the spot, and put an ear on himself, listening to what they would say.

Scarcely had they gathered into the rath till they all began shouting, and screaming, and talking amongst themselves; and then each one of them cried out: "My horse, and bridle, and saddle! My horse, and bridle, and saddle!" and Guleesh took courage, and called out as loudly as any of them: "My horse, and bridle, and saddle! My horse, and bridle, and saddle!" But before the word was well out of his mouth, another man cried out: "Ora! Guleesh, my boy, are you here with us again? How are you coming on with your woman? There's no use in your calling for your horse to-night. I'll go bail you won't play on us again. It was a good trick you played on us last year!"

"It was," said another man, "he won't do it again."

"Isn't he a prime lad, the same lad! to take a woman with him that never said as much to him as, 'how do you do?' since this time last year!" says the third man.

"Perhaps he likes to be looking at her," said another voice.

"And if the *omadawn* only knew that there's an herb growing up by his own door, and to boil it and give it to her and she'd be well," said another voice.

"That's true for you."

"He is an omadawn."

"Don't bother your head with him, we'll be going."

"We'll leave the *bodach* as he is."

And with that they rose up into the air, and out with them of one *roolya-boolya* the way they came; and they left poor Guleesh standing where they found him, and the two eyes going out of his head, looking after them, and wondering.

He did not stand long till he returned back, and he thinking in his own mind on all he saw and heard, and wondering whether there was really an herb at his own door that would bring back the talk to the king's daughter. "It can't be," says he to himself "that they would tell it to me, if there was any virtue in it; but perhaps the sheehogue didn't observe himself when he let the word slip out of his mouth. I'll search well as soon as the sun rises, whether there's any plant growing beside the house except thistles and dock-ings."

He went home, and as tired as he was he did not sleep a wink until the sun rose on the morrow. He got up then, and it was the first thing he did to go out and search well through the grass round about the house, trying could he get any herb that he did not recognize. And, indeed, he was not long searching till he observed a large strange herb that was growing up just by the gable of the house.

He went over to it, and observed it closely, and saw that there were seven little branches coming out of the stalk, and seven leaves growing on every branch*een* of them, and that there was a white sap in the leaves. "It's very wonderful," said he to himself, "that I never noticed this herb before. If there's any virtue in an herb at all, it ought to be in such a strange one as this."

He drew out his knife, cut the plant, and carried it into his own house; stripped the leaves off it and cut up the stalk; and there came a thick, white juice out of it, as there comes out of the sow-thistle when it is bruised, except that the juice was more like oil.

He put it in a little pot and a little water in it, and laid it on the fire until the water was boiling, and then he took a cup, filled it half up with the juice, and put it to his own mouth. It came into his head then that perhaps it was poison that was in it, and that the good people were only tempting him that he might kill himself with that trick, or put the girl to death without meaning it. He put down the cup again, raised a couple of drops on the top of his finger, and put it to his mouth. It was not bitter, and, indeed, had a sweet, agreeable taste. He grew bolder then, and drank the full of a thimble of it, and then as much again, and he never stopped till he had half the cup drunk. He fell asleep after that, and did not wake till it was night, and there was great hunger and great thirst on him.

He had to wait, then, till the day rose; but he determined, as soon as he should wake in the morning, that he would go to the king's daughter and give her a drink of the juice of the herb.

As soon as he got up in the morning, he went over to the priest's house with the drink in his hand, and he never felt himself so bold and valiant, and spirited and light, as he was that day, and he was quite certain that it was the drink he drank which made him so hearty.

When he came to the house, he found the priest and the young lady within, and they were wondering greatly why he had not visited them for two days.

He told them all his news, and said that he was certain that there was great power in that herb, and that it would do the lady no hurt, for he tried it himself and got good from it, and then he made her taste it, for he vowed and swore that there was no harm in it.

Guleesh handed her the cup, and she drank half of it, and then fell back on her bed and a heavy sleep came on her, and she never woke out of that sleep till the day on the morrow.

Guleesh and the priest sat up the entire night with her, waiting till she should awake, and they between hope and unhope, between expectation of saving her and fear of hurting her.

She awoke at last when the sun had gone half its way through the heavens. She rubbed her eyes and looked like a person who did not know where she was. She was like one astonished when she saw Guleesh and the priest in the same room with her, and she sat up doing her best to collect her thoughts.

The two men were in great anxiety waiting to see would she speak, or would she not speak, and when they remained silent for a couple of minutes, the priest said to her: "Did you sleep well, Mary?."

And she answered him: "I slept, thank you."

No sooner did Guleesh hear her talking than he put a shout of joy out of him, and ran over to her and fell on his two knees, and said: "A thousand thanks to God, who has given you back the talk; lady of my heart, speak again to me."

The lady answered him that she understood it was he who boiled that drink for her, and gave it to her; that she was obliged to him from her heart for all the kindness he showed her since the day she first came to Ireland, and that he might be certain that she would never forget it.

Guleesh was ready to die with satisfaction and delight. Then they brought her food, and she eat with a good appetite, and was merry and joyous, and never left off talking with the priest while she was eating.

After that Guleesh went home to his house, and stretched himself on the bed and fell asleep again, for the force of the herb was not all spent, and he passed another day and a night sleeping. When he woke up he went back to the priest's house, and found that the young lady was in the same state, and that she was asleep almost since the time that he left the house.

He went into her chamber with the priest, and they remained watching beside her till she awoke the second time, and she had her talk as well as ever, and Guleesh was greatly rejoiced. The priest put food on the table again, and they eat together, and Guleesh used after that to come to the house from day to day, and the friendship that was between him and the king's daughter increased, because she had no one to speak to except Guleesh and the priest, and she liked Guleesh best.

He had to tell her the way he was standing by the rath when the good people came, and how he went in to the Pope, and how the sheehogue blew fire out of his mouth, and every other thing that he did till the time the good people whipt her off with themselves; and when it would be all told he would have to begin it again out of the new, and she never was tired listening to him.

When they had been that way for another half year, she said that she could wait no longer without going back to her father and mother; that she was certain that they were greatly grieved for her; and that it was a shame for her to leave them in grief, when it was in her power to go as far as them. The priest did all he could to keep her with them for another while, but without effect, and Guleesh spoke every sweet word that came into his head, trying to get the victory over her, and to coax her and make her stay as she was, but it was no good for him. She determined that she would go, and no man alive would make her change her intention.

She had not much money, but only two rings that were on her hand, when the sheehogue carried her away, and a gold pin that was in her hair, and golden buckles that were on her little shoes.

The priest took and sold them and gave her the money, and she said that she was ready to go.

She left her blessing and farewell with the priest and Guleesh, and departed. She was not long gone till there came such grief and melancholy over Guleesh that he knew he would not be long alive unless he were near her, and he followed her.

(The next 42 pages in the Leabhar Sgeuluigheachta are taken up with the adventures of Guleesh and the princess, on their way to the court of France. But this portion of the story is partly taken from other tales, and part is too much altered and amplified in the writing of it, so that I do not give it here, as not being genuine folk-lore, which the story, except for a very little embellishment, has been up to this point. The whole ends as follows, with the restoration of the princess and her marriage with Guleesh.)

It was well, and it was not ill. They married one another, and that was the fine wedding they had, and if I were to be there then, I would not be here now; but I heard it from a birdeen that there was neither cark nor care, sickness nor sorrow, mishap nor misfortune on them till the hour of their death, and that it may be the same with me, and with us all!

Hallowe'en: How to Celebrate It

Martha Russell Orne, 1898

As has already been noted, the Victorians were fond of parties, and small pamphlets on entertaining were popular. Thus, it was probably inevitable that the first book to be dedicated entirely to Hallowe'en would be a 48-page booklet focused largely on party-giving.

Martha Russell Orne's *Hallowe'en: How to Celebrate It* begins with a brief history of the holiday, one that is overall reasonably accurate. Orne's other published works were mainly plays and a grammar textbook, so it's doubtful that she was intimately acquainted with the holiday's history prior to writing this pamphlet (strangely, though, her information doesn't coincide with most of the popular histories of the holiday such as those presented in Brand's *Popular Antiquities* or Chambers's *Book of Days*). She is, however, obviously well acquainted with Halloween poetry, since she makes frequent reference to Burns, Gay, and Charles Graydon. Note also that Orne repeats the four-line verse about "Murtagh's evil" that's also quoted in William Sharp's article "Halloween: A Threefold Chronicle," but Orne's version has somehow transmogrified the name to "Mustaph's evil," which may be a typo, or may be a deliberate change reflecting certain western prejudices against Middle Eastern names.

The original price of the book, by the way, was 35 cents.

HALLOWE'EN:

ITS ORIGIN AND
HOW TO CELEBRATE IT WITH APPROPRIATE
GAMES AND CEREMONIES

By Martha Russell Orne

CONTENTS.
ORIGIN OF HALLOWE'EN
SUGGESTIONS FOR HALLOWE'EN PARTIES
FORMS OF INVITATION
PROGRAMS FOR HALLOWE'EN
HALLOWE'EN GAMES
HALLOWE'EN FORTUNE-TELLING

ORIGIN OF HALLOWE'EN.

All-Hallow Eve falls on the last day of October, the day following being All-Saints' Day, or All-Hallows.

This is the date of the last of three festivals held by the Druids, who in olden times were scattered over northern Europe. Those festivals were observed on May 1st, the time of sowing; June 21st, the season of the ripening of the crops; and October 31st, the harvest season.

One of the religious rites of the Druids consisted in maintaining throughout the year immense fires on stone altars erected upon eminences in honor of the Sun-God. On the night of October 31st, the Druids assembled at the altars in their snow-white robes, and at a given signal, during absolute silence on the part of the multitude gathered to witness the ceremony, they solemnly extinguished the fires. New fires were then kindled, and as the flames leaped heavenward, the people raised a mighty shout, and then, obtaining live embers from the altars, they returned to their homes to extinguish the old fires left burning on their hearths, and kindle them anew with the sacred embers of the priests. This new fire was believed to protect each homestead from peril so long as it remained burning.

HALLOWE'EN

ITS ORIGIN AND
HOW TO CELEBRATE IT WITH APPROPRIATE
GAMES AND CEREMONIES

BY

MARTHA RUSSELL ORNE

FITZGERALD PUBLISHING CORPORATION
SUCCESSOR TO
DICK & FITZGERALD
18 Vesey St.,   New York

Original title page of *Hallowe'en: How to Celebrate It.*

As the Druidic faith faded in the light of Christianity, the heathen festivals lost much of their grandeur and former significance, and assumed a lower character. Gradually the simple country folk came to believe that on October 31st the fairies forsook their hiding-places to dance in the forest glades, while witches, goblins, and other evil spirits held revels in deserted abbeys, or plotted against mankind in the shadows of ruinous castles and keeps.

By a very natural transition the Hallowe'en fire came to be looked upon as a charm against evil spirits; and even as late as the seventeenth century we learn that it was customary for the farmer to make the circuit of his acres, brandishing a lighted torch, and chanting or singing some doggerel rhyme to protect his farm from evil during the coming year.

From the fact that these supernatural agents seemed so near at this season, Hallowe'en was supposed to be the night of all nights for prying into the mysteries of the future; and this is probably the origin of those games and ceremonies by which it is claimed that one's fate may be learned, at the same time providing a great deal of innocent fun and flirtation for youths and maidens of every degree at a Hallowe'en celebration.

An attempt is made in this little book to gather in those games and ceremonials which are popular among Hallowe'en celebrants; a few of them, however, can only be carried out successfully in country and farming districts where the special conditions exist for their performance.

Suggestions for a Hallowe'en Party.

The kitchen, in which many of the games are played, and other rooms where it is practicable, should be grotesquely decorated with Jack-o'-lanterns made of apples, cucumbers, squashes, pumpkins, etc., the pulp having been removed, incisions made for eyes, nose, and mouth, and a lighted candle placed within.

Green branches, autumn leaves, apples, tomatoes, and corn should also play an important part in the adornment of the rooms, and with a few yards of red and yellow scrim or cheese-cloth make very effective and inexpensive decorations.

Invite only unmarried friends; married couples are rather *de trop* on such occasions; and especially avoid all formality.

Let the invitations, if possible, be sent out a week previous to the festivity. Appropriate forms of invitation will be found elsewhere in the book.

With regard to refreshments, individual taste must prevail to a great extent; in the centre of the table, however, should be placed the "fortune cake." This is made much like a birthday cake, the chief difference being that in the batter of the fortune cake are dropped a ring, a thimble, and a dime. Care should be taken in the cutting and eating of this cake; for a wedding will soon be the fate of him (her) who finds the ring. The thimble denotes celibacy; the dime, a legacy. The "Hallowe'en pie" is also a pleasing feature of the repast, and should contain souvenirs for every one, representing gnomes, witches, black cats, brownies, etc.

Although, as has been previously stated, all appearance of formality must necessarily be dispensed with on this occasion, the host or hostess should nevertheless have in mind a well-arranged program. If there be any misgivings as to the guests' entering into the spirit of the occasion, the following suggestions may be helpful:

They may be received by some one covered with a sheet, who conducts them through a dimly lighted hall to an apartment where they are requested to lay aside their wraps, while groans and raps and other strange noises are heard on every side. The conversation of the "ghost" should be somewhat in this vein: "This is the room where I died seven years ago. These groans proceed from my ancestors, who cannot rest in their graves because I have returned to earth to spend Hallowe'en!" etc.

The guests themselves may be furnished with sheets and introduced to one another after this fashion: "This is my great-uncle who died in 1798; he was an intimate friend of George Washington; he caught a severe cold while crossing the Delaware in 1776, and died twenty-two years later from the effects;" or, "This is my beloved aunt, who died forty years ago from drinking pale ale and eating too much plum-pudding," etc., etc.

Shadow pantomimes representing witches, fairies, gnomes, cats, ghosts, bats, and other weird forms, may be made very amusing. Fortune-telling as described at the close of this book should certainly be one of the features of the evening.

To pair off the guests for supper or for games, place in walnut shells, from which the meat has been removed, some seeds, such as beans, peas, nasturtiums, raisins, celery, all-spice, nutmegs, etc., using only two of each kind and placing but one in each shell. Tie the shells with ribbon and place one of each kind in a box for the ladies, and the same assortment in another box for the gentlemen. Each guest takes his (her) choice of the nuts; then, picking out the seed, each gentleman goes in search of the lady who has its mate.

Another very good plan is to select pieces of calico of different patterns, a small apron and a bow being made of each pattern. As the guests remove their wraps, each lady is presented with an apron, and each gentleman with a bow, which they wear. The gentleman then seeks out the lady who wears the apron corresponding with his bow.

Conundrums with answers may be put into peanut shells, and placed beside each plate at the table; each guest in turn reads his (her) conundrum and gives the others an opportunity to guess the answer; if they fail, he (she) reads the answer.

Hallowe'en vegetables on an early postcard.

The success of the evening greatly depends upon unflagging interest in the proceedings being maintained. To this end the order of exercise contained in the program should be carried out in quick succession. A game must be stopped the moment it ceases to absorb attention, preferably even sooner. Everything should be provided beforehand in readiness for use in games requiring previous preparation.

Suggestions for programs will be found in their proper place.

FORMS OF INVITATION TO HALLOWE'EN PARTIES.

The invitations should be strictly informal, and may be somewhat like the following:

253 EUCLID AVE.

My dear Miss Cromwell:

On Saturday, October 31st, I shall celebrate Hallowe'en, and hope that you and your cousin Francis will be able to come. The Spirits are expected to arrive at eight o'clock.

Yours cordially,

ADELAIDE BALDWIN.

33 HIGHLAND AVE.

Dear Sadie:

I shall expect to see you at my Hallowe'en Party, Saturday, October 31st, at eight-thirty o'clock. Do not disappoint me. Many choice Spirits will be there; so come prepared to learn your fate.

Yours truly,

MARION WENTWORTH.

519 LAKEVIEW AVE.

Dear Ethel:

I am going to give a Hallowe'en Party, Monday, October 31st, for the benefit of the new Chapel. The leading feature of the evening will be the Hallowe'en Fortune-Teller. Come prepared to have your fortune told, and to cross the palm of the fortune-teller with what you feel like giving toward a good cause. Come at eight-thirty o'clock.

Yours cordially,

SEVILLE O. NEWHALL.

441 COLUMBUS AVE.

Dear Bessie:

Witches and Choice Spirits of Darkness will hold high carnival at my home Tuesday, October 31st, at eight-thirty o'clock. You are invited to be present.

Yours for a good time,

MABEL SWEETLAND.

PROGRAMS FOR HALLOWE'EEN PARTIES.

1. RECEPTION AND INTRODUCTION OF GUESTS.
2. INSTRUMENTAL MUSIC.
3. READING: "THE GOBLE-UNS 'LL GIT YOU, EF YOU DON'T WATCH OUT."

4. GUESTS TELL GHOST STORIES.
5. FORTUNE-TELLING WITH THE HALLOWE'EN FORTUNE-TELLER.
6. GAMES.
7. SUPPER.
8. GAMES.

PROGRAM NO. 2.

1. RECEPTION AND INTRODUCTION OF GUESTS.
2. MUSIC: "COMIN' THRO' THE RYE."
3. A RECITATION, SELECTED.
4. MUSIC: "MY SWEETHEART'S THE MAN IN THE MOON."
5. SUPPER.
6. FORTUNE-TELLING.
7. GAMES.

HALLOWE'EN GAMES.
PULLING THE KALE.

> Then first and foremost, through the kale,
>   Their stocks maun a' be sought once;
> They steek their een, an' graip an' wale,
>   For muckle anes and straight anes.
>
> BURNS.

In country districts a leading ceremony of Hallowe'en is by each one pulling a stock or plant of kale or cabbage. The participants must go out in couples hand in hand, with eyes shut, and pull the first stock they come to. Its being big or little, straight or crooked, is prophetic of the size and shape of the grand object of all their spells — the husband or wife. If any earth stick to the root, it is a fortunate omen; and the state of the heart of the stem (whether sweet, sour, brittle, hard, etc.) is indicative of the disposition or natural temper of the future mate.

> "One, two, three, and up to seven;
> If all are white, all go to heaven;
> If one is black as Mustaph's evil,
> He'll soon be screechin' wi' the devil."

In the old Scottish Hallowe'en game, each took home his (her) stock and laid it behind the outer door, and the first person to enter next morning was to be the future wife or husband. Or, should the first person to enter be already married, the first letter in his (her) name was to be the initial letter of the name of the future spouse of the owner of the kale-stock.

NAMING CHESTNUTS.

Roast three chestnuts before the fire, one of which is named for some lady (or gentleman); the other two, for gentleman (or ladies). If they separate, so will those for whom they are named; those jumping toward the fire are going to a warmer climate; those jumping from the fire, to a colder climate; if two gentlemen jump toward one another, it means rivalry.

THE PEANUT HUNT.

Peanuts are previously hidden in every conceivable place in the rooms to which the guests have access. The finder of the greatest number receives a prize.

THE PERPLEXING HUNT.

In this game the seeker for a prize is guided from place to place by some such doggerels as the following, and is started on his hunt with this rhyme:

"Perhaps you'll find it in the air;
If not, look underneath your chair."

Beneath his chair he finds the following:

"No, you will not find it here;
Search the clock and have no fear."

Under the clock he finds:

"You will have to try once more;
Look behind the parlor door."

Tied to the door-knob he discovers:

"If it's not out in the stable,
Seek beneath the kitchen table."

Under the kitchen table he finds another note, which this time reads:

"If your quest remains uncertain,
You will find it 'neath a curtain."

And here his quest is rewarded by finding the prize.

THE MIRROR.

Walk backward several rods out of doors in the moonlight with a mirror in your hand, or within doors with a candle in one hand and a mirror in the other, repeating the following rhyme, and the face of your future companion in life will appear in the glass:

"Round and round, O stars so fair!
Ye travel and search out everywhere;
I pray you, sweet stars, now show to me
This night who my future husband (wife) shall be!"

COMBING THE HAIR BEFORE A MIRROR.

Stand alone before a mirror, and by the light of a candle comb your hair; in due time the face of your future conjugal companion will appear in the glass, peeping over your shoulder. No young man would disappoint her at such a critical opportunity.

APPLE-PARING INITIAL.

Pare an apple; swing the unbroken paring around your head, and let it drop on the floor. A letter thus formed shows the initial of your future spouse's name.

> "I pare this pippin round and round again,
> My shepherd's name to flourish on the plain;
> I fling th' unbroken paring o'er my head,
> Upon the grass a perfect L is read."

SNAPDRAGON.

The dragon consists of one half-pint of brandy or alcohol poured into a dish, and the brandy is then ignited; as soon as the brandy is fairly in flame, all lights must be extinguished, and salt freely sprinkled into the dish; this will impart a corpse-like pallor to every countenance. Candied fruits, figs, raisins, sugared almonds, etc., are then thrown in, and the guests snap for them with their fingers; the person securing the most prizes from the flames will meet his or her true love within the year.

Or, wrap tightly in tin-foil slips of paper upon which verses are written, and place them in the dish. Then pour on the brandy and ignite it. The verse each individual gets is supposed to tell his (her) fortune.

The burning dish should be placed in the middle of a bare table, for drops of burning spirits are often splashed about.

MELTING LEAD.

Each person melts some lead and pours it through a wedding-ring or key into a dish of water. The lead will cool in various shapes, supposed to be prophetic. Any ingenious person will interpret the shapes, and furnish much amusement for his listeners; thus, a bell-shaped drop indicates a wedding within the year; a drop resembling a torch or lamp signifies fame; a pen or ink-bottle, that the future companion is to be an author; a horn of plenty, wealth; a bag or trunk, travel; etc.

THE NEEDLE GAME.

Each person takes a greased needle and floats it in a basin of water. Impelled by attraction of gravitation, the needles will behave very curiously: some will cling together, others will rush to the margin and remain there. The manner in which one person's needle behaves toward another's causes much amusement, and is supposed to be suggestive and even prophetic.

BOBBING FOR APPLES.

In bobbing for apples, the hands of the contestants are tied behind them. In the heart of each apple a name may be placed, carefully encased in tin-foil, or an initial letter cut in the skin. Each player draws two apples with his (her) teeth from the tub of water in which they are floating. The apples should be stemless.

In some localities the winner of the greatest number of apples gets a prize.

THE THREE DISHES.

Take three dishes, one of which shall contain clear water, one soapy water, and the other nothing. Blindfold one of the party and lead him (her) to the table on which the three dishes are arranged; with the left forefinger he (she) tries to dip into one of the dishes: should it be the empty dish, he (she) will remain single; if into the soapy water, he (she) will marry a widow (widower); if into the clear water, the future companion will be both young and handsome.

WALNUT BOATS.

Open a number of English walnuts, remove the meat, and in each half-shell fasten short pieces of differently colored Christmas candles. These are each to be named for a member of the party, and, after lighting, set afloat in a large pan or tub of water.

The behavior of these tiny boats reveals the future of the youths and maidens for whom they are named. If two glide on together, their owners have a similar destiny; if they glide apart, so will their owners. Sometimes the candles will huddle together as if talking to one another, while perchance one will be left alone, out in the cold, as it were. Again, two will start off and all the rest will follow in close pursuit. The one whose candle first goes out is destined to be an old bachelor or maid.

These nut-shell boats may also be made by pouring melted wax into halves of walnut-shells in which are short strings for wicks.

THE ALPHABET GAME.

Cut the alphabets from a newspaper and sprinkle on the surface of water; the letters floating may spell or suggest the name of the future husband or wife.

THE CANDLE AND THE APPLE.

At one end of a stick eighteen inches long fasten an apple; at the other end, a short piece of lighted candle. Suspend the stick from the ceiling by a stout cord fastened on the centre of the stick so that it will balance horizontally, and while it is revolving allow the players to try to catch the apple with their teeth. If desirable, a prize may be placed in the heart of the apple.

THE RAISIN RACE.

A raisin is strung in the middle of a thread a yard long, and two persons take each an end of the string in his (her) mouth; whoever by chewing the string reaches the raisin first has the raisin, and will be the first to be wedded.

THE BARREL-HOOP.

Take a barrel-hoop, suspend it from the ceiling, and on its circumference fasten alternately at regular intervals apples, cakes, candies, and candle-ends. The players gather in a circle around it, and as it revolves each in turn tries to bite one of the edibles; the one who is so unfortunate as to seize a candle pays a forfeit.

TO TRY ONE'S LUCK.

In a dish of mashed potatoes place a ring, a dime, and a thimble. Each guest is provided with a spoon with which to eat the potatoes; whoever gets the ring is to be married within a year; the thimble signifies single blessedness, while the dime prophesies riches or a legacy.

Some canny lassies have been known to get the ring into one of their very first spoonfuls, and have kept it for fun in their mouths, tucked snugly beneath the tongue, until the dish was emptied. Such a lass was believed to possess the rare accomplishment of being able to hold her tongue, but nevertheless tricky.

CYNIVER.

A play in which the youth of both sexes seek for an even-leaved sprig of ash; the first of either sex that finds one calls out *cyniver*, and is answered by the first of the opposite sex that succeeds; and these two, if the omen fails not, are to be joined in wedlock.

APPLE SEEDS.

Name two wet apple seeds and stick them on the forehead. The first seed to fall indicates that the love of him (her) whose name it bears is not steadfast.

THE HALLOWE'EN SOUVENIR GAME.

Suspend apples by means of strings in the doorway or from the ceiling at the proper height to be caught between the teeth. The first successful player receives a prize. These prizes should be Hallowe'en souvenirs, such as emery cushions of silk representing tomatoes, apples, pears, pickles, or radishes; or pen-wipers representing witches, cats, bats, brooms, or other appropriate devices.

THREADING THE NEEDLE.

Sit upon a round bottle laid lengthways upon the floor, and try to thread a needle. The one first rewarded with success will be the first to be married.

WINNOWING CORN.

Steal out into the barn or garden alone and go three times through all the motions of throwing corn against the wind. The third time an apparition of your future spouse will pass you; in some mysterious manner, also, you may obtain an idea of his (her) employment and station in life.

THE RING AND THE GOBLET.

Tie a wedding-ring or key to a silken cord and hold it suspended within a goblet, then begin to repeat the alphabet slowly; whenever the ring strikes the goblet, begin the alphabet again, and in this way spell out the name of your future mate.

BLIND NUT-SEEKERS.

Let several of the guests be blindfolded. Then hide nuts or apples in various parts of the room or house. The seeker finding the greatest number of nuts or apples wins a prize.

THE GAME OF FATE.

All the guests take part in this game, being seated in a circle. Three "Fates" are then chosen, one of whom whispers to each individual in turn the name of his (her) future sweetheart. The second "Fate" follows, whispering to each where he (she) will next meet his (her) sweetheart; as, "You will meet on a load of hay," or "at a picnic," or "at church," or "on the river," etc. The third "Fate" then reveals the future; as "You will marry him (her) next Christmas," or "You will be separated many years by a quarrel, but will finally marry," or "Neither of you will ever marry," etc. Each guest must remember what is said to him (her) by each of the "Fates"; then each in turn should repeat aloud what has been told him (her). For example: "My future sweetheart's name is Obednego; I shall meet him next Wednesday on the Moonlight Excursion, and we shall be married within a week."

THE WATER EXPERIMENT.

A laughable experiment consists in filling the mouth with water and walking around the house or block without swallowing or spilling a drop during the walk; the first person of the opposite sex you meet is your fate.

A clever hostess will send two unsuspecting lovers by different doors; they are sure to meet, and not unfrequently settle matters then and there.

A SURE TEST.

Take water and meal and make a dough. Let the young men write on slips of paper the names of several of their fair friends, roll them up in balls of the dough, and drop them into a basin of water. In a short time the balls will melt apart, and the papers that first become visible will be watched with breathless interest. Young ladies may also adopt the same means to determine the name of their future husbands.

THE LOAF CAKE.

A loaf cake is often made, and in it are placed a ring and a key. The former signifies marriage, and the latter a journey, and the person who cuts the slice containing either must accept the inevitable.

THE DUMB CAKE.

If a dumb cake is wished for a charm, the young ladies must meet, between the hours of ten and eleven, in the kitchen. Each of them places a handful of wheat flour on a sheet of white paper and sprinkles it over with as much salt as she can hold between her finger and thumb. Then one of the party must make it into a dough, being careful not to use spring water. Each young lady must then roll up a portion of the dough, spread it out thin and flat, and mark her initials upon it with a new pin. The cakes having been placed fore the fire, all must take a seat as far from it as possible. This must all be done before eleven P.M., and between that time and midnight each one must turn her cake once. When the clock strikes twelve the future husband of her who is to be married first will enter and lay his hand upon the cake marked with her name. Throughout the whole proceeding not a word must be spoken. Hence the name "dumb cake." This is a grand opportunity for a gentleman to covertly pop the question.

THE BOWL OF FLOUR.

A bowl is filled tightly with flour. During the process of filling, a wedding ring is inserted vertically in some part of it. The bowl, when full, is inverted upon a dish and withdrawn, leaving the mound of flour on the dish. Each guest cuts off with a knife a thin slice which crumbles into dust. The guest who cuts off the slice containing the ring will be married first.

THE MIRROR AND APPLE.

The young woman who reads her lover's heart aright, though he may not as yet have confessed his passion, may lead him to betrayal if she will stand in front of a mirror in a dimly lighted room while she eats an apple. If her lover has spirit enough to be worthy of her he will step softly in, peep over her right shoulder, and ask for a slice of the fruit. It would be manifestly unfair to detail any more of the pretty drama.

THE MAGIC STAIRS.

If a maiden wants to tempt the future, let her walk down-stairs backward, holding a lighted candle over her head. Upon reaching the bottom, if she turns suddenly, lo! before her will stand the wished-for one. He would be remiss indeed if he was not there.

THE LIME-KILN TEST.

If a maid would know the name of the man she is to marry, let her on All-Hallowe'en steal out to a lime-kiln and throw therein a clue of blue yarn, still holding on to the other end. Presently the end in the kiln will be sharply pulled. Then the maid must say, "Who holds?" Whereupon the voice of her future husband will pronounce his name, both the Christian and surname.

In the absence of a lime-kiln the lads and lassies can easily agree upon a substitute; and he would be a booby, indeed, who would not take advantage of the means thus afforded of determining his standing in the affections of his lady-love.

THE BOGIE.

A pumpkin is carefully hollowed out until nothing but the shell of the rind remains. One side of it is punctured with holes for the mouth, eyes, and nose, and made as nearly as possible to resemble a human face. A lighted candle is then fastened within, the eyebrows are put on with burnt-cork, and a demon-like expression given to the features. Sometimes horns are stuck on, and the bogie made to look like Satan, whose Sabbath All-Hallowe'en is. The bogie is put in a dark room, where the young people may stray on it unawares, or it is hidden away in the grounds in some secluded nook to which each swain must some time or other lead his sweetheart for "a good scare," taking pains to see that no real bogies are around, and then availing himself to the full of the privilege of consoling her half-feigned terrors.

THE TRUE-LOVER TEST.

Two hazel-nuts are thrown into the hot coals by a maiden. She secretly gives a lover's name to each. If one of the nuts bursts, then that lover is unfaithful; but if it burns with a steady glow until it becomes ashes, she knows that her lover's faith is true. Sometimes it happens, but not often, that both nuts will burn steadily, and then is the maiden's heart sore perplexed.

Two hazel-nuts I throw in the flame,
And to each nut I give a sweetheart's name;
This, with the loudest bounce me sore amazed;
That, in a flame of brightest color blazed.
As blazed the nut so may thy passion glow,
For 't was thy nut that did so brightly glow.

                                        GAY.

The Dreamer.

If a maid wishes to know to what manner of fortune she shall be married,—if to a gentleman, a tradesman, or a traveler,—let her, on All-Hallowe'en, take a walnut, a hazelnut and nutmeg; grate and mix them up with butter and sugar into pills, which must be taken when she goes to bed; and then, if her fortune be to marry a gentleman, her sleep will be filled with golden dreams; if a tradesman, she will dream of odd noises and tumults; if a traveler, there will be thunder and lightning to disturb her. It is safe to assume that in the medley of dreams that is sure to follow, any young girl with first-class dreaming machinery can easily find her own true love.

The Crowning Test.

The mysterious rites of Hallowe'en are not complete when the merrymaking is done and "good-night" is said. Each young lady, in order to complete the charms of the night, on reaching her home must take two pink roses with long stems, naming one for herself and the other for her lover. She must then go directly to her sleeping-room without speaking to any one, and kneeling beside her bed, must twine together the stems of the two roses and repeat the following lines, gazing meanwhile intently upon the lover's rose:

"Twine, twine, and intertwine;
Let my love be wholly mine,
If his heart be kind and true,
Deeper grow his rose's hue."

If her swain be faithful, the color of the rose will appear darker; if unfaithful, it will grow paler.

Apple-Pip Test.

Cut open an apple and pick out the seeds or pips from the core. If only two pips are found, it portends an early marriage; three imply a legacy; four, great wealth; five, a sea voyage; six, great fame as an orator or singer; seven, the possession of any gift most desired by the finder.

Wood and Water.

A quaint old book of charms, published in Edinburgh in 1690, entitled, "Old Father Time's Bundle of Faggots Newly Bound Up," declares that an infallible means of getting a view of your future husband or wife is to go to bed on Hallowe'en with a glass of water, in which a small sliver of wood has been placed, standing on a table by your bedside. In the night you will dream of falling from a bridge into a river, and of being rescued by your future wife or husband, whom you will see as distinctly as though viewed with waking eyes. This charm is thus alluded to by the poet Gay:

> "Last Hallow Eve I looked my love to see,
> And tried a spell to call her up to me.
> With wood and water standing by my side,
> I dreamed a dream and saw my own sweet bride."

AROUND THE WALNUT TREE.

Of all the many Hallowe'en spells and charms associated with nuts, one of the oldest is that which prevails in some of England's northern counties, and which is to the effect that if a young man or woman will go at midnight on Hallowe'en to a walnut tree and walk around it three times, crying out each time, "Let him (her) that is to be my true love bring me some walnuts," the future wife or husband will be seen in the tree gathering its fruit. The poet Gay thus refers in his "Pastorals" to this custom:

> "Last Hallow Eve I sought a walnut tree,
> In hopes my true Love's face that I might see.
> Three times I called, three times I walked apace;
> Then in the tree I saw my true Love's face."

WHERE DWELLS MY LOVER?

A very old Hallowe'en divination, formerly much practised by English rustics, to tell from what quarter of the compass the future husband or wife will come, is performed by stealing out unobserved at midnight, plucking a small lock of hair from one's head, and casting it to the breeze. Whatever direction it is blown toward is believed to be the location of the future matrimonial partner. This divination is also mentioned by Gay in his "Pastorals," as follows:

> "I pluck this lock of hair from off my head
> To tell whence comes the one that I shall wed.
> Fly, silken hair, fly all the world around
> Until you reach the spot where my true love is found."

THE LOVERS' TEST.

A maid and a youth place each a chestnut to roast on the fire, side by side. If one of them hisses and steams, it indicates a fretful temper in the owner of the chestnut; if both equally misbehave in that manner, it augurs strife. If one or both pops away, it means sure separation; but if both consume to ashes tranquilly side by side, a long life of undisturbed happiness will be the favored lot of the owners.

Charles Graydon fitly defines these portentous omens in the following lines:

> "These glowing nuts are emblems true
> Of what in human life we view;
> The ill-matched couple fret and fume,
> And thus in strife themselves consume;
> Or from each other wildly start,
> And with a noise forever part.
> But see the happy, happy pair,
> Of genuine love and truth sincere;
> With mutual fondness while they burn,
> Still to each other kindly turn;
> And as the vital sparks decay,
> Together gently sink away;
> Till life's fierce trials being past,
> Their mingled ashes rest at last."

HALLOWE'EN FORTUNE-TELLING.

These fortunes may be written with milk on white paper, and, after being allowed to dry, placed in walnut shells from which meat has been removed. Each guest selects his (her) own walnut, and placing his (her) paper where it will receive sufficient heat to brown the milk, will be surprised to see his (her) fortune stand out on what appeared to be blank paper: or

They may be selected by number and read by one who is fantastically dressed to represent a witch or gypsy fortune-teller: or

The hostess may assign to each number the name of a flower. Each guest may then select his (her) favorite flower, and his (her) fortune will be that of the corresponding number: or

The fortune may be written with French chalk upon a mirror and gently erased. The guest is told to breathe gently on the mirror, when the writing will appear.

The numbers run from one to forty inclusive.

THE HALLOWE'EN FORTUNE-TELLER.

No. 1.

You will marry before the end of another year; of silver and gold you will have more than enough. You will travel extensively, see a great deal of society and of the world. Your companion through life will be an artist. Three beautiful children will be born to you, and your family will be a happy one.

No. 2.

It will be your fate to serve others; but your calling will be a high one. You will never suffer from want or hunger, and many will bless you. There are sorrows in your life, but the closing years will be bright and happy.

No. 3.

Your career will be a brilliant one, and many will envy you. You have great genius,

"The Lovers' Test" on Hallowe'en — burning nuts.

but are inclined to be selfish. Remember the fate of Napoleon, and let not ambition ruin you. You will marry in four years. Eventually you will become wealthy, but there is a long, steep hill to climb before you reach the consummation of your desires.

No. 4.

Your life resembles a broad stretch of prairie; no elevations of happiness, no vales of sorrow or despair. Your companion in life will ever be true. You will have a competency. Your two children will be a comfort and a blessing to you; and if you should ever be the subject of envy, it will be on your children's account.

No. 5.

Your occupation in life will be of a mercantile nature. You will always find plenty to do; more than one public institution will be indebted to your philanthropy, and when you die a whole city will mourn your loss. Few sorrows, but much happiness, are in store for you and yours.

No. 6.

It is your lot to bear other people's burdens. In a few years you will be married, and then your troubles will begin. You could not escape them, however, should you remain single. One year of your life will show you what poverty is, but after that will come bright and happy days. Your companion will be a true helpmeet, and you will never have cause to regret your marriage.

No. 7.

You will live in a land where the palm-tree grows. Dusky faces will crowd around you to listen to your teachings. Peace and joy will be your portion and that of your true-hearted, noble-minded companion. You will be married in less than a year.

No. 8.

You will know much of the ocean, and your wealth will come from the sea. Twice will you be rescued from shipwreck. You will visit many foreign coasts, but will settle eventually in an inland town in California. Many young faces will grace your board, and one of your children will be an honor to his country.

No. 9.

You will be a successful teacher. At the end of five years you will marry a teacher, and six years later will change your profession for one more lucrative and agreeable. Success will attend you through life, though a jealous rival, at one period of your career, will make you extremely unhappy. You will live to see the day when this rival will apply to you for influence and aid.

No. 10.

Your coming will be heralded from city to city; you will be presented to kings and queens who deem it an honor to know you. Yet, notwithstanding all this pomp and honor, you will often sigh for rest, and for one who could not follow your wanderings. You will die suddenly, away from home and friends, but kings and princes will follow you to the grave.

No. 11.

The busy thoroughfares of a city will see much of you and your work; your name will be given to a city, and you will not be forgotten many generations hence. You will never marry, but your life will be happy and useful beyond the ordinary lot of mankind.

No. 12.

Science will owe a great discovery to you, and the world will be enriched thereby, and mankind benefited. You will have as many enemies as friends, but the influence of your friends will prevail and finally place you above the machinations and calumnies of your enemies. The world will be your workshop. You will be married to the one your heart has already selected, and the marriage will be a happy one.

No. 13

Early in life your business will take you from door to door; later, people will come to you. You will become immensely wealthy. You have already met your companion in life, and will be wedded one year from to-day. Your married life will not be a specially happy one, though as happy as the majority. Remember that as much depends upon you as on any one to make it happy.

No. 14.

The rattle of musketry, the boom of cannon, and the terrible scenes of war will be familiar to you. Although you will not take part in any battle, you will care for the sick, wounded, and disabled. Your entire life will be an unselfish one, and many will bless you with their last breath. You cannot but be happy.

No. 15.

A disappointment will befall you within a year which will prove to be the best thing that could happen to you. You will lose all interest in your employments of the past, and seek forgetfulness in a new occupation. You will not become wealthy, but will never want; and in the new place you make for yourself, you will find a companion worthy of you.

No. 16.

The rumble of machinery will be constantly in your ears; but to you it will be music. Five years hence, you will receive a promotion at the hands of your employers that will place you above want. Fortunate investments in real estate will make you wealthy. Your companion will be in every way worthy of you, though there will be much opposition to your marriage.

No. 17.

Your life will be spent among flowers, and the music of birds will ever greet your ears. You will be neither rich nor poor in this world's goods. You have a jealous rival; you will marry young and will be happy if you succeed in making those about you happy.

No. 18.

Beware of false friends and be true to yourself. You have already had a fair sample of what your life will be unless you put forth more effort than you are doing at present. Do not be afraid of work. Do not be in a hurry to get married. You can be and do what you will if you show energy and perseverance. Your success in life depends on yourself.

No. 19.

The greater part of your life will be spent on an island. You will know what want and privations are for three years, but it will be good training for you; if you take it in the right spirit, it will prepare you for future successes. Do not give in to trifles or discouragements. The latter part of your life will be bright, and many children will bless you.

No. 20.

You have a mission to which you have already been called. Do not hesitate. Your choice lies between two undertakings, but your conscience tells you which you should select. You will see much of the world. You will not meet your companion in life for ten years. Never engage in speculations of any kind.

No. 21.

The happiest period of your life will be spent near the sea in a beautiful villa. Liveried servants will attend you, and every luxury will be yours; but death will rob you of one you love, and for several years life will lose all charms for you. The latter years of your life will be devoted to the poor and needy, and many will bless you.

No. 22.

You will marry young and will live in the country, where you will experience the regular routine of life of the farm. You will live in peace and plenty. Many friends will come and go, and many happy and contented faces will gather around your bountiful board.

No. 23.

Your mission in life will be to attend the sick. You will have two strong temptations at the beginning of your career that will influence your entire life. If you overcome these two evils, your career will be a brilliant one; if not, your life will be a failure. Your marriage will take place soon and will be a happy one.

No. 24.

Your mission in life is to administer justice. Much care will devolve upon you. Your companion in life will be true and noble, the possessor of many rare qualities and virtues. Your home will be not only happy, but a model of culture and refinement.

No. 25.

Many high dignitaries will bow before you, and your influence will be worth more than gold or silver. You will marry soon, but will know little of home life. You will reside in a great city with long, broad avenues, but your power will extend far beyond the city limits. Two years will be spent at a foreign court and two in travel. A younger rival will finally succeed you in office, but your influence will be felt for many years after.

No. 26.

You will be the central figure of a circus within a year. The plaudits of the crowd will follow you wherever you go. You will marry a dashing rider and be twice divorced.

No. 27.

You are a rover by nature; take heed lest you become a tramp. You will marry, but will not settle down until you are obliged to do so.

No. 28.

You will keep a peanut stand, and speculate in bananas. You will become rich, but no one will suspect it except yourself.

No. 29.

Music is your forte. Your whole life will be devoted to it; for you will travel from door to door with a hand-organ and monkey. You will never marry, in spite of the fact that you think your matrimonial prospects are most excellent at the present time. You will never regret it, however.

No. 30.

Neatness is a hobby with you, and your occupation in life will be to gather up all the old rags, bottles, and useless pieces of iron, etc., which are always to be found in a large city.

No. 31.

Honesty is such a virtue with you that you will make it a business to return all the umbrellas which come in your way. In addition to that, you will restore broken ribs and handles and recover them for their owners.

No. 32.

You will be admitted to the grandest houses in the land. The wealthiest and most cultured ladies will invite you to their homes — to wash their windows and cleanse their furniture.

No. 33.

The enlightenment of the masses is your mission in life; with this end in view, you will climb many a lofty electric pole. You will marry young.

No. 34.

That "economy is the road to wealth" is a favorite maxim with you. Therefore you assist people along the road by cobbling their shoes, laying by a trifle occasionally to help yourself along.

No. 35.

You made up your mind long ago that you would never work for a living, and you will not. Work requires brains. You will simply wait upon others while they do the work and reap the reward.

No. 36.

You are a keen observer of human nature. You have concluded, after a careful review of the lives of many noted, influential, and successful men, that they owe their success largely to "soft soap." You will go into the manufacture of that article on a lavish scale, and will soon be a noted dealer in the commodity.

No. 37.

You will be successful at nothing until you settle down to hard, determined work. Neither wealth nor fame is obtained for the asking. Let your motto be "hard work," and live up to it, and fortune will smile upon you. One year from New Year's Eve you will be married.

No. 38.

Life has many ups and downs for you during the next two years, as you are soon to become a professional bicycle-rider.

No. 39.

You will receive a large legacy within the year, will marry happily, and outlive most of your friends.

No. 40.

For the next ten years, yours will be a checkered life, made up of sunshine and sorrow, success and failure. After this period you will receive a legacy which will enable you to carry out certain schemes you have in mind. You will travel extensively, marry within two years, and live to a good old age.

Fortune Telling by the Grounds in a Tea or Coffee Cup

Pour the grounds of tea or coffee into a white cup; shake them well about, so as to spread them over the surface, reverse the cup to drain away the superfluous contents, and then exercise your fertile fancy in discovering what the figures thus formed represent. Long, wavy lines denote vexations and losses — their importance depending on the number of lines. Straight ones, on the contrary, foretell peace, tranquility, and long life. Human figures are usually good omens, announcing love affairs and marriage. If circular figures predominate, the person for whom the experiment is made, may expect to receive money. If these circles are connected by straight, unbroken lines, there will be delay, but ultimately all will be satisfactory. Squares foretell peace and happiness; oblong figures, family discord; whilst curved, twisted, or angular ones are certain signs of vexations and annoyances, their probable duration being determined by the number of figures. A crown signifies honor; a cross, news of death; a ring, marriage — if a letter can be discovered near it, that will be the initial of the name of the future spouse. If the ring is in the clear part of the cup, it foretells a happy union; if clouds are about it, the contrary; but if it should chance to be quite at the bottom, then the marriage will never take place. A leaf of clover, or trefoil, is a good sign, denoting if at the top of the cup, speedy good fortune, which will be more or less distant in case it appears at or near the bottom. The anchor, if at the bottom of the cup, denotes success in business; at the top and in the clear part, love and fidelity; but in the thick, or cloudy parts, inconstancy. The serpent is always the sign of an enemy, and if in the cloudy part gives warning that great prudence will be necessary to ward off misfortune. The coffin portends news of a death, or long illness. The dog, at the top of the cup, denotes true and faithful friends; in the middle, that they are not to be trusted; but at the bottom, that they are secret enemies. The lily, at the top of the cup, foretells a happy marriage; at the bottom, anger. A letter signifies news; if in the clear, very welcome news; surrounded by dots, a remittance of money; but if hemmed in by clouds, bad tidings, and losses. A heart near it denotes a love letter. A single tree portends restoration to health; a group of trees in the clear, misfortunes which may be avoided; several trees, wide apart, promise that your wishes will be accomplished; if encompassed by dashes, it is a token that your future is in its blossom, and only requires care to bring to maturity; if surrounded by dots, riches. Mountains signify either friends or enemies, according to their situation. The sun, moon, and stars, denote happiness, success. The clouds, happiness or misfortune, according as they are bright or dark. Birds are good omens, but quadrupeds, with the exception of the dog, foretell trouble and difficulties. Fish imply good news from across water. A triangle portends an unexpected legacy; a single straight line, a journey. The figure of a man indicates a speedy visitor; if the arm is outstretched, a present; when the figure is very distinct, it shows that the person expected will be of dark complexion, and vice versa. A crown near a cross indicates a large fortune, resulting from a death. Flowers are signs of joy, happiness, and peaceful life. A heart, surrounded by dots, signifies joy, occasioned by the receipt of money; with a ring near it, approaching marriage.

THAT'S ALL!

(A weird story suitable to be related when called upon to tell a ghost story. It will be more effective if the person telling the story has the lights turned down and has the listeners gathered about him or her — then tell the story as dramatically as possible.)

Mrs. Smith and her neighbor thought they would like to know the sensation of hanging, so they decided to go up in the attic and try it out. Mrs. Smith wanted to try first, so she stood on a chair with a rope around her neck. They decided the chair would be taken away, and when Mrs. Smith wanted to come down she was to wiggle her feet, and the chair would be put back. When all was ready, the chair was taken away. Just then the telephone rang and the neighbor ran down stairs to answer it. When she came back Mrs. Smith was dead!! This of course frightened the neighbor very much, as she thought she would be held for murder. After thinking it over she decided to carry Mrs. Smith down stairs and sit her up in a chair by the window, and put her sewing in her hands, so that when her husband comes home he would think she died of heart trouble. She arranged Mrs. Smith as natural as she could and left her. After a short time the husband came home, and seeing his wife in the window, whistled and waved his hand. Finally when he could not draw her attention, he picked up a pebble and threw it in the window. It happened to hit her in the head and she fell over. When he came into the house and found her dead, he thought he had killed her and became panic stricken. He did not know what to do, so in his terror he grabbed her up, ran down stairs and put her in the buggy. Not knowing just what the outcome would be, he sat her up and made her look as natural as possible and then started the old horse going. He just drove wildly around corners and in and out of streets as fast as he could, praying for something to happen. At last the horse became frightened, ran up on the sidewalk and the buggy overturned, throwing the poor woman down an area-way into a basement where a shoemaker was mending shoes and using one of those things you make holes in the shoes with — you know — one of those — what do you call them now? *(Some one will no doubt say "an awl" and you say — "Yes — that's all!")*

"The Young Man in the Fairy Knoll"

From *Superstitions of the Highlands & Islands of Scotland Collected Entirely from Oral Sources,* John Gregorson Campbell, 1900

"The Young Man in the Fairy Knoll" is a wonderful short Scottish Halloween tale, one that involves both fairy mythology and a moral warning. It also makes use of the mythology of needles or metal and their use against fairies (in another folk belief, for example, on Halloween night a needle inserted into the sleeve of a jacket could keep a traveler safe from malicious fairies).

An early postcard with a Scottish Hallowe'en theme.

128

"The Young Man in the Fairy Knoll"

Two young men, coming home after nightfall on Hallowe'en, each with a jar of whisky on his back, heard music by the roadside, and seeing a dwelling open and illuminated, and dancing and merriment going on within, entered. One of them joined the dancers, without as much as waiting to lay down the burden he was carrying. The other, suspecting the place and company, stuck a needle in the door as he entered, and got away when he liked. That day twelvemonths he came back for his companion, and found him still dancing with the jar of whisky on his back. Though more than half-dead with fatigue, the enchanted dancer begged to be allowed to finish the reel. When brought to the open-air he was only skin and bone.

This tale is localized in the Ferintosh district, and at the Slope of Big Stones (*Leathad nan Clacha mòra*) in Harris. In Argyllshire people say it happened in the north. In the Ferintosh story only one of the young men entered the brugh, and the door immediately closed. The other lay under suspicion of having murdered his companion, but, by advice of an old man, went to the same place on the same night the following year, and by putting steel in the door of the Fairy dwelling, which he found open, recovered his companion. In the Harris story, the young men were a bridegroom and his brother-in-law, bringing home whisky for the marriage.

Celtic Folklore:
Welsh and Manx

Excerpt from Volume I, Sir John Rhys, 1901

This Hallowe'en section from Rhys's book provides not only a look at a specifically Welsh celebration of Hallowe'en, but is also one of the more frightening entries on the holiday, featuring references to "the cutty black sow" and various seasonal demons.

Rhys's lengthy etymological footnotes have been omitted from this excerpt.

... A bonfire was always kindled on the farm called Cromlech on the eve of the Winter Calends or *Nos Galan Gaeaf*, as it is termed in Welsh; and the like were to be seen in abundance towards ILithfaen, Carnguwch, and ILanaelhaearn, as well as on the Merioneth side of the bay. Besides fuel, each person present used to throw into the fire a small stone, with a mark whereby he should know it again. If he succeeded in finding the stone on the morrow, the year would be a lucky one for him, but the contrary if he failed to recover it. Those who assisted at the making of the bonfire watched until the flames were out, and then somebody would raise the usual cry, when each ran away for his life, lest he should be found last. This cry, which is a sort of equivalent, well known over Carnarvonshire, of the English saying, 'The devil take the hindmost,' was in the Welsh of that county—

Yr hwch du gwta
A gipio'r ola';

that is to say, 'May the black sow without a tail seize the hindmost.'

The cutty black sow is often alluded to nowadays to frighten children in Arfon, and it is clearly the same creature that is described in some parts of North Wales as follows:—

Hwch du gwta	A cutty black sow
Ar bob camfa	On every stile,
Yn nydu a chardio	Spinning and carding
Bob nos G'langaea.'	Every Allhallows' Eve.

In Cardiganshire this is reduced to the words:—

| *Nos Galan Gaea'* | On Allhallows' Eve |
| *Bwbach ar bob camfa* | A bogie on every stile. |

130

Welsh people speak of only three Calends — *Calan-mai*, or the first of May; *Calan-gaeaf*, the Calends of Winter, or Allhallows; and *Y Calan*, or The Calends *par excellence*, that is to say, the first day of January, which last is probably not Celtic but Roman. The other two most certainly are, and it is one of their peculiarities that all uncanny spirits and bogies are at liberty the night preceding each of them. The *Hwch du gwta* is at large on Allhallows' Eve, and the Scottish Gaels have the name 'Samhanach' for any Allhallows' demon, formed from the word *Samhain*, Allhallows. The eve of the first of May may be supposed to have been the same, as may be gathered from the story of Rhiannon's baby and of Teyrnon's colt, both of which were stolen by undescribed demons that night — I allude to the *Mabinogi* of Pwyll, Prince of Dyfed.

Halloween bogies — a witch, black cats and bats — on a 1911 postcard.

"Samhain, Hallowmas"

Excerpt from *Witchcraft & Second Sight in the Highlands & Islands of Scotland*, John Gregorson Campbell, 1902

This excerpt offers up both some interesting variations on traditional Halloween activities and a wonderful description of Halloween bonfires (compare this with Hardy's account of the Fifth of November bonfires from *The Return of the Native*).

Samhain, Hallowmas,

is the first day of winter, and is also known as All-Saints' Day (*Latha nan uile Naomh*), Nov. 1–13. It was a sign of a bad winter if it fell upon a Wednesday, according to the saying: "When Hallowmas is on Wednesday, it is afflictive after it" (*Nuair is Di-ciadàin an t-samhainn is iargaineach na dèigh*).

The coming of winter was hailed with more fun and merriment than any other season of the year. The cold was now fairly set in, the fruits of the summer, down to the very nuts, were gathered, and the young became desirous of learning their fate with regard to that subject of anxiety in every age, their future husbands and wives. This natural welcoming of winter explains the ceremonies of the day, and the games of the evening. Hardly any of them have reference to the practices or deities of the nations of antiquity or to Scripture, and this explanation must be sought for in Pagan times.

On the last day of autumn children gathered ferns, tar-barrels, the long thin stalks called *gàinisg*, and everything suitable for a bonfire. These were placed in a heap on some eminence near the house, and in the evening set fire to. The fires were called *Samhnagan*. There was one for each house, and it was an object of ambition who should have the biggest. Whole districts were brilliant with bonfires, and their glare across a Highland loch, and from many eminences, formed an exceedingly picturesque scene. Some find in them traces of the worship of the invariable Baal, but there is no reason to look upon them otherwise than as the natural and defiant welcome of the season, in which fires are most required, when the heat of the year is departed, and cold and frost and rushing winds cover all things with gloom. Bonfires are kindled on all occasions of public rejoicing, or excitement, and Hallowmas fires are a natural expression of the change of season.

A young woman attempts a divination involving hemp seed sowing in this early postcard.

It is possible a deity was originally associated with the practice, but there is now no trace of him in name or practices of this day.

As the evening wore on, the young people gathered to one house, and an almost endless variety of games (*cleasan*) were resorted to, with the object in every case of divining the future lot of the company. Were they to marry or not, was it to be that year or never, who was to be married first, what like the future husband or wife was to be, their names, trade, colour of hair, size, property, etc.? were questions of great importance, and their answer was a source of never-failing entertainment. The modes of divination are of interest, from the light they throw on the character of the people among whom they prevailed, and from an antiquarian point of view, as remains of Pagan times.

A shoe caught by the tip and thrown over the house, fore-indicates the future by its position on the ground on the other side. In whatever direction the toe points, the thrower will go before long, and it is very unlucky if the shoe be found with the sole uppermost, misfortune is "making for" him. A thin, fine shoe, used in this manner, led the man, fished up from the Green Island, to remark, after some years of silence:

> "A thin shoe, little valued,
> It is hard to say who will wear it."[1]

He might well say so, for the owner of the shoe died in a few days.

The white of eggs, dropped in a glass of pure water, indicates by certain marks how many children a person is to have. The impatience and clamour of the children often made the housewife perform this ceremony for them by daylight, and the kindly mother, standing with her face to the window, dropping the white of an egg into a crystal glass of clean water, and surrounded by a group of children, eagerly watching her proceedings, formed a pretty picture.

When the fun of the evening had fairly commenced, the names of eligible, or likely as possible matches, were written on the chimney place, and the young man, who wished to essay his fortune, was blindfolded and led up to the list. Whatever name he put his finger one would prove to be that of his future wife.

Two nuts were put on the fire beside each other, representing two individuals, whose names were made known to the company. As they burned together, or flared up alone, or leaped away from each other, the future marriage of the pair, or haughty rejection of each other, was inferred.

A dish of milk and meal (*fuarag*, Scot. Crowdie), or of beat potatoes, was made, and a ring was concealed in it. Spoons were given to the company, and a vigorous attack was made on the dish. Whoever got the ring would prove to be the first married. This was an excellent way of making the taking of food part of the evening's merriment.

Apples and a silver sixpence were put in a tub of water. The apples floated on the top, but the coin lay close the bottom. Whoever was able to lift either in his mouth, and without using his teeth, was counted very lucky, and got the prize to himself.

By taking an apple and going to a room alone, dividing it there into nine pieces

1. Bròg thana, 's i gun mheas,
   Gun fhios co chaitheas i.

against the name of the Father and the Son, eating eight pieces with the back to a looking glass and the face looking over the left shoulder, and then throwing the ninth piece over the same shoulder, the future husband or wife was seen in the glass coming and taking the piece of apple away.

A person, going in the devil's name to winnow in a barn alone, will see his future partner entering the door.

An unmarried woman, taking a ball of thread and crossing a wall on her way, went to a kiln or other out-house. Here, holding one end of the thread, she threw the ball in the dark into the eye of the kiln (*sùil àth*), or over one of the rafters or a partition wall, in the name of a sweetheart whom she had before fixed on in her mind, and calling out "who is down there at the end of my little rope?" (*co so shìos air ceann mo ròpain?*), at the same time she gave the thread a gentle pull. In reply, some one or something pulled the thread at the other end, and a voice called out the name of her future husband. There is a story of a tailor having hid himself in anticipation of this mode of divination being resorted to, and when the ball was thrown he caught it and gave the thread a tug. In answer to the question "who is this at the end of my little rope?" he said, "I am the devil." (*Tha mise, 'n deamhan*), and the woman to whom this frightful answer was given never tried divination again.

Young women sowed hemp seed (*fras lìn*) over nine ridges of plough land, saying "I sow hemp seed, and he who is to be my husband, let him come and harrow it." (*Tha mi cur fras lìn, 's am fear bhios na fhear 'dhomh, thigeadh e 's cliathadh e*). On looking back they saw the figure of their future husband. Hallowe'en being the night preceding the first day of a lunar month was always dark, and this ceremony was rendered more awful by a story that a woman once saw herself coming after her, and never recovered from the effects of the vision.

By dipping his shirt sleeve in a well to the south (*tobar mu dheas*), and then pulling off the shirt and placing it to dry before the fire, the anxious youth, if he does not oversleep himself, will see his sweetheart entering through the night and turning the shirt.

On putting an odd number of keys in a sieve, going to a barn alone, and there riddling them well "with the wrong hand turn" (*car tuaitheal*), the destined one will come and put the odd key right.

By holding a mouthful of water in the mouth, and going to listen (*farcluais*) at a neighbour's window, the first name overheard will prove to be that of one's intended.

The same knowledge was obtained by biting a piece of the last cart that sent in the corn, and with it in the mouth going, without speaking, to listen (*farcluais*) under a neighbour's window.

A common practice was to go and steal kail stocks. Unless the plants are pulled surreptitiously, without the knowledge or consent of their owner, they are of no use for the purpose of divination. A number of young people go together, and having cautiously and with difficulty made their way into a kailyard, pull each one the first stock that comes to hand after bending down. It must be the first that the hand meets. The plant is then taken home and examined by the light, and according to its height, straightness, colour, etc., will be the future husband or wife. A quantity of soil adhering to it signifies money and property. When put for the night above the lintel of the door, it affords indications by the first person entering below it in the morning; and, put below the pillow, it is excellent to dream over.

A straw, drawn at random from a stack, indicates by the number of grains upon it what family a person is to have.

Three ears of corn similarly pulled and placed below the pillow for the night, will cause dreams of the future husband reaping them.

A plate of clean water, one of dirty water, and one empty being placed on the floor, and a napkin thrown over the eyes, the dish in which the person blindfolded puts his forefinger, indicated a maid, or widow, or none at all.

A piece of flesh being buried this night, if any living creature was found in it in the morning, the person burying it would be married; but if not, he never would.

If water, in which the feet had been washed, were kept in the house this night,[1] (and the Fairies were apt to enter the house when that was the case), a person putting a burning peat in it will see the colour of his sweetheart's hair in it.

If a mouthful of the top sod of the house wall (*foid fail na h-anainn*), or a mouthful from the clod above the lintel of the door (*àrd-dorus*) be taken into the house in one's teeth and any hair be found in it, it is of the same colour as that of the future wife of the person who performs the rite.

One of the chief performances of the evening was for young women to go to a Boundary Stream (*allt crìche*), (if between two neighbouring proprietors so much the better,) and with closed eyes to lift from it three stones between the middle finger and thumb, saying these words:

> "I will lift the stone
> As Mary lifted it for her Son,
> For substance, virtue, and strength;
> May this stone be in my hand
> Till I reach my journey's end."[2]

The stones were for putting below the head when going to sleep.

Many other modes of divination were practiced too tedious to mention, by slices from the plough, different metals, eating a stolen raw salt herring, sprinkling corn in front of the bed, etc., etc. These observances can hardly be characterised as superstitions; they proceeded from a spirit of fun more than from any belief in their efficacy. There are in every community many weak and simple people who are easily imposed on, and made to believe almost anything; but the divinations of Hallowe'en left an abiding impression on few minds.

---

1. Campbell's *Superstitions of the Scottish Highlands*, p. 260.

2. Togaidh mise chlach,
   Mar a thog Moire da Mac,
   Air bhrìgh, air bhuaidh, 's air neart;
   Gun robh a chlachsa am dhòrn,
   Gus an ruig mi mo cheann uidhe.

"More Folklore from the Hebrides"

Excerpt from *Folk-Lore, Volume XIII*, A. Goodrich-Freer, 1902

Located thirty miles off the northwest coast of Scotland, the Hebrides islands offer a folklore history that is heavily Scottish and yet also unique, with interesting variants on such traditional Halloween divinations as the luggie bowls and the dumb cake.

... Hallowe'en is of course the great time for looking into the future, and it may be interesting to quote such methods as we have met with, for the sake of comparison with similar customs elsewhere. The following notes have all been taken at first hand from those who have practised or seen in practice the divinations in question.

There is a saying:

> "Hallowe'en will come, will come,
> Witchcraft [or divination] will be set agoing,
> Fairies will be at full speed,
> Running in every pass.
> Avoid the road, children, children."

On Hallowe'en six plates were placed on the floor each with separate contents, and the girl of the house came blindfolded. The first she touched foretold her fate. 1. Pure water portended an unexceptionable husband. 2. Salt, a sailor. 3. Meal, a farmer. 4. Earth, a death. 5. Dirty water, a disreputable husband. 6. An empty plate, no husband.

Another Hallowe'en divination is known as the *Pollag na Samkna* = the little hole of Hallowe'en. The person seeking a revelation of the future digs a little hole in the ground about the size of a saucer, and then loosely replaces the earth, which he removes again next morning. If he find a live worm in it, it is a sign he will be alive next Hallowe'en, if a dead one, that his career is ended. A girl called Kate, who had found a dead worm in her hole, had recently died of measles within the year. In some places the Pollag is turned to another account. Three are dug, representing three eligible young men, or maids, as the case may be. The one in which a live worm is found indicates the name of the sweetheart assigned by fate.

The "Luggie bowl" method of fortune-telling is displayed on this 1909 postcard.

Another method is to take a glass half full of water and an egg perforated at the bottom, through which the white is allowed to drop into the water. If it falls to the bottom and remains there, ill-luck will follow; if it rises, it rises slowly, and the method is to hold the glass between the eye and the light and divine the future according to the shapes it may assume. If little round globules come up they should be counted, for they indicate the number of the future family. A variant was, to break an egg into the water, and then, closing the tumbler with the palm of the hand, to turn it quickly upside down and back again, and then watch the forms assumed while the egg is in movement.

Another custom was for young women to go to a stream that was a boundary, and to wash or dip their shifts into the stream and afterwards place them at the fire to dry. All must be done in strict silence, and the man of whom they dreamt, or whose image they saw as from time to time they turned the garment at the fire, was the man they would marry.

Another custom was to go alone to the kiln where grain is dried (nothing gets much chance to dry naturally in such a climate as Uist), taking a coil of heather rope, of which one end was inserted down the flue. The girl then asked, "Who is that at the end of my rope?" and the name given in answer was that of the future husband.[1]

If a girl went to a house and listened at the door, the first man whose name she heard would be her husband.

There is a mysterious method of divination which consists in carrying an apple on a

1. There was a somewhat similar custom in the Lowlands, where the girls on Hallowe'en used to put their garters outside the window, and pulling them in gently would ask in the same way, "Who is at the end of my garters?"

fork *against the Father, the Son, and the Holy Ghost* on Hallowe'en, the first person met to be considered one's fate. The custom was quoted with much expression of horror and fate explained as an importation, not a local practice, which, as forks and apples are alike modern innovations, is very probable.

A favourite dish on Hallowe'en is called *Fuarag*, and suggests the Yorkshire frumenty or furmenty. It is made of churned cream, oatmeal, and sugar. A ring is put into it — on the same principle as into a plum-pudding in England.

A salt cake called *Bonnach Salainn* is eaten on Hallowe'en to induce dreams of the future in store. Not a word must be spoken after taking it, not even prayers if they don't happen to have been said previously, and no water must be drunk. The cake is made of common meal, with an inordinate quantity of salt. A variant on this is to eat a salt herring roasted on the fire. It must be consumed in three bites, bones, fins, and all, and the same conditions observed.

There is one custom observed on Hallowe'en of which unless it be the survival of some ceremony of *blessing*, one does not see the import. It was thus described. The boys of the house, urged by their parents, take a peat from the fire, and proceed round the house, the stackyard, and the barn, sunwise. In going round the stackyard one must enter, and place a stone on each stack on the inside of the heather rope going round the stack.

The girls too have their special game, which has probably some interesting historical origin, if one did not know it. They call it *Mathair M'hor*, "the big mother." All but one sit in a row inside the house, one at the end acting The Big Mother. The remaining child hops in on one foot, and the Mother asks what she has come for. The reply is: "*Dioja, Dioja, Diasgan*" (nonsense words, pronounced *Cheeka, Cheeka, Chelusgan*), "Macleod sent me to ask for a piece of pork." The game is to see how many times this can be said on one leg. It should be remembered that the true Highlander scorns pork, and even when (which is still not often, and was formerly yet more rare) he keeps pigs, it is usually for sale, not for his own use.

"A European Custom of Pagan Times Brought Over to America (Halloween at Chicago)"

From *Internationaler Amerikanisten-Kongress*, Jonkheer L. C. van Panhuys, s'Gravenhage, 1904

This quaint paper provides a Dutch insight into the early 20th-century American Halloween (albeit an insight which does include a few fanciful errors, such as listing November 1st as the date of All Souls Day, which of course actually occurs on November 2nd); but it's perhaps most worthwhile for including one of the earliest first-person accounts of an embryonic form of trick-or-treat, in which an urban child attempts to frighten the narrator (although of course the actual phrase "trick or treat" is still some years from popular usage, as is the offering of candy to the trickster).

Those of the Americanists who, at the close of the Congress of New York in 1902, made the most interesting trip, which was graciously offered to them by the American Museum of Natural History, to various cities in the United States, and arrived the 31th of October at Chicago, may like the narrator, in the evening of that day, have been struck by a festivity, called Halloween, which took place especially among young people, and was commented and spoken of in the news papers of the town.

> We will meet on Halloween
> That night when the spooks and ghosts are seen
> Be sure you arrive a half hour before eight
> For the spirits grow lively before very late...etc.

So ran the invitation of the girls basket ball master for three schools, in a news paper. In another paper we were told how apples and nuts, perhaps with a ring cake, had to be the "menu" for the evening, how Halloween was a maiden festival and in which way the girls could try to get an insight in the character of their intended.

In the neighborhood of the Hotel de Prado groups of children walked round with

A youngster celebrates Hallowe'en with a noisemaker, a stalk of corn and a jack-o'-lantern in this early postcard.

Venetian lanterns and a young child with a sly face came with a toy at my window, to play ghost. I duly returned that attention by hiding myself much terrified to her great delight behind an easy chair.

So we meet in America with a curious custom, sprung, as we may see by comparison with the same custom in Europe, from the old pagan belief, — that during the night the souls of the dead are walking round (the souls from Purgatory) and that eatables, eaten by the living, will put the ghosts into a cheerful mood.

Much information is given about the custom in England in Observations on the Popular Antiquities of Great-Britain by John Brand, revised by Ellis, new Edition, Vol. I, 1883, in the chapter Allhallow Eden (sic), vulgarly Halle'een (sic), pag. 377–396. On pag. 389 the origin of Druidism is pleaded.

G. F. Northall, in English Folk-rhymes, Collection of traditional verses relating to places and persons, customs, superstitions, London, 1892, says about the word *halloween* that it derives from the Saxon *haligan*, holy, and gives a rhyme about the custom in Shropshire.

In the Netherlands the custom is, as far as I know, out of use; in Flanders they may still bake the "zieltjes koekjes" (cakes for the little souls) and, as many souls will be delivered from Purgatory as cakes will have been eaten with religious sense and prayer.

The Gaules, on All Souls day, the first of November, covered tables with eatables in order that the souls of the dead might partake of the same. Bosc and Bonnemere assure us that even untill now the Bretons earnestly believe that in that night the souls of relations and friends do enter their house. In Schraders Reallexikon der Indogermanischen

Altertumskunde, 1901, is mentioned, sub Ahnencultus, that still to this time in Tyrol milk is put on the table on All Saints day and oil is put in the lamp to dress the wound of the poor souls from Purgatory (Meyer, Deutsche Volkskunde, S. 275) and to refresh them.

In my lecture I will explain shortly that it was probably by the English, and not by the old Dutchmen, that the custom was brought over from Europe to the United States. For those who are interested not only in the spreading but also in the arising of Thought in different places on earth, I will conclude with the following extract from the *Journal de la société des Americanistes de Paris*, Nouvelle Serie, Tome I, no I, Etudes sur le Indiens de la region de Riobamba, par le Dr. Rivert, pag. 76:

"Les Indiens, au siecle des Incas, offraient aux morts des liqueurs et des aliments, pour que ceux-ci puissent boire et manger. Leurs descendants ont conserve cette coutume. Le jour des Morts, ils s'asseoient au milieu de l'eglise, une bouteilie de chicha ou d'aguardiente devant eux; autour d'eux, de petits pains qu'ils arrosent conscienceieusement. Ils donnent a manger aux ames, tout en priant pour elles: offrande et priere, paganisme et christianisme!"

May the Chicago children keep long their interesting and innocent feast, a token of the folk poetry of former ages.

To our sketch as it was read at Stuttgart we have to add a few facts for the Proceedings of the Congress. Only a few, our subject leading too quickly from American Folklore into the dominion of European History of Civilisation. That the mentioned customs were brought over to Chicago by colonists of Celtic blood is proved by the same customs still existing in Celtic countries. Compare f. i. the Halloween customs given by E. J. Guthrie (Old Scottish Customs, London dan Glasgow, Hamilton, Adams and Co, 1885) as: an insight in futurity, burning nuts, cutting an apple, perhaps also: dipping the shirt sleeve and pricking the egg etc. The feasts on the evening of October 31st and on November 1st were one and the same, as will be explained at the end.

As origin of the festivity we find back the feast of the sun god; Combined with the ground idea of Fear for the spirits of the dead. The connexion between these two ideas is shown in the following quotation. Prof. Rhys writes: "Halloween night was the Saturnalia of all that was hideous and uncanny in the world of spirits. It had been fixed at the time of all others when the sun god, whose power had been gradually falling off since the great feast associated with him on the first of August, succumbed to his enemies, the powers of darkness and of winter. It was their first hour of triumph after an interval of subjection, and the popular imagination pictured them stalking abroad with more than ordinary insolence and aggressiveness.[1]

The idea of eating cakes for the souls was there for no other than putting the spirits[2] by an offering into a cheerful mood. Guthrie, 1. c. pag. 66 gives some more explanation

---

1. Rhys. *Celtic Folklore*. Welsh and Manx. Oxford 1901, page. 226.

2. Spirits of relatives supposedly were considered as a rule benevolent, but gave trouble and caused sickness when not propitiated; anyhow a spirit, even of a departed household dead became a stranger, who is, in the belief of all primitive people, synonymous with an enemy.

about the feast of the Sun. All fires, save those of the Druids, were extinguished from whose altars alone the holy fire had to be purchased. The bon fires (bon means bone) of Halloween bleeze were surrounded in Scotland with a circular trench, symbolical of the Sun.

In the different names we find also an explanation. The first of November, still called New-Years day on the island of Man, was the new years day on the beginning of the winter half year among Fins, Scottish, Danes, Swedish, Britons and Germans[1]; and called *Calan gaeaf*, i.e. the Calends of winter, by the Welsh and Manx, *Samhanach* and *Samhein*, the feast of the sun, by Scottish and Irish.[2] *Hollantide* (Hallow-tide) was the English name in Manx. In Whitby and Cleveland the Halloween evening is called according to the surviving custom Nut crack night. A rhyme in Cleveland says:

Nutty crack Neet Ah mount forget
Near neets afvoar Mart' mas day
We hav' a feast o' happles an' nuts
An how we krack away![3]

As happened with many others the heathen feast of November 1st was proclaimed by the clergy to be a Christian one. The heathen ideas associated with it were altered into a feast to the memory of the souls of the Saints of the Christian Church. The people kept the custom to remember on the 1st November their dead relatives, but gave up the heathen idea of fear for the dead. To leave room for a feast to the memory of All Saints as well as to the memory of dead relatives, an All Souls day is held in several countries on the 2nd November. With great care and foresight the Fathers of the Church succeeded in purifying those feasts from all heathen reminiscences.[4] Of course no obstacle was made against the continuance of old customs when they were no longer associated with anti-christian ideas.

The old custom of beginning a feast the evening before, called in English wake (in Dutch also wake, pronounce wauke), in Latin vigilia, was interdicted by the Concilium of Autisiodorum (Auxerre) in 586. This interdiction seems to have had little or no influence in Celtic Countries from where the Halloween evening has been brought over on American soil.

1. Finn Magnusen. *Den Förste November en Historik-Kalendarisk Undersögelse*. Tidskrift for Nordisk Old-kyndighed, 2 bind. Kjöbenhavn 1829, translated by Jhr. M. Hottema D. C. L., Leeuwarden, Fr. Schier-beck, 1835, pag. 2.

2. Rhys, l. c. page. 316, 317 etc.

3. *County Folklore* Vol. II. Published by the Folklore Society. London 1901. Examples collected by Mrs. Gutch., pag. 266.

4. Beugnot. *Histoire de la destruction du Paganisme en Occident*. Paris Firmin, Didot Frères, 1835. Tome II, Livre XII.— Buddingh. Verhandeling over het Westland. Leyden. 1844. Bls. 377–379, 398–399.

"The Ignis Fatuus, Its Character and Legendary Origin"

From *The Journal of American Folklore*, Vol. 17, No. 65, William Wells Newell, 1904

If Halloween can be said to have one single outstanding symbol or icon — its Santa Claus, if you will — that figure would undoubtedly be the jack-o'-lantern. While most contemporary Halloween celebrants could tell you that the jack-o'-lantern is a carved pumpkin with a candle placed within it, all designed for eerie effect, few could offer any explanation as to the background behind this most popular of Halloween traditions.

Although it makes no specific references to Halloween, this 1904 piece by William Wells Newell is one of the most comprehensive collections of Jack-o'-lantern legends ever gathered. It compares and contrasts Jack-o'-lantern and Will-o'-the-wisp legends from America, the British Isles and Europe, and shows how the legend of Jack ties into the mysterious lights glimpsed around bogs and marshes.

The next time you sit down on Halloween to transform the pumpkin into a glowing, grinning face, remember these tales of the wily Jack and how his trickery eventually led him to wander the dark earth with only a glowing hell ember to light his way.

A TALE OF MARYLAND NEGROES AND ITS COMPARATIVE HISTORY.

The legend below printed was obtained by Miss Mary Willis Minor of Baltimore, from the recitation of a Negro servant, and forms part of the collections of the Baltimore Folk-Lore Society, to be hereafter published as the Ninth Memoir of the American Folk-Lore Society.[1]

JACK-O'-MY-LANTERN.

Once dey wuz a man name Jack. He wuz a mighty weeked man, an' treat he wife an' chil'en like a dawg. He did n' do nuttin' but drink from mawin' tell night, an' 'twarn'

---

1. In regard to the dialect, I give the spelling as communicated by Miss Anne W. Whitney, Secretary of the Baltimore Society.

no use to say nuttin' 'tall to 'im 'cause he wuz jes' ex ambitious ez a mad dawg. Well suh, he drink an' he drink tell whiskey could n' mek 'im drunk; but et las' hit bu'n 'im up inside; an' den de Debble come fur 'im. When Jack see de Debble, he wuz so skeart he leettle mo'n er drapt in de flo'. Den he bague de Debble to let 'im off jes' a leetle while, but de Debble say, —

"Naw Jack, I ain' gwine wait no longer; my wife, Abbie Sheens, is speckin' yo'."

So de Debble start off pretty bris' an' Jack wuz 'bleeged to foller, tell dey come to a grog shop.

"Mr. Debble," said Jack, "don' yo' wan' a drink?"

"Well," said de Debble, "I b'leeve I does, but I ain' got no small change; we don keep no change down dyah."

"Tell yo' wotcher do, Mr. Debble," said Jack. "I got one ten cent en my pocket; yo' change yo'sef inter nurr ten cent, an' we kin git two drinks, an' den yo' kin change yo'sef back agin."

So de Debble change hisse'f inter a

The jack-o'-lantern seems to be the king of Hallowe'en in this early postcard.

ten cent, an' Jack pick 'im up; but stid o' gwine in de grog shop, Jack clap de ten cent in he pocket-book dat he had n't took outen he pocket befo', 'cause he did n' wan' de Debble to see dat de ketch wuz in de shape ob a cross. He shet it tight, an' dyah he had de Debble, an' 'twarn' no use fur 'im to struggle, 'cause he could n' git by dat cross. Well suh; fus' he swar and threat'n Jack wid what he wuz gwine do to 'im, an' den he begun to bague, but Jack jes' tu'n roun' an' start to go home. Den de Debble say, -

"Jack, ef yo'll lemme out o' hyah, I'll let yo' off fur a whole year, I will, fur trufe. Lemme go Jack, 'cause Abbie Sheens is too lazy to put de bresh on de fire, an' hit 'll all go black out ef I ain' dyah fo' long, to ten' to it."

Den Jack say ter hisse'f, "I gret mine to let 'im go, 'cause in a whole year I kin 'pent and git 'ligion an' git shet on 'im dat er way."

Den he say, "Mr. Debble, I'll letcher out ef yo' 'clar fo' gracius yo' won' come after me fur twel munt."

Den de Debble promise befo' Jack undo de clasp, an' by de time Jack got he pocket-book open he wuz gone. Den Jack say to hisse'f, "Well, now I gwine to 'pent an' git 'ligion sho'; but 't ain' no use bein' in no hurry; de las' six munt will be plenty o' time. Whar dat ten cent? Hyah 't is. I gwine git me a drink." When de six munt wuz gone, Jack 'lowed one munt would be time 'nuff to 'pent, and when de las' munt come, Jack say he gwine hab one mo' spree, an' den he would have a week er ten days lef' an' dat wuz plenty o' time, 'cause he done hearn o' folks 'penting on dey death bade. Den he went on a spree fo' sho', an' when de las' week come, Jack had 'lirium trimblins, an' de fus' ting he knowed dyah wuz de Debble at de do', an' Jack had to git outen he bade and go 'long wid 'im. After a while dey pas a tree full o' gret big red apples.

"Don' yo' wan' some apples, Mr. Debble?" said Jack.

"Yo' kin git some ef yo' wan' em," said de Debble, an' he stop an' look up in de tree.

"How yo' speck a man wid 'lirium trimblins to climb a tree?" said Jack. "Yo' cotch hole de bough, an' I'll push yer up in de crotch, an' den yo' kin git all yo' wants."

So Jack push 'im in de crotch, an' de Debble 'gin to feel de apples to git a meller one. While he wuz doin' dat, Jack whip he knife outen he pocket, an' cut a cross in de bark ob de tree, jes' under de Debble, an' de Debble holler, -

"Tzip! Sumpi' nurr hut me den. Wotcher doin' down dyah, Jack? I gwine cut yo' heart out."

But he could n' git down while dat cross wuz dyah, an' Jack jes' sot down on de grars, an' watch 'im ragin' an swarin' an' cussin'. Jack kep' 'im dyah all night tell 'twuz gret big day, an' den de Debble change he chune, an' he say, -

"Jack, lemme git down hyah an' I'll gib yo' nurr year."

"Gimme nuttin'!" said Jack, an stretch hisse'f out on de grars. Arfter a while, 'bout sun up, de Debble say, -

"Jack, cut dis ting offen hyah an' lemme git down, an' I'll gib yo' ten year."

"Naw surree," said Jack, "I won' letcher git down less yo' 'clar fo' gracious dat yo' won' nuver come arfter me no mo.'"

When de Debble fine Jack wuz hard ez a rock, he 'greed, an' 'clared fo' gracious dat he woudn' nuver come fur Jack agin, an' Jack cut de cross offen de tree, and de Debble lef' widout a word. Arfter dat Jack nuver thought no mo' 'bout 'pentin', 'cause he warn' feared ob de Debble, an' he did n' wan' to go whar day warn' no whiskey. Den he lib on tell he body war out, an' he wuz' bleeged to die. Fus' he went to de gate o' heaven, but de angel jes' shake he hade. Den he wen' to de gate o' hell, but when wud come dat Jack wuz dyah, de Debble holler to de imps.

"Shet de do' an' don' let dat man come in hyah; he done treat me scanlous. Tell 'im to go 'long back whar he come frum."

Den Jack say, -

"How I gwin fine my way back in de dark? Gimme a lantern."

Den de Debble tek a chunk outen de fire, an' say, -

"Hyah, tek dis, and dontcher nuver come back hyah no mo'."

Den Jack tek de chunk o' fire an' start back, but when he come to a ma'sh, he done got los,' an' he ain' nuver fine he way out sence.

This Negro legend is of European origin; before citing parallels, it will be necessary to consider the nature of the phenomenon which goes by the name of *ignis fatuus*.

More than one writer has observed the manner in which American negroes have appropriated the superstition. Speaking of Jack-o'-the-Lantern, W. Wirt Sikes observes: "The Negroes of the southern seaboard states of America invest the goblin with an exaggeration of the horrible peculiarly their own. They call it Jack-muh-lantern, and describe it as a hideous creature five feet in height, with goggle-eyes and huge mouth, its body covered with long hair, which goes leaping and bounding through the air like a gigantic grasshopper. This frightful apparition is stronger than any man and swifter than any horse, and compels its victims to follow it into the swamp, where it leaves them to die."[1] Mary A. Owen mentions similar beliefs as prevalent among aged negresses in Missouri, who relate extravagant tales respecting "Jacky-mi-Lantuhns" or "Wuller-Wups." There is, she explains, both a "man-jacky" and a "woman-jacky"; persons unfaithful in the marriage relation are tied by the devil in bladders and flung into the swamp, where they endeavor to drown the victims who by magical influence are compelled to follow their steps. Such spirits often issue from churchyards, and the notion is mingled with superstitious ideas answering to those concerning vampires. They are as tall as cottonwood trees.[2]

The Negro conceptions are not so peculiar as has been asserted, but on the contrary do not essentially differ from ideas current in Europe, whence they have doubtless been derived.[3]

Even with persons scientifically inclined, the *ignis fatuus* still passes for an external reality. Thus the Century Dictionary defines the word: "A meteoric light that sometimes appears in summer and autumn nights, and flies in the air a little above the surface of the earth, chiefly in marshy places near stagnant waters, and in churchyards. It is generally supposed to be produced by the spontaneous combustion of small jets of gas (carbureted or phosphuretted hydrogen) generated by the decomposition of vegetable or animal matter.... Before the introduction of the general drainage of swamplands, the *ignis fatuus* was an ordinary phenomenon in the marshy districts of England." Murray's Dictionary uses corresponding language, and adds: "It seems to have been formerly a common phenomenon, but is now extremely rare. When approached, the *ignis fatuus* appears to recede, and finally to vanish, sometimes reappearing in another direction. This led to the notion that it was the work of a mischievous sprite." The most recent encyclopædist of meteorology remarks: "Many have expressed doubts concerning the actuality of the phenomenon, yet the accounts of its appearance are so well attested that its reality must be conceded." He gives a number of mentions, beginning with an elaborate account of 1807, but rejects chemical explanations, assuming spontaneous combustion of illuminating gases as out of line with correct theory.[4] On the other hand, many observers, after taking all possible pains, have failed to satisfy themselves in regard to the existence of the gleams. I am not aware that phenomena of the sort have attracted attention in the United States; at least, in a marshy district where I spend much of my time I have not heard of any comment on similar displays.

The truth seems to be, that the credit given to the *ignis fatuus* is in great measure

1. *British Goblins*, London, 1880, p. 18.

2. *Voodoo Tales*, New York, 1893, c. xviii.

3. In Switzerland the eyes of an *irrlicht* are compared to fiery bushel-baskets. E. L. Rochholz, *Schweitzersagen aus der Aargau*, 1856, ii. 84. Their size is variable, from dwarfish to gigantic; they may be as tall as forest trees. F. Schönwerth, *Aus der Oberpfalz*, Augsburg, 1858, ii. 90. Untrue women walk after death; if an adulterous man meet them, he must dance with them until he sinks exhausted. A. Wuttke, *Deutsche Volksaberglaube*, 2d ed., Berlin, 1869, p. 445. The motion of *ignes fatui* by leaps and bounds is everywhere usual.

4. S. A. Arrhenius, *Lehrbuch der kosmischen Physik*, Leipzig, 1903, pp. 879–90. Arrhenius does not mention the observations of J. Allies, who succeeded in finding the *ignes fatui*, which he describes as rising several feet and falling to earth, as moving horizontally like the flights of the green woodpecker, being bluer than a candle, and some as large as Sirius. *On the Ignis-Fatuus, or Will-o'-the-wisp, and the Fairies*, London, 1839.

owing to the imposing Latin title which gives it an air of verisimilitude. Whatever illuminations may occasionally be perceived, and whether these be electrical or chemical, those accredited by folk-lore are not referable to actual occurrences, but are either purely imaginary, or else fanciful interpretations of every-day happenings.

This proposition becomes clear, when the belief is taken in connection with kindred opinion in which similar lights play a part. These are divisible into several categories. First may be mentioned the so-called "corpse-candles," supposed to precede and prognosticate a death. If luminous appearances of the sort issue from the room of a sick person, and are seen to enter the churchyard, it is taken for granted that the illness will be fatal, and that the sufferer will shortly be borne to his rest along the path followed by the apparition. The movement of the flame answers to that which may be expected from the living man; if the pace be brisk, as that of a youth skipping or running, the death of a child is indicated; if slow and even, of an elderly person. In this case the vision is, so to speak, a present reflection of the future event; inasmuch as it formerly was usual to inter by night, and in consequence torches or candles were borne by the mourners, such lamps belong to the funeral procession, which appears in an anticipatory reflex. So another sort of flames, those indicating the presence of buried treasure, may represent the flickering of the funeral pyres anciently employed in cremation; the dead was laid in the barrow with his goods about him, whence a bold hand might win riches. Lights, again, may be expected in any meeting with ghosts, since the astral body of a spirit is in itself luminous.[1]

According to early religious conceptions, the cultivated land, the farm and croft, belongs to mankind and to the deities whose homes have therein been established; beyond this territory lies the wilderness, where dwell spirits who in the desert pursue a life similar to that of humanity, live by the produce of the forest, and have to wild animals a relation answering to that which man bears to the flocks and herds. Mountain and bog are supposed to abound in spiritual neighbors, often hostile and always capricious, who live like men in communities and families, have proper names, individual form, character, and function, yet remain unknown, save in so far as accident brings some particular being into contact with the villagers. Mysterious gleams perceived in untilled ground are interpreted as evidencing the presence of such strangers, who may be of any age and either sex, will be engaged in tasks and enterprises answering to those which would employ the perceiver, will be taken for friendly or malevolent as the impression dictates, and in general take toward the farmer and his community about the same attitude as the latter have to the distrusted inhabitants of the adjoining village. The presence of such neighbors will be indicated by the same signs which ordinarily mark the approach of human wanderers; the spirits will need and use lights for all tasks in which lights are needed, while the nature of the lamp will answer to that which is common in the locality, torch, rush-candle, or lantern; the bearer will naturally often be accompanied by others of his supernatural kind, with whom he will engage in games, revels, and industries; if busy with toils of agriculture, he may be desirous of profiting by human experience, and after the general habit of tillers of the soil borrow the tools he requires.

1. For the subject of ghostly lights, see several papers in recent volumes of *Folk-Lore* (London); M. J. Walhouse, vol. v. (1894), pp. 293–99; H. F. Feilberg, vi. (1895), 288–300; R. C. Maclagan, "Ghost Lights of the West Highlands," viii. (1897), 203–56.

In this manner arise innumerable variations of appearance and possibilities of conception, in different localities associated with different presentations of such imagined existences.

As for the external cause which supplies the perception, this is a matter of secondary consequence. The flash of a firefly, or a watery reflection of a star, the sunset-gleam returned from a window, moonlight in the forest, the flight of a luminous insect, or simply the reaction of the eyeball against extreme darkness, will be all-sufficient to create elaborate and circumstantial visions, of which the intellectual element is projected from the fancy. Imagination creates experience; during the period of its existence a superstitious belief never lacks the support of ocular testimony, and is never discredited by failure to observe a corresponding reality. The *ignis fatuus* is one aspect of a universal faith; that it alone has continued to pose as a separate entity is an example of the way in which a high-sounding title promotes recognition.

For these lights, names are numerous. *Ignis fatuus* is universal in European literature, but has the appearance of a relatively modern and rationalistic designation. English testimonies are from the sixteenth century; the word is explained as meaning "foolish" or "false" fire. The term "fool's fire" is also English. Corresponding, but in what manner is not perfectly clear, is the French *feu follet*. Another Latin title is *ignis erraticus*, to which answer the English "wandering fire," "walking fire," German *irrlicht*.[1]

For the ghostly fire English literature has accepted two proper names, Jack-of-the-lantern (Jack-a-lantern, lantern-Jack, etc.) and Will-o'-the-wisp (Will-a-wisp, Will-in-a-wisp, etc.). But to the light belongs many other personal names: Jenny-with-the-lantern, Peg-a-lantern, Hob-with-a-lantern (Hoberdy's lantern, etc.), Kit-with-the-canstick, Kitty-candlestick, Joan-in-the-wad, Jacket-a-wad, Gillion-a-burnt-tail. We perceive that the sprite might have any common Christian name, out of which two have found literary reception, and, as usual, superseded and extinguished less favored appellations.[2]

The *ignis fatuus* may also be named from locality, as in the English example of "Syleham lights." Such title implies a story, the nature of which may be conjectured from an Irish instance. In Scottish islands the phenomenon has been called "Uist Light" (*Solus Uithist*), a name derived from a legend variously told. A girl from Benbecula is said, by misconduct, to have brought on her head the maternal curse. She disappeared (being probably drowned), and her spirit becomes a "great fire" (*teine mhor*).[3]

The idea underlying these personal and local appellations is that wandering flames belong to the souls of persons well known and recently deceased, of whom can be related

---

1. For the English words, see testimonies in Murry, *New English Dictionary*, and the *Stanford Dictionary*. Italian uses especially the plural, *fuochi fatui*. The Old French *folet* signifies elf, fairy; *feu follet*, therefore, ought to mean fairy fire, corresponding to the English elf-fire (seventeenth century), Welsh *ellyldân* (E. Owen, *Welsh Folk-Lore*, Oswestry, 1887–96, p. 112), Gaelic *teine sîth* (J. G. Campbell, *Witchcraft and Second-Sight in the Highlands and Islands of Scotland*, Glasgow, 1902, p. 171). *Feu follet*, therefore, may be the original from which, by mistranslation, has come *ignis fatuus*. *Folet* I take to be from *fol*, causatively, as a being that befools (by spiritual possession); *feu follet* may have once carried such connotation, a befooling fire.

2. For names of the *ignis fatuus*, see the learned paper of G. L. Kittredge, "The Friar's Lantern and Friar Rush," *Publications of the Modern Language Association of America*, xv. (1900), 415–41. Kittredge shows that Rush had nothing to do with the lantern-bearing friar of Milton's *L'Allegro*. Also, C. P. G. Scott, "The Devil and his Imps," *Transactions of the American Philological Association*, xxvi, (1895), 79–146.

3. Campbell, *op. cit.*, p. 171; Maclagan, *op. cit.*, p. 227; J. MacRury, in *Transactions of the Gaelic Society of Inverness*, xix. (1893), 158–171; *Folk-Lore*, xiii. (1902), 43.

histories explanatory of the reason which caused them to undergo such transformation.[1] Among an infinite number of such tales, certain ones, because of their intrinsic interest, attained a circulation beyond the limits of the neighborhood, and became widely famous, as is the case with the particular narrative of which we have an American version from the lips of a Maryland Negro. It should be added that such legends are generally not of local invention, but far-wandered beliefs which here and there strike independent root, develop into a new species, and in their turn travel and vary.

The extent to which the fiery apparitions vary in aspect is indicated by the English names. In the cases of Jack and Will, we have only spectral men who carry lanterns or torches, as sensible people do on dark nights. In all countries nocturnal gleams are similarly interpreted.[2] But the glow may proceed from the person of the wanderer, in a number of different ways.[3] Gill-of-the-burnt-tail evidently draws the flaming streak behind her.[4] As for Joan-in-the-wad, the flaming bundle of cloth envelops her person, so that she must appear as a pyramid of fire; just so *revenants* who come from Hell or Purgatory are dressed in blazing garments.

Being ghosts, the night-roamers are likely to be closely connected with their mortal remains; if the Will-o'-the-wisp be seized, only a bone is left in the grasp.[5] A particularly weird manner of conception is that the skeleton should walk with a light in the breast, so that the ribs are darkly silhouetted on the radiance, and are therefore compared to baskets containing a lamp.[6] In Ireland, such a skeleton is thought of as winged, and wings are elsewhere assigned to an *ignis fatuus*.[7] In general, it may be said that the local element of the descriptions is relatively limited; West European ideas so closely coincide that an observation in Norway, Germany, the Low Countries, France, Brittany, or England will probably have had parallels in the other lands, and after dialectic variation and divergence of name is allowed for, observations from one region may be cited as likely to hold in all. If English folk-lore does not furnish examples of all the different ways of imaging

1. Thus in Aarau, Switzerland, the illumination was thought to be the soul of a miller deceased twenty years before. Rochholz, *op. cit.*, ii. 84.

2. Among examples of ecclesiastics who carry a "friar's lantern" may be added that of the *éclaireur* in Upper Brittany, who is always looking for the sacramental wafer which he has dropped in water. Such illuminators may be asked to give light, with a formula:

> Eclaire-moi, Foirard;
> J'vas t'donner deux liards.

P. Sébillot, *Traditions et superstitions de la Haute-Bretagne*, Paris, 1882, i. 150.

3. The evil spirit appears as a horse with fiery tail. *Folk-Lore*, x. (1899), 362. Perhaps Gill may have had an equine form.

4. Fiery men show themselves as all fire, spitting fire, or bearing fire on the back, as a burning parcel of straw or fiery column, drawing a streak of flame, or as a fiery skeleton, with head under arm. Rochholz, *op. cit.*, p. 446.

5. A. Kuhn and W. Schwartz, *Norddeutsche Sagen*, etc., No. 260.

6. So regularly in Swiss belief, Rochholz, *loc. cit.*; like Irish representation, Maclagan, 229; the fire is in the heart of the girl; the same comparison to a basket.

7. For the lights as winged, Irish, Maclagan, *loc. cit.*, Campbell, *op. cit.*, p. 171. In Flanders, *les lumerottes* are souls of infants who die unbaptized, and appear as a bird which bears in its beak a diamond whence proceeds the light. J. Lemoine, *Le folk-lore Wallon*, Ghent, 1892, p. 131. The idea rests on the general representation of such souls as birds. A. Le Braz, *La légende de la mort en Basse-Bretagne*, Paris, 1883, p. 270; Grimm, *Teutonic Mythology*, 829, 916.

the lustres, such deficiency is to be set down to poverty of record much more than to any original difference; in this respect, as in others, West European folk-lore forms a body of popular knowledge which is nearly uniform.

Since *ignes fatui* are only illuminated spirits, and every spiritual being may at one time or another be lustrous, it is only natural that many classes of supernatural beings should be represented among the nocturnal light-givers whom the Latin name *ignis fatuus* has grouped in one family.

Flaming wanderers may be gods or saints, as with Maria *stella maris* and Saint Elmo, to whom the British mariner formerly attributed the "composant" ("corpus sant," *corpo santo*) whose shining was regarded as protective.[1]

Or, on the other hand, the incandescence may be considered as demonic, proceeding from the devil,[2] or from goblins,[3] or diabolic animals.[4]

However, the light-bearers with whom I am especially concerned, and who play the more extensive part in European records, are neither celestial nor devilish, but those spirits of the departed which, according to universal European popular belief, are denied entrance equally to heaven and the inferno, and compelled to perform their penance by long wanderings on earth. For such destiny the reasons might be either ethical or ritual.

If the soul of the deceased had in life committed any wrong which might be undone, or undertaken any vow possible to carry out, it would probably be unable to repose until atonement had been made. A crime of this sort, from Babylonian antiquity

1. These fires, as is known, were by Hellenic antiquity attributed to the Dioscuri Castor and Pollux, and their sister Helena; the name of the latter survives in Saint Elmo, Herme, etc.; in Brittany still Saint Helena. See P. Sébillot, *Légendes, croyances et superstitions de la mer*, Paris, 1886, ii. Pp. 87 ff.; F. S. Bassett, *Legends and Superstitions of the Sea and of Sailors*, Chicago, 1885, pp. 302–320. These lustres have, I believe, always been considered as interpretations of a particular electric marine phenomenon; but this doctrine will not hold; application to such supposed illuminations is at the most only secondary; the fires of St. Elmo are not to be distinguished from the *ignis fatuus*, of which they form a single species. According to Pliny, the starry lights manifested themselves also on the heads of favored individuals; a relic of such superstition survives in the Italian *fuochi fatui lambenti*. (Dictionary of Tommaseo and Bellini.) Sébillot observes that in Treguier the *feux follets* of marshes are subject to identical superstitions, p. 107. That a spirit of the marsh may be active also at sea is shown in the case of the Irish "Bog-sprite" or "Water-skeerie," an *ignis fatuus* who is thought to wave a wisp of lighted straw. Some think him a disembodied spirit and guardian of hidden treasures. He exhibits all the transitions common to such spirits, flies, stands still, becomes extinct, revives, is seen in churchyards, but also by mariners on the masts, spars, or sails. "Lageniensis" (J. O'Hanlon), *Irish Folk-Lore*, Glasgow, 1870, p. 170. The recorder adds that a single apparition is considered to betoken danger, two or more safety. The same belief is mentioned by Pliny, *Nat. Hist.* ii. 37 (see Brand, *Antiquities*, iii. 349). A Sicilian legend explains the fire of St. Elmo as the shining of a lantern given by Christ through St. Christopher. G. Pitrè, *Usi a costumi del popolo Siciliano*, Palermo, 1889, iii. 66. In Cornwall "Jack Harry's lights" appear on a phantom vessel resembling that of which the loss is indicated (instead of on the ship of the navigators). M. A. Courtney, *Cornish Feasts and Folk-Lore*, Penzance, 1890, p. 134. Again, on the same coast, a wreck is foreshown by the appearance at sea of a lady who carries a lantern, and who is supposed to be in search of her drowned child. Courtney, p. 135. In Italian and Spanish, Santelmo, according to the dictionaries, is used as a name of the *ignis fatuus*, appearing on trees as well as on the water. It will be seen that the maritime lights cannot be taken by themselves, but are only a modification of the terrestrial superstition.

2. A Hessian legend explains the *irrwisch* as the body of a dead usurer, whom the devil flays, stuffs with straw, and makes fly as a burning wisp. Wolf's *Zeitschrift für Deutsche Mythologie*, i. (1853), 246.

3. Light proceeds from pixies with shining heads on fire, like the rising moon. *Folk-Lore*, xi. 1900, 214.

4. The light is ascribed to wehrwolves, fire-drakes, etc. Kittredge, *op. cit.*, p. 431.

especially abhorred, was the removal of the boundary stones which determined the own-
ership of land. A Swiss legend relates that a youth, who at nightfall happens to pass by
the edge of a wood, sees a "burning man" in whom he recognizes his godfather Gotti.
On the morrow with pick and shovel he resorts to the spot, and, aided by the ghost, is
able to restore the stone to its original site; the fiery soul obtains peace and is seen no
more, while the lad, who has been promised Paradise as his guerdon, shortly expires.[1]
Again, the person who had hidden away a treasure must roam until he can find means of
restoring it to his heirs.

For ritual reasons, the *revenants* who shine at night are those who have not received
the offices of the church, have been cast out uninterred, been drowned or otherwise
irregularly disposed of. A touching belief sees among such the souls of children who have
died unbaptized; these are not hopelessly exiled, but under certain circumstances may
attain salvation. If buried under the eaves of the church (according to German ideas), the
rain which falls during the christening of a living infant will serve for their water of bap-
tism. These spirits have such object always in mind, and particularly approach their parents in order to sue for their aid. So in the case of older persons who are buried out of
holy ground, and therefore have become "burning men," the carrying of the cross which
marks their burial-place into "God's acre" will be enough to deliver the sufferer. If
English folk-lore does not exhibit similar features, the absence, I suppose, is owing solely
to the impression on popular fancy produced by the Protestant reformation; mediæval
notions were the same in England as in France and Germany.[2]

The usual fluctuation in folk-thought appears in the manner of conceiving the
activity of similar beings. Their malice or good-nature would of course depend on the
character of the particular man who had become a fiery ghost.

Ignes fatui share with other spirits the habit that they are influenced by sacrifices,
and demand in return for their service some present, though it may be a very small one,
as a small coin, or even a crumb. For the purpose of imploring their aid are used formu-
las, much the same in all countries of Western Europe; an English example is: -

Jack of the lantern, Joan of the lub,

Light me home, and I'll give you a crub (crumb).[3]

After the service has been rendered, the proper expression is: "Thank 'ee, Jack."
Here the German has better preserved the original intention; the person assisted should
say "*Gelts Gott*,"[4] on which the soul undergoing purgation is likely to be released, the
idea being that merit and earning the gratitude of men shortens the term of penance.

On the other hand, there is a class of malicious ghosts, of whom salvation can
hardly be predicted, and who take an evil pleasure in misleading night-wanderers; and it
is this character which has prevailed in literature, and is reflected in the history of Jack or

1. Rochholz, p. 78. In Brittany souls of rich men who have made bad gains, thieves, etc., must wander
until restoration is made. Le Braz, *op. cit.*, p. 388.

2. As testimonies, I may refer to the citations made by Brand, *Antiquities*, edition of W. C. Hazlitt, 1870,
iii. 348, from works published in 1704 and 1723, to the effect that the people believed *ignes fatui* to be
souls in a flame, come from purgatory, to move others to pray for their entire deliverance.

3. In Devon, *Folk-Lore*, xi. (1900), 212. Grimm, *Teutonic Mythology*, 1801; Schönwerth, ii. 100. For French
formula, see above.

4. Schönwerth, ii. 94.

Will. Experience showed that those who followed the lanterns of the sprites and were lost in the bog were likely to be persons fond of the bowl; as like seeks like, this led to the conclusion that the ghost was that of a drunken person; thus Will-o'-the-wisp is said to have a face like a brandy-bottle;[1] and this is the character given the spirit in the legend now in question.

After this brief exposition, necessary in order to render the matter intelligible, I proceed to trace the comparative history of the Maryland narrative.

Of the legend in England, I have met only with an abbreviated version, credited to Shropshire.

"There came to a blacksmith's shop late one night a traveller, whose horse had cast a shoe, and he wanted the blacksmith to put it on for him. So Will (that was the man's name) was very ready, and he soon had it on again all right. Now the traveller was no other than the Apostle St. Peter himself, going about to preach the Gospel; but before he went away, he told the smith to wish a wish, whatever he chose, and it should be granted him. 'I wish,' says Will, 'that I might live my life over again.' So it was granted him, and he lived his life over again, and spent it in drinking and gambling, and all manner of wild pranks. At last his time came, and he was forced to set out for the other world, thinking of course that he would find a place in hell made ready for him; but when he came to the gates, the Devil would not let him in. No, he said, by this time Will had learnt so much wickedness he would be more than a match for him, and he dared not let him in. So away went the smith to heaven, to see if St. Peter, who had been a good friend to him before, would find him a place there; but St. Peter would not, it wasn't very likely he would! and Will was forced to go back to the Old Lad again, and beg and pray for a place in hell. But the Devil would not be persuaded even then. Will had spent two lifetimes in learning wickedness, and now he knew too much to be welcome anywhere. All that the Devil would do for him, was to give him a lighted coal from hell-fire to keep himself warm, and that is how he comes to be called Will-o'-the-wisp. So he goes wandering up and down the moors and mosses with his light, wherever he can find a bit of boggy ground that he can 'tice folks to lose their way in the bog and bring them to a bad end, for he is not a bit less wicked and deceitful now than he was when a blacksmith."[2]

The Shropshire narrative shows the essential features, lost in the American version, according to which the three wishes are conferred by Christ, in exchange for hospitality offered to the Lord and his Apostles, in the course of their earthly wanderings.

I think it likely that the remnant of another English version is to be found in an Irish story attributed to Carleton, regarding one Billy Dawson, who is regarded as a notorious and an incorrigible scamp who lived a riotous and drunken life. This caused his nose to become very inflammable, and when an arch-enemy seized it with red-hot tongs, a flame at once burst forth. This continued to burn on, winter and summer; while a bushy beard which he wore helped to feed the fuel. Hence, the northern country peo-

1. *Folk-Lore*, xi. 214. In Brittany, *Paotik he shod tan* (Boy with the lighted torch) flies like a butterfly over prairies and marshes, misleading and even drowning drunken folk, or rash persons who pursue him. F. M. Luzel, *Veillées bretonnes*, Morlaix, 1879, p. 64.

2. C. S. Burne, *Shropshire Folk-Lore*, London, 1883, pp. 34–5. Taken from the *Shrewsbury Journal*, 1877.

Early postcard showing a Hallowe'en prankster fleeing through a field of jack-o'-lanterns.

ple say that Billy Dawson has been christened Will of the Wisp, and that he plunges into the coldest quagmires and pools of water to quench the flames emitted from his burning nose. It is a remnant of his mischievous disposition, however, to lead unthinking and tipsy night-travellers into bogs, where they are likely to be drowned.[1]

The tale has obtained currency in Gaelic speech, being localized in the Hebrides. A poor smith, who has vainly striven to support his family, is reduced to such despair that he professes himself willing to accept help from God or the Devil. A little old man, with feet like pig's hoofs, calls at the smithy, and promises aid, on condition that the smith shall be ready to go with him at the end of a year; meanwhile he shall always find gold in his right pocket, and silver in his left. During the interval another man calls, is hospitably entertained, and as a reward grants the smith three wishes. The latter desires that any one who helps him at the forge must remain during his pleasure, that whoever sits on his chair shall not remove until given leave, and that any piece of money in his pocket must remain there until he takes it out. The stranger says the desires shall be granted, but it is a pity the wisher had not asked mercy for his soul. At the end of the year Satan appears; the smith induces him to work at the forge, where the demon remains fixed, and is obliged to grant another year; on a second visit the fiend is made to sit in the chair, with a like result; on a third visit, Satan is challenged to prove his power by turning himself into a sixpence which the smith pockets; the coin is restless, and the smith has it hammered at the forge, till the purse is reduced to dust, and the devil goes up the chimney in sparks of fire. The hero of the tale is now free, but, though no longer pestered, goes down in the world, and at death is cast out unburied; knowing that it would be useless to apply at the gate of heaven, his soul takes the road to hell, but the Devil refuses admittance: "There is not," said he, "your like within the bounds of my kingdom; I light a fire never to be quenched in your bosom. And I order thee to return to the earth, and wander up and down until the day of judgment. Thou shalt have rest neither day nor night. Thou shalt wander on earth among every place that is wetter, lower, lonelier, and more dismal than another. And thou shalt be a disgust to thyself, and a harm to every living creature thou seest."

From the smith, whose name is Sionnach (Fox), the "great fire" is called *teine Sionnachain.*[2]

That the history has been current in Wales is shown by a distorted version. Sion Dafydd (John David) of the Bwlch of Ddauafen in the Arvon hills has converse with demons, quarrels with them and beats two devils in a bag which flies to pieces; the fiends take refuge in the village of Rhiwgyfylchi, which from that time has an evil repute. In return for present riches, he sells himself, with the condition that he may escape provided that he has the power to adhere to anything; when the demon comes after him, he asks leave to get into his apple-tree, and hangs on in despite of all efforts to pull him away. After death he is changed into a *Jac-y-lantern.*[3]

No doubt other Welsh versions could have been found which would have precisely answered to the English.

---

1. "Lageniensis," *op. cit.*, p. 170. I have in vain sought for the passage in the works of William Carleton to which I have access.

2. Maclagan, *op. cit.*, p. 233.

3. *Cymru fu*, Wrexham, 1862, p. 385, from oral tradition. Abstracted by Wirt Sikes, *op. cit.*, p. 204.

With numerous variations, the tale is everywhere current in Europe.[1]

A Norwegian version recites that a smith makes a bargain with the Devil, in which he agrees to belong to the fiend at the end of seven years, provided that in the interval he may be the most skilful of his craft. In the course of wanderings, Christ and St. Peter enter the forge; as a recompense for his free service, the smith is granted three wishes. Neglecting intimations that he ought to request eternal peace, the smith, who has been troubled by thieves, desires that whoever climbs his pear-tree may be unable to descend without permission, that whoever sits in his chair must remain, and that aught which enters his steel purse must stay there. The Devil is caught, and obliged to grant successive respites. The details are related with much humor, and application of old proverbs. The Devil is induced to enter the purse in order to examine its links, and reports them sound; but the smith remarks that it is well to be slow and sure, and proceeds to weld a doubtful link. In the sequel the smith dies, is turned away from hell, and goes to heaven, where he finds the door ajar, and throws his hammer into the crack; if he did not get in, the narrator knows not what became of him.[2]

The smith debarred from heaven and hell, and hence obliged to wander eternally, is known also in numerous German versions. In the Upper Palatinate it is related that a smith gives work to an applicant, apparently a poor journeyman, but who proves so skilful that he is able to detach the foot of a horse, adjust the shoe, and restore the leg to its original condition.[3] When the time comes for parting, the former servant grants his master three wishes. The smith has been annoyed by thieves who steal the nails from his bag, defile his stone, and rob his apple-tree; he therefore desires that whoso inserts a hand in the bag may be unable to remove it, that a man who sits on the stone may stick there, and that any one who climbs his apple-tree cannot get down. After the departure of his servant, the smith falls into poverty, and makes a compact with the Devil (in the form of a green man), in virtue of which he is to be enriched, on condition of an enigmatical cession; the object to be yielded proves to be his unborn son. After seven years, the Devil sends subordinate demons to obtain the price, and take the smith, who has offered his own life to redeem that of the child. The three fiends are successively shut in the bag, fastened to the stone, and attached to the tree, and in each case well hammered by the smith and his men. The principal devil then comes in person, and carries off the smith; but on the way to hell he meets a priest carrying the sacrament to a sick person, and in order to hide himself from the terrifying presence of the halidome, creeps into the bag, where he is detained, and obliged to promise the captive immunity. When the smith comes to die, he is rejected at the gates of heaven and hell; he does indeed obtain temporary admission into a former place, but by a stratagem is cast out. He is obliged to roam between the homes of rest and torment; some persons call him the Wandering Jew (*Der ewige Jude*).[4]

The three comical wishes of the tale seem originally to have been that thieves might be

1. Grimm, *Kinder- und Hausmärchen*, Nos. 81, 82, and Notes; R. Köhler, *Kleinere Schriften*, Weimar, 1898, i. 67 *et al.*, see index; A. Voigt, *Zeitscrift für vergleichende Litteraturgeschichte*, v. (1892), 62.

2. S. W. Dasent, *Popular Tales from the Norse*, Edinburgh, 1859, No. 16.

3. The tale has been "contaminated" by the story of the Master-smith (the legend of St. Eloi). See Köhler, *op. cit.*, p. 296.

4. Schönwerth, *op. cit.*, iii. 77.

imprisoned respectively in the sack, the chair, and the fruit-tree. Instead of the chair, a variety substituted a pack of winning cards; thus, in a Roman story, a host who has liberally entertained Jesus and his disciples is promised whatever gift he may desire; however, as the beneficiary is a person of a contented mind, who has no family and a thriving trade, he is at a loss to know what he should ask. At last it occurs to him that he is fond of cards, and he desires that he may be able always to win. Two wishes remain, and St. Peter performs his duty by making his usual suggestion, namely, that the proper course is to request the salvation of the asker's soul; but unheeding this intimation, the host desires that, inasmuch as his figs are always stolen, whoever climbs the tree may be obliged to remain until liberated, and that he may have a life of four-hundred year. Finally, at the advice of the saint, he does run after the Lord, and request his soul's salvation, which is granted as a fourth boon. After the term has expired, Death arrives, but is caught in the tree, and forced to cede another four hundred years. When these are expired, Death takes the man, and according to the final promise of the Saviour is about to convey him to Paradise, but on the way (according to a common mediæval conception) is obliged to pass the gate of Hell, where the Devil is standing. The innkeeper proposes a game of cards, the stake being his own soul, against that of the damned who had just been admitted; by virtue of the winning pack, he gains all the souls, with which he repairs to the gate of heaven. "Who's there?" asks St. Peter. "He of the four hundred years." "And what's all that rabble behind you?" "Souls that I have won for Paradise." "Oh, that won't do tall, here," replies St. Peter. In the end, the saint consents to refer the matter to Christ, who orders that the innkeeper only is to be admitted; but when the Latter sends word that when the Lord had applied for lodging at his inn, he himself had never made difficulty by reason of disciples following, orders are given for the reception of the whole party.[1] Another version names the host as the priest Olivo.[2]

The same history is related, with witty touches, in a poem of the eighteenth century, by D. Batacchi: The priest Ulivo entertains Jesus and his followers with remarkable liberality, the cuisine being described *con amore*. For guerdon the priest is allowed a wish, and desires to live six hundred years. St. Peter reproves him for lack of good sense, and advises him to try again (thus intimating that the only proper desire of man should be for eternal felicity). Ulivo does not follow this suggestion; as he has a tree from which he never gets pears, he asks that any thief may be detained until he grants leave to come down; since he is fond of playing cards after the hour at which his companions are impatient for bed, he begs that any one who sits on a certain chair may not rise till he pleases, and also that his cards may win. The host, therefore, has spent his three wishes without obtaining salvation, which nevertheless the saint promises. Ulivo, by means of the chair and the pear-tree, is twice enabled to arrest Death, with whom he makes contracts which insure him a life extended nearly down to the present time. The ending answers to the modern Roman legend.[3]

The version of Batacchi explains in what manner the hero may have acquired the repute which, in a tale of Grimm, has given him the name of Jack the Gambler.[4] Some narrator suggested that an inveterate gamester might use the magic chair for insuring a

1. R. H. Bush, *Roman Legends*, Boston, 1877, p. 178.

2. Busk, p. 183.

3. *Novelle*, Milan, 1879, p. 5

4. Grimm, No. 82, *Spielhansl*.

supply of adversaries who were not permitted to leave the card-table; the next step was to borrow from other histories the trait that a holy personage might always be able to win in the game.[1] Thus, in a celebrated *fabliau*, we learn that a minstrel who has shared the usual fate of his profession, and gone naked and hungry till Death releases him, is captured by an inexperienced demon and taken to hell, which he finds the only warm and comfortable place he has known. Fondness for heat makes him a suitable person to stoke the fire for heating the kettle in which are boiling souls of the damned. Satan and his troop go out hunting, leaving the singer at his duty. St. Peter perceives the opportunity, descends from heaven, and has no difficulty in awakening the former passion for dice; the singer sets as his stake the souls, with the result that he loses them, as Peter always throws one higher. The returning fiend, who finds hell empty, in his rage expels the singer, and beats the devil who had been careless enough to fetch in such booty; from that time there has been no hell for poets. We do not learn what became of the minstrel; but the *fabliau* must have had for basis a popular narration which must have offered some explanation, and may have been akin to the legend with which I am concerned.[2]

Another sub-species of the history is distinguished by the traits that the wishes are granted in exchange for alms rather than for hospitality, and that the bag takes the character of a wishing-sack, in which the owner is able to carry off whatever he pleases. From a mere variant this type has developed into a narration widely different, to the extent of being quite unrecognizable except through comparative examination.

Only slightly deviating from the mother-form is an Irish story. A traveling smith, Seâgahn Tinceâr (Jack the Tinker), takes service in Kildare; on the way, in passing a bridge, he has stumbled, and wishes that the Devil may break his neck, if ever again he take that road. Returning after four years with the earnings of his labor, he meets an aged beggar who asks alms in the name of God; this happens three times, and Jack gives away all his money. On each occasion he obtains a wish, and desires, first, to confine anything disagreeable in the bottle he carries, secondly to detain any offender in his bag, and thirdly to keep thieves in his apple-tree. Forgetful of his vow, Jack does once more cross the bridge, and is accosted by the Devil, whom he wishes into his bag, and afterward causes the fiend to be beaten at a smithy. The Devil returns, but is induced to mount the tree, where he remains seven years, till Jack picks him off in gathering a fagot for his wife; the third time the persecutor is shut in the bottle.[3] The story lacks the proper ending, having instead annexed another legendary tale of kindred character.[4]

Wider is the deviation in a Gascon narrative. A peddler, who is neither a good nor a bad man, carries his wares in the bag on his back. He is solicited for charity, first by a lame old man, then by a female beggar, and gives away what little he possesses. These mendicants, however, are only transformations of St. Peter, on whom the alms have been bestowed, and who, in guerdon, asks the liberal benefactor to name his wish, at the same time commanding him to discard his present possessions. The peddler accordingly

---

1. In case of necessity, a saint could throw sevens (by the breaking of a die). *Hist. litt. de la France*, xxiii, 112.

2. Montaiglon and Raynaud, *Recueil general*, Paris, 1883, v. 65.

3. D. Hyde, *An Sgéaluide Gaedhealach*, London, No. 3.

4. That of "Godfather Death," Grimm, No. 44; Köhler, i. 291.

throws away his sack; but having his chief happiness and content in his trade, he can think of nothing better to ask for than a new bag. This the saint bestows, with the addition that the recipient is at liberty to wish into the sack anything he desires to obtain. The peddler now has a merry life, seeing that he is able to appropriate without compensation any delicacy that suits his palate; the temptation proves too strong for his principles, and he obtains in this manner the wife he seeks. When he comes to die and makes application at the gate of heaven, this liberty becomes ground for rejection. However, the peddler is not to be daunted; he lingers at the entrance until he has opportunity to fling in the bag, and then wishes himself inside; once in heaven, he insists on remaining.[1]

The gayety and reckless humor belonging to this form of the story gave it an attraction which procured circulation through all Europe.[2] A Spanish version relates the discomfiture of Death by the aid of the fruit-tree and wishing-bag, but adds the feature that Juan the Soldier wishes St. Peter himself into the sack, and so secures heaven by force.[3] An episode uses the bag in such manner as to effect the disenchantment of a castle; a Russian variant, enlarging this episode, becomes a mere recital of fantastic adventures, in which the legend resolves itself into a fairy-tale.[4]

That the history enjoyed mediæval popularity is shown by numerous literary reworkings of the sixteenth and following centuries.

In 1526 the Venetian Cintio dei Fabrizii, having occasion to explain the origin of popular proverbs, used the tale to illustrate the adage, "Envy never dies." In order to satisfy himself as to the degree of justice in the murmurings of mankind, in company with Mercury, Jupiter descended to earth, and obtained lodging from Envy (*Invidia*). In recompense for kindness, the god, on departure, asks her to name a wish. She requests protection for her apple-tree, which is frequently visited by thieves, and Jupiter gives it the property that none who climbs may descend without the owner's permission. When Death comes for Envy, she asks him, as a last favor, to pluck an apple from her tree. Death is thus fixed in the boughs, where he is detained until Jupiter, desiring his release, promises Envy immortality.[5]

In 1551 Hans Sachs gave the history a rhymed form. In return for shelter, St. Peter grants a peasant three wishes; these are, that he may know Death when he sees him, and that whoever blows his fire must continue until told to stop. Death is thus caught, and compelled to grant a respite. Finally, when Death is again imprisoned, and no man dies, St. Peter descends to earth, and offers the farmer a hundred years of life if he will set the destroyer free.[6]

Before 1582 an anonym wrote the history of one Sanctus, in which he freely used the legend, which he combined with other similar material. Sanctus, pursued by Death,

1. Cénac Moncaut, *Littérature populaire de la Gascogne*, Paris, 1868, p. 57.

2. See R. Köhler, *op. cit.*, i. pp. 83, 111; also A. Leskien and K. Burmann, *Litauische Volkslieder und Märchen*, Strassburg, 1882, No. 17, note (in which are mentioned Russian, Polish, Czech, and Moravian versions).

3. F. Wolf, *Beiträge sur spanischer Volkspoesie aus den Werken F. Caballeros*, Vienna, 1859, p. 74.

4. Afanasief, *Skaski*, v. 43.

5. *Jahrbuch für Romanische und Englishe Litteratur*, i. (1859) 310.

6. C. Lützelberger, *Album des literarischen Vereins in Nürnberg*, 1864, 232, "Der Tod auf dem Stule." I have not found the piece in the collected works of Sachs.

makes a truce by accepting him as godfather of his son,[1] and obtains an extension of his earthly term. He resolves to lead a good life, but is tempted by the Devil, and yields (as Jack in the American version) on the ground that there is plenty of time left for repentance. When the period expires, he flies, and arrives in heaven, where he misconducts himself and is expelled, but promised that three wishes may be accomplished. Death, who has used up seven hundred pairs of shoes in seeking him, wishes to carry him off, but the expedient of the tree is used, and no man dies, whence results great distress. Sanctus at last himself grows weary of life, and seeks Death, whom he invites to descend. As the remaining two wishes he desires salvation and remembrance on earth.[2]

The version of Attanasy von Dilling, printed in 1691, more closely resembles the modern forms. Christ and St. Peter lodge with a smith, and are kindly treated by the good wife of the host. On leaving the woman is offered a wish, and desires only heaven. The husband, who is promised four wishes, in spite of repeated suggestions on the part of St. Peter that he ought to desire his soul's salvation, selects the usual detention in the cherry-tree at the forge and bellows, and finally, that his green cap shall remain his own property, and he may not be parted from it. After Death has twice failed, the Devil comes, and is kept at the bellows until he vows never to have anything to do with the smith. Finally, the smith's guardian angel is sent to take him, and carries him to hell, where the Devil, on perceiving the new-comer, hastily shuts the window from which he is looking. The smith is next escorted to heaven, where St. Peter is equally unwilling to accept his visitor; but in virtue of the fourth wish, the dead smith is still provided with his cap, which he throws in, and remains seated on his property.[3]

More popular than any other literary form has been that in which the legend has been put to an allegorical use, in a different sense from that of the Venetian author; instead of Envy, it is Misery that never dies. Such is the conclusion of a French chap-book, "L'Histoire du bonhomme Misère," which from the beginning of the eighteenth century has had an enormous circulation in successive editions. Peter and Paul, who rove the earth as needy vagrants, in the first instance apply at the door of Wealthy (*Richard*), by whom they are refused; they proceed, and are taken in by Misery, who entertains as well as he may his visitors, to whom he abandons his couch of straw! On departing, the guests ask Misery to desire what he pleases. The poor man, who is out of spirits because his pear-tree has been robbed, can think of nothing better than any one who climbs it shall be unable to come down without permission. In this manner he catches a thief whom he pardons. When Death arrives, he succeeds in enticing him into the tree, and refuses release until Death promises never again to come after him, and moralizes: "You can boast, good man, to be the first living man who ever vanquished Death. Heaven ordains that with thy consent I quit thee, and return not until the day of the universal judgment, after I shall have achieved my great work, the destruction of the human race. See it thou shalt, I warrant thee; without hesitancy, suffer me to descend, or fly hence; at the distance of a hundred leagues, a widow awaits me in order to depart." From that day

---

1. With reference to the tale of "Godfather Death," above noted.

2. J. Bolte, "Die Historia von Sancto," *Zeitschrift für Deutsche Philologie*, xxxii. (1892) 369.

3. Vulpius, *Curiositäten*, Weimar, 1813, iii. 422. See Grimm, Note to No. 82, who gives an account also of the version of Trömer, "Der Schmied von Jüterbogk."

Misery has dwelt in the same poverty, near his beloved tree, where, according to the pledge of Death, he shall remains as long as world is world.[1]

The name of Misery as chief actor appears also in a number of traditional versions, which, however, seem to me to have borrowed the appellation (though not the plot) from the chap-book.[2]

The undying Misery has an analogy to the Wandering Jew, which has not been overlooked by ballad-makers. A Breton *gwerz* (ballad) makes *Misère* meet Isaac the Wanderer, with whom he has a discussion in alternate rhymes. Isaac, who can boast only seventeen hundred years, is a child compared to Misery, who was born when Adam went into exile. The former is furious against the latter as the author of his distresses; but the song has a moral turn; Misery remarks that those who desire to avoid him have only to shun prodigality and be industrious.[3]

The name is used as the basis of an allegory by an author whose rather stupid work is given in the "Bibliothèque Bleue." Obstinate, in company with Passion, Patience, and Reason, is seeking the way to the house of Happiness. Misery appears a little and decrepit man, with a chain on his leg, carrying a burden; influenced by Hope, he is on his way to the land of Happiness, where he expects soon to arrive. Obstinate is anxious to follow, until he is shown by what impossible paths the journey is made.[4]

It will be observed that in the older versions of the legend it is Death, not the Devil, who is the enemy to be overcome; internal evidence favors the view that this was the original form of the story, that the hero of the action did become exempt from death, but that the resultant evils compelled providential interference. The version of von Dilling shows in what manner, as a substitute for Death, the Devil may have been introduced into the narration.

The Maryland variant presents numerous variations from the recorded English and Irish tales, yet as a rule such differences find parallels in European forms of the story, and are therefore likely to have been imported; of anything distinctively negro there is nothing, except the dialect, and the singular name given to the wife provided for the fiend.[5]

The legend presents a striking example of the variation incident to traditional narratives, which, after the manner of a living organism, alter in such wise as to fill every vac-

1. J. F. H. Champfleury, *Recherches sur l'origine et les variations du Bonhomme Misère*, Paris, 1861; reprinted in *Histoire du l'imagerie populaire*, Paris, 1869, pp. 105–88.

2. Italian, "Compar Miseria," A. de Gubernatis, *Le novelline di Santo Stefano*, Turin, 1869, No. 32; T. F. Crane, *Italian Popular Tales*, Boston, 1885, p. 221. Misery, having entertained Jesus and St. Peter, is granted three wishes, which are magic chair, the fig-tree, salvation. In the end, Death abandons the attempt to capture Misery, who never dies. The inconsistency of the desire for salvation with the trait of deathlessness, shows sufficiently the hybridization of the tale. The author of the story in the chap-book says it came from Italy; this may have been only a *façon de parler*. The writer used a legend in which Christ was made to apply first at the house of a rich man (*Richard*), afterwards at that of a poor one; this trait does not appear in "Compar Miseria," nor in the Bohemian tale given by Waldau, *Slavische Blätter*, 1865, 598, "Gevatter Elend." See, also, the Breton tale below cited, and Köhler, *op. cit.*, i. 103, 349.

3. Champfleury, p. 164, after the communication of F. M. Luzel.

4. Champfleury, p. 175.

5. The Devil is detained in the fruit-tree by the power belonging to the sign of the cross; so in a Breton variant, he is imprisoned in the box by holy nails, and in the tree by bars of iron which have been sprinkled with holy water. P. Sébillot, *Littérature orale de la Haute-Bretagne*, Paris, 1881, p. 175, "Misère."

uum. The adversary is either Death, or the Devil, or both; the hero either becomes deathless, or obtains a long life; when he does finally pass away, his spirit either reaches heaven, or remains in an intermediate state; in the latter case he either wanders as a ghost, or changes into an *ignis fatuus*.

The diffusion of folk-tales is also illustrated. Out of a single narration variants are seen to arise, establish themselves as sub-species, circulate without obstruction by barriers of race or language, in fresh soil strike independent root, and in each region assume appropriate personal reference and local color.

It is not necessary to suppose that in all instance such evolution requires a very long period of time. As already remarked, there is reason to assume that the forms of the story in which the Devil figures are modern rather than mediæval; yet their recency has not prevented the attainment of European circulation, and in such manner that any one district is likely to present several such variants. The special narration which makes the overcomer of Satan turn into a wandering fire may be of English origin, yet has been accepted in Wales and Ireland.

Though the legend, in all its varieties, considered as a particular tale, is hardly ancient, yet it belongs to a genus which can be traced into antiquity; such geneaological inquiry must be reserved for a future occasion.[1]

---

1. Since these pages were in type, I have learned from a friend (Dr. W. A. Farabee of Harvard University) that belief in the *ignis fatuus*, as a supernatural phenomenon, is still widely spread among whites through the United States. In Pennsylvania hunters observed that they were followed by a light, which paused when they concealed themselves, and retreated when pursued; this they took to be a Jack-a-lantern (see Journal of American Folk-Lore, ii. (1889), 35). In Dallas County, Missouri, where many persons were occupied with dreams of buried treasure (coin having actually been concealed during the civil war), a light said to have been observed for years on marshy though elevated ground, was taken to be a Jack-a-lantern, which served as the token of such hidden wealth; when investigation proved unavailing, the sign was presumed to have another meaning.

As to the more ancient form of the legend under discussion, in which Death is the adversary to be encountered, D. Hyde (see note 41) observes that there are Irish variants, in which Seâghan Tinnceâr overcomes Death instead of the Devil. No doubt English versions of corresponding form formerly existed.

For negro superstitions concerning the *ignis fatuus*, see this Journal, i. (1888), 139.

"Hallowmass"

From *Faiths and Folklore: A Dictionary of National Beliefs, Superstitions and Popular Customs, Past and Current, with Their Classical and Foreign Analogues, Described and Illustrated*, Volume I, W. Carew Hazlitt, 1905

The entry on Hallowmass from Hazlitt's *Dictionary* is separate from his listing on "Hallow E'en," and more interesting since it addresses the custom of "souling," or begging on All Saints' Day for small cakes. There's been some conjecture that English and Irish souling may have been an early precursor to American trick-or-treating (see, for example, how Jack Santino traces the history of Halloween mumming in his article "Halloween: The Fantasy and Folklore of All Hallows" at the website for the Library of Congress), and Hazlitt's entry provides a fascinating look at some of the very early practices associated with Halloween, including bell-ringing and (in the entry on "Hallowmass in Scotland," which is also included here) offerings at the Isle of Lewis to a sea-god named Shony.

Hallowmass. — In the "Festyvall," 1511, is the following passage: "we rede in olde tyme good people wolde on All halowen days bake brade and dele it for all crysten soules." On Allhallows' Day, or Hallowmass, it was an ancient English custom for poor persons and beggars to go a-souling, which signified to go round asking for money, to fast for the souls of the donors of alms or their kinsfolk. In the "Two Gentlemen of Verona," Shakespear makes Speed speak of some one puling, "like a beggar at Hallowmass." But the usage is referred to by Scot in his "Discovery of Witchcraft," 1584. In Shropshire (and perhaps elsewhere) the children still go souling, as they did in Aubrey's day, on Hallowmass, and they sing the following verses, for which I am indebted to a correspondent of "Notes and Queries":

> "Soul! soul! for a soul-cake;
> Pray, good mistress, for a soul-cake.
> One for Peter, two for Paul,
> Three for them that made us all.

This turn-of-the-century postcard shows a Hallowe'en fortune-telling cake.

> Soul! soul! for an apple or two;
> If you've got no apples, pears will do.
> Up with your kettle, and down with your pan
> Give me a good big one, and I'll be gone.
>   Soul! soul! &c.
> An apple or pear, a plum or a cherry,
> Is a very good thing to make us merry.
>   Soul! soul! &c.

Some of the richer sorts of persons in Lancashire and Herefordshire (among the papists there) used to give cakes of oaten bread to the poor on this day; and they, in retribution of their charity, hold themselves obliged to say this old couplet:

> —"God have your Saul,
> Beens and all."

In the Cleveland country these loaves are called similarly Sau-mas Loaves. In the Whitby Glossary, they are described as "sets of square farthing cakes with currants in the centre, commonly given by bakers to their customers; and it was usual to keep them in the house for good luck." In this last respect they resembled the Good Friday bread and cross-buns. Mr. Brand's servant, who was a native of Warwickshire, told him that seed-cakes at Allhallows were also usual in that country. Harvey, the Dublin conjurer, states that, on this Eve, which he characterizes as an "anile, chimerical solemnity," his servants demanded apples, ale, and nuts, and left him alone, while they went to enjoy themselves.

In the Churchwardens' Accounts of Heybridge, Essex, under 1517, are the following items: "Payed to Andrew Elyott, of Maldon, for newe mendynge of the bell knappelle agenste Hallowmasse, £0 1s. 8d. Item, payed to John Gidney, of Maldon, for a new bell-rope agenste Hallowmasse, £0 0s. 8d." In the time of Henry VIII, "the Vigil and ringing of bells all the night long upon Allhallow day at night," was abolished. In the appendix also to Strype's "Annals," the following injunction, made early in the reign of Elizabeth, occurs: "that the superfluous ringing of bels, and the superstitious ringing of bels at Alhallown tide, and at All Souls' Day with the two nights next before and after, be prohibited." It is stated in Kethe's Sermon preached at Blandford, 1570, that "there was a custom, in the papal times, to ring bells at Allhallow-tide for all Christian souls." No. 130 of "Mery Tales and Quicke Answers," 1567, however, is "Of the gentilman that checked his seruant for talke of ryngyng." "A Gentilman, brought vp at London in an In of court, was maryed, and kepte an house in the countrey; and as he sate at supper with his neyghbours aboute hym, vpon an alhalow daie at night, amonge other communication, he talked of the solemne ringing of the belles (as was the vsage than)." The feast of Allhallows is said to drive the Finns almost out of their wits.

Hallowmass in Scotland. — Martin, speaking of the Isle of Lewis, says that it was long before the minister there could persuade the people to relinquish a ridiculous custom they had of going by night on Hallow-tide to the Church of St. Mulvay, whence one of their number went into the sea up to his waist, with a cup of ale brewed for the occasion with malt contributed by the inhabitants (each family giving a peck), and pouring the liquid into the water, addressed a propitiatory allocution to a sea-god called Shony, who was supposed to have an influence over the crops. They then returned to church, observed a moment's dead silence, then extinguished at a given signal the candle on the altar, and proceeded to the fields, where the rest of the night was spent in revelry.

"Hallowe'en"

From *The School Arts Book, Volume Five,*
Emma Woodman, 1906

This entry from a 1906 collection of articles and letters by and for teachers may strike a note of wry amusement with some contemporary readers, since it seems that there have always been those who found Halloween objectionable in some way and were certain they knew how to fix it. Fortunately, Ms. Woodman's notion of "benevolent" jack-o'-lanterns never caught on.

"Who carried off the gates of Gaza?" demanded the Sunday School teacher. "It wasn't me," declared the small urchin, apprehensively, "I didn't go out with the boys hallowe'en."

This Scotch festival of the fairies and witches dates back to the eighteenth century, when the peasants kept vigil with bonfires on the eve of All Saints' Day, November first. To the boyish heart it is still a carnival of fun not easily given up. People endure the soaped windows and "tick tacks" with more or less resignation to the inevitable; but at times, even the police fails to prevent ruthless destruction of property. Young people of the highest standing will indulge in the prevailing pranks.

"Upon that night, when Fairies light,
On Cassilis Downans dance,"

as Robert Burns says in the beginning lines of "Hallowe'en."

The problem for parents and teachers is this: How can all this overflowing energy be utilized to the best advantage? Our plan has proved most pleasant and helpful to all concerned.

In October many sketches were made in preparation for Hallowe'en posters to illustrate "A Good Joke." The literal meaning of this title was adhered to, and any suggestion otherwise became unpopular. The sixth, seventh and eighth grades took a keen interest in figure study with all its requirements, to be able to express with life-like effect the scene: A moonlight night, an humble cottage, boys and girls placing baskets of good things on the steps or hanging warm garments on the clothes line, then running away to prevent their left hands' knowing what their right hand had been doing, and lastly, the surprise of the poor people to find a *benevolent* Jack-o-lantern beaming upon them from a clothes post.

Early photo postcard showing the morning-after results of Hallowe'en pranking in an east Iowa town: Note carts, gates, and even a bathtub gathered in the town's main street!

By the way, why should these carved faces always be made so ugly? And why should the drawings of them be hung before a room full of children ready to reflect expressions?

Besides the drill afforded in sketching from the pose, for the hallowe'en posters, there was much interest shown in the study of lights and shadows from the harvest moon, the lantern, and the lamp shining out of the window or door. Each was attempted separately in practice work, till the problem of three lights showing at once was solved.

The originality called for in portraying "good" jokes did much to make later work independent; while the space relations, values of color, and perspective involved strengthened all these lines.

To be sure, when the eventful evening arrived some of the novelty of playing hallowe'en pranks had worn off; but the interest awakened in needy neighbors bore fruit, and will continue to in the lives of the boys and girls.

Shakespeare speaking of this festival in Richard II says,

> "She came adorned hither like sweet May
> Sent back for Hallowmass or shortest day."

Like the happy custom of hanging May baskets, the observance of hallowe'en should bring pleasure to everybody, and by wise planning it will.

"Hallowe'en"

From *Plea of the Negro Soldier and a Hundred Other Poems*, Corporal Charles Frederick White, 1908

Corporal Charles Frederick White served with distinction (as did so many other African-American soldiers) in the Spanish-American War, which concluded in 1898; upon their return home, these men were briefly celebrated (principally by the poet Paul Laurence Dunbar, in "The Conquerors"), then forgotten and returned to the often brutal living conditions of African-Americans at the time (as White describes eloquently in his preface to *Plea of the Negro Soldier*).

White's collection is a mix of spirituals, love poems, meditations on his life as a serviceman and an African-American, and seasonal poems. His "Hallowe'en" is a delightful (and fairly detailed) ode to holiday mischief. Compare to Burns's poem of the same title, penned more than a century earlier, and note how Halloween has transformed from a Scottish celebration centered on fortune-telling to an American festival when boys test their daring with displaced gates (earning the holiday the temporary name of "Gate Night") and "ticktacks" (noisemakers).

HALLOWE'EN

(To a Friend)

Last night was Hallowe'en, you know;
   The cowbells rang, the horns did blow,
The goblins stalked o'er stones and planks
   And small boys played their annual pranks.

The women dressed in men's attire;
   The small girl, too, quenched her desire
To get into her brother's pants:
   The hollow pumpkin had its chance.

The sidewalks creaked, the street cars balked,
   The sign boards moved, the lamp posts mocked,

Mischief-makers steal a gate on Hallowe'en night (1911 postcard).

The wagons went to roof resorts
    And front gates climbed poles of all sorts.

The Indians at tobacco stores
    Went on the warpath by the scores.
The ticktacks played on window panes
    And stuffed men mounted weather vanes.

The larger boys played other tricks;
    They tied dogs' tails to large-sized bricks;
Pinned placards on policemen's coats
    And set fire to the tails of goats.

They masked themselves as spooks and ghosts
    And stood behind trees and big posts;
They set logs 'gainst some folk's front doors,
    Then knocked and ran away, of course.

They put torpedoes on the rails
    For streetcars, and painted cats' tails;
And many more such things as these
    They did, which you may name with ease;

For, if you were not once a boy,
    I'm rather sure you did enjoy,
At some time, hearing stories told
    Of how the boys did do of old.

But boys must have their fun and play,
   Although they often have to pay
Quite dearly for their tricks and sport,
   Which sometimes wind up in a court.

Yet, boys can play their pranks and jokes
   On numerous good-natured folks
Who think that boys must have their fun,
   E'en though they sometimes have to run.

So Hallowe'en may come and go,
   And cranky folk may often show
Their temper, but the boys don't care;
   For what's a boy who will not dare?
                                   Nov., 1904.

"The Hallowe'en Fires"

From *The Golden Bough, Part VII: Balder the Beautiful, Volume I: The Fire-Festivals of Europe and the Doctrine of the External Soul*, Sir James G. Frazer, 1913

The first lengthy examination of Hallowe'en traditions and folktales was provided by Sir James G. Frazer in his massive study of mythology and folklore, *The Golden Bough*. Although Frazer's classic is probably best known to contemporary readers in one- or two-volume editions (which include no more than a scant few paragraphs of Hallowe'en information), his full 13-volume edition of *The Golden Bough* features an entire 20-page chapter entitled "The Hallowe'en Fires," in which Frazer gathered together an amazing amount of data on fire traditions, fortune-telling games, and folk stories. Frazer's study of Hallowe'en would remain unsurpassed until Ruth Kelley's *The Book of Hallowe'en* was published six years later, and that book drew heavily from Frazer's entry.

"The Hallowe'en Fires" as presented here has been edited slightly to exclude recreations of articles or tales that are presented in their original form elsewhere in this book. However, I have left some material herein that may be redundant, since Frazer's comments on and juxtaposition of information are often revealing.

---

6. The Hallowe'en Fires

From the foregoing survey we may infer that among the heathen forefathers of the European peoples the most popular and widespread fire–festival of the year was the great celebration of Midsummer Eve or Midsummer Day. The coincidence of the festival with the summer solstice can hardly be accidental. Rather we must suppose that our pagan ancestors purposely timed the ceremony of fire on earth to coincide with the arrival of the sun at the highest point of his course in the sky. If that was so, it follows that the old founders of the midsummer rites had observed the solstices or turning-points of the sun's apparent path in the sky, and that they accordingly regulated their festal calendar to some extent by astronomical considerations.

But while this may be regarded as fairly certain for what we may call the aborigines throughout a large part of the continent, it appears not to have been true of the Celtic

An Irish Hallowe'en is celebrated with bobbing for apples and snap-apple in this 1888 engraving.

peoples who inhabited the Land's End of Europe, the islands and promontories that stretch out into the Atlantic ocean on the North-West. The principal fire–festivals of the Celts, which have survived, though in a restricted area and with diminished pomp, to modern times and even to our own day, were seemingly timed without any reference to the position of the sun in the heaven. They were two in number, and fell at an interval of six months, one being celebrated on the eve of May Day and the other on Allhallow Even or Hallowe'en, as it is now commonly called, that is, on the thirty-first of October, the day preceding All Saints' or Allhallows' Day. These dates coincide with none of the four great hinges on which the solar year revolves, to wit, the solstices and the equinoxes. Nor do they agree with the principal seasons of the agricultural year, the sowing in spring and the reaping in autumn. For when May Day comes, the seed has long been committed to the earth; and when November opens, the harvest has long been reaped and garnered, the fields lie bare, the fruit-trees are stripped, and even the yellow leaves are fast fluttering to the ground. Yet the first of May and the first of November mark turning-points of the year in Europe; the one ushers in the genial heat and the rich vege-tation of summer, the other heralds, if it does not share, the cold and barrenness of win-ter. Now these particular points of the year, as has been well pointed out by a learned and ingenious writer,[1] while they are of comparatively little moment to the European husbandman, do deeply concern the European herdsman; for it is on the approach of summer that he drives his cattle out into the open to crop the fresh grass, and it is on the approach of winter that he leads them back to the safety and shelter of the stall. Accord-

1. E.K. Chambers, *The Mediaeval Stage* (Oxford, 1903), i. 110 *sqq.*

ingly it seems not improbable that the Celtic bisection of the year into two halves at the beginning of May and the beginning of November dates from a time when the Celts were mainly a pastoral people, dependent for their subsistence on their herds, and when accordingly the great epochs of the year for them were the days on which the cattle went forth from the homestead in early summer and returned to it again in early winter.[1] Even in Central Europe, remote from the region now occupied by the Celts, a similar bisection of the year may be clearly traced in the great popularity, on the one hand, of May Day and its Eve (Walpurgis Night), and, on the other hand, of the Feast of All Souls at the beginning of November, which under a thin Christian cloak conceals an ancient pagan festival of the dead.[2] Hence we may conjecture that everywhere throughout Europe the celestial division of the year according to the solstices was preceded by what we may call a terrestrial division of the year according to the beginning of summer and the beginning of winter.

Be that as it may, the two great Celtic festivals of May Day and the first of November or, to be more accurate, the Eves of these two days, closely resemble each other in the manner of their celebration and in the superstitions associated with them, and alike, by the antique character impressed upon both, betray a remote and purely pagan origin. The festival of May Day or Beltane, as the Celts called it, which ushered in summer, has already been described;[3] it remains to give some account of the corresponding festival of Hallowe'en, which announced the arrival of winter.

Of the two feasts Hallowe'en was perhaps of old the more important, since the Celts would seem to have dated the beginning of the year from it rather than from Beltane. In the Isle of Man, one of the fortresses in which the Celtic language and lore longest held out against the siege of the Saxon invaders, the first of November, Old Style, has been regarded as New Year's day down to recent times. Thus Manx mummers used to go round on Hallowe'en (Old Style), singing, in the Manx language, a sort of Hogmanay song which began "To-night is New Year's Night, *Hog-unnaa!*"[4] One of Sir John Rhys's Manx informants, an old man of sixty-seven, "had been a farm servant from the age of sixteen till he was twenty-six to the same man, near Regaby, in the parish of Andreas, and he remembers his master and a near neighbour of his discussing the term New Year's Day as applied to the first of November, and explaining to the younger men that it had

1. In Eastern Europe to this day the great season for driving out the cattle to pasture for the first time in spring is St. George's Day, the twenty-third of April, which is not far removed from May Day. See *The Magic Art and the Evolution of Kings*, ii. 324 *sqq.* As to the bisection of the Celtic year, see the old authority quoted by P.W. Joyce, *The Social History of Ancient Ireland* (London, 1903), ii. 390: "The whole year was [originally] divided into two parts — Summer from 1st May to 1st November, and Winter from 1st November to 1st May." On this subject compare (Sir) John Rhys, *Celtic Heathendom* (London and Edinburgh, 1888), pp. 460, 514 *sqq.*; *id., Celtic Folk-lore, Welsh and Manx* (Oxford, 1901), i. 315 *sqq.*; J.A. MacCulloch, in Dr. James Hastings's *Encyclopaedia of Religion and Ethics*, iii. (Edinburgh, 1910) p. 80.

2. See below, p. 225.

3. Above, pp. 146 *sqq.*; *The Magic Art and the Evolution of Kings*, ii. 59 *sqq.*

4. (Sir) John Rhys, *Celtic Folk-lore, Manx and Welsh* (Oxford, 1901), i. 316, 317 *sq.*; J.A. MacCulloch, in Dr. James Hastings's *Encyclopaedia of Religion and Ethics*, iii. (Edinburgh, 1910) *s.v.* "Calendar," p. 80, referring to Kelly, *English and Manx Dictionary* (Douglas, 1866), *s.v.* "Blein." Hogmanay is the popular Scotch name for the last day of the year. See Dr. J. Jamieson, *Etymological Dictionary of the Scottish Language*, New Edition (Paisley, 1879–1882), ii. 602 *sq.*

always been so in old times. In fact, it seemed to him natural enough, as all tenure of land ends at that time, and as all servant men begin their service then."[1] In ancient Ireland, as we saw, a new fire used to be kindled every year on Hallowe'en or the Eve of Samhain, and from this sacred flame all the fires in Ireland were rekindled.[2] Such a custom points strongly to Samhain or All Saints' Day (the first of November) as New Year's Day; since the annual kindling of a new fire takes place most naturally at the beginning of the year, in order that the blessed influence of the fresh fire may last throughout the whole period of twelve months. Another confirmation of the view that the Celts dated their year from the first of November is furnished by the manifold modes of divination which, as we shall see presently, were commonly resorted to by Celtic peoples on Hallowe'en for the purpose of ascertaining their destiny, especially their fortune in the coming year; for when could these devices for prying into the future be more reasonably put in practice than at the beginning of the year? As a season of omens and auguries Hallowe'en seems to have far surpassed Beltane in the imagination of the Celts; from which we may with some probability infer that they reckoned their year from Hallowe'en rather than Beltane. Another circumstance of great moment which points to the same conclusion is the association of the dead with Hallowe'en. Not only among the Celts but throughout Europe, Hallowe'en, the night which marks the transition from autumn to winter, seems to have been of old the time of year when the souls of the departed were supposed to revisit their old homes in order to warm themselves by the fire and to comfort themselves with the good cheer provided for them in the kitchen or the parlour by their affectionate kinsfolk.[3] It was, perhaps, a natural thought that the approach of winter should drive the poor shivering hungry ghosts from the bare fields and the leafless woodlands to the shelter of the cottage with its familiar fireside.[4] Did not the lowing kine then troop back from the summer pastures in the forests and on the hills to be fed and cared for in the stalls, while the bleak winds whistled among the swaying boughs and the snow drifts deepened in the hollows? and could the good-man and the good-wife deny to the spirits of their dead the welcome which they gave to the cows?

But it is not only the souls of the departed who are supposed to be hovering unseen on the day "when autumn to winter resigns the pale year." Witches then speed on their errands of mischief, some sweeping through the air on besoms, others galloping along the roads on tabby-cats, which for that evening are turned into coal-black steeds.[5] The

---

1. (Sir) John Rhys, *Celtic Folk-lore, Welsh and Manx*, i. 316 *sq.*

2. Above, p. 139.

3. See *Adonis, Attis, Osiris*, Second Edition, pp. 309–318. As I have there pointed out, the Catholic Church succeeded in altering the date of the festival by one day, but not in changing the character of the festival. All Souls' Day is now the second instead of the first of November. But we can hardly doubt that the Saints, who have taken possession of the first of November, wrested it from the Souls of the Dead, the original proprietors. After all, the Saints are only one particular class of the Souls of the Dead; so that the change which the Church effected, no doubt for the purpose of disguising the heathen character of the festival, is less great than appears at first sight.

4. In Wales "it was firmly believed in former times that on All Hallows' Eve the spirit of a departed person was to be seen at midnight on every cross-road and on every stile" (Marie Trevelyan, *Folk-lore and Folk-stories of Wales*, London, 1909, p. 254).

5. E. J. Guthrie, *Old Scottish Customs* (London and Glasgow, 1885), p. 68.

A Hallowe'en witch, with broom and owl (1909 postcard).

fairies, too, are all let loose, and hobgoblins of every sort roam freely about. In South Uist and Eriskay there is a saying:—

> *"Hallowe'en will come, will come,*
> *Witchcraft [or divination] will be set agoing,*
> *Fairies will be at full speed,*
> *Running in every pass.*
> *Avoid the road, children, children."*[1]

In Cardiganshire on November Eve a bogie sits on every stile.[2] On that night in Ireland all the fairy hills are thrown wide open and the fairies swarm forth; any man who is bold enough may then peep into the open green hills and see the treasures hidden in them. Worse than that, the cave of Cruachan in Connaught, known as "the Hell-gate of Ireland," is unbarred on Samhain Eve or Hallowe'en, and a host of horrible fiends and goblins used to rush forth, particularly a flock of copper-red birds, which blighted crops and killed animals by their poisonous breath.[3] ... wicked fairies are apt to carry off men's wives with them to fairyland; but the lost spouses can be recovered within a year and a day when the procession of the fairies is defiling past on Hallowe'en, always provided that the mortals did not partake of elfin food while they were in elfinland.[4]

1. A. Goodrich-Freer, "More Folklore from the Hebrides," *Folk-lore*, xiii. (1902) p. 53.

2. (Sir) John Rhys, *Celtic Heathendom* (London and Edinburgh, 1888), p. 516.

3. P.W. Joyce, *A Social History of Ancient Ireland* (London, 1903), i. 264 *sq.*, ii. 556.

4. Ch. Rogers, *Social Life in Scotland* (Edinburgh, 1884–1886), iii. 258–260.

...

In all Celtic countries Hallowe'en seems to have been the great season of the year for prying into the future; all kinds of divination were put in practice that night. We read that Dathi, a king of Ireland in the fifth century, happening to be at the Druids' Hill (*Cnoc-nan-druad*) in the county of Sligo one Hallowe'en, ordered his druid to forecast for him the future from that day till the next Hallowe'en should come round. The druid passed the night on the top of the hill, and next morning made a prediction to the king which came true.[1] In Wales Hallowe'en was the weirdest of all the *Teir Nos Ysbrydion*, or Three Spirit Nights, when the wind, "blowing over the feet of the corpses," bore sighs to the houses of those who were to die within the year. People thought that if on that night they went out to a cross-road and listened to the wind, they would learn all the most important things that would befall them during the next twelve months.[2] In Wales, too, not so long ago women used to congregate in the parish churches on the night of Hallowe'en and read their fate from the flame of the candle which each of them held in her hand; also they heard the names or saw the coffins of the parishioners who would die within the year, and many were the sad scenes to which these gloomy visions gave rise.[3] And in the Highlands of Scotland anybody who pleased could hear proclaimed aloud the names of parishioners doomed to perish within the next twelve months, if he would only take a three-legged stool and go and sit on it at three cross-roads, while the church clock was striking twelve at midnight on Hallowe'en. It was even in his power to save the destined victims from their doom by taking with him articles of wearing apparel and throwing them away, one by one, as each name was called out by the mysterious voice.[4]

But while a glamour of mystery and awe has always clung to Hallowe'en in the minds of the Celtic peasantry, the popular celebration of the festival has been, at least in modern times, by no means of a prevailingly gloomy cast; on the contrary it has been attended by picturesque features and merry pastimes, which rendered it the gayest night of all the year. Amongst the things which in the Highlands of Scotland contributed to invest the festival with a romantic beauty were the bonfires which used to blaze at frequent intervals on the heights. "On the last day of autumn children gathered ferns, tar-barrels, the long thin stalks called *gàinisg*, and everything suitable for a bonfire. These were placed in a heap on some eminence near the house, and in the evening set fire to. The fires were called *Samhnagan*. There was one for each house, and it was an object of ambition who should have the biggest. Whole districts were brilliant with bonfires, and their glare across a Highland loch, and from many eminences, formed an exceedingly picturesque scene."[5] Like the Beltane fires on the first of May, the Hallowe'en

1. P.W. Joyce, *Social History of Ancient Ireland*, i. 229.

2. Marie Trevelyan, *Folk-lore and Folk-stories of Wales* (London, 1909), p. 254.

3. (Sir) John Rhys, *Celtic Heathendom*, pp. 514 *sq.* In order to see the apparitions all you had to do was to run thrice round the parish church and then peep through the key-hole of the door. See Marie Trevelyan, *op. cit.* p. 254; J. C. Davies, *Folk-lore of West and Mid-Wales* (Aberystwyth, 1911), p. 77.

4. Miss E. J. Guthrie, *Old Scottish Customs* (London and Glasgow, 1885), p. 75.

5. The Rev. John Gregorson Campbell, *Witchcraft and Second Sight in the Highlands and Islands of Scotland* (Glasgow, 1902), p. 282.

bonfires seem to have been kindled most commonly in the Perthshire Highlands. Travelling in the parish of Moulin, near Pitlochrie, in the year 1772, the Englishman Thomas Pennant writes that "Hallow Eve is also kept sacred: as soon as it is dark, a person sets fire to a bush of broom fastened round a pole, and, attended with a crowd, runs about the village. He then flings it down, heaps great quantity of combustible matters on it, and makes a great bonfire. A whole tract is thus illuminated at the same time, and makes a fine appearance."[1] The custom has been described more fully by a Scotchman of the eighteenth century, John Ramsay of Ochtertyre. On the evening of Hallowe'en "the young people of every hamlet assembled upon some eminence near the houses. There they made a bonfire of ferns or other fuel, cut the same day, which from the feast was called *Samh-nag* or *Savnag*, a fire of rest and pleasure. Around it was placed a circle of stones, one for each person of the families to whom they belonged. And when it grew dark the bonfire was kindled, at which a loud shout was set up. Then each person taking a torch of ferns or sticks in his hand, ran round the fire exulting; and sometimes they went into the adjacent fields, where, if there was another company, they visited the bonfire, taunting the others if inferior in any respect to themselves. After the fire was burned out they returned home, where a feast was prepared, and the remainder of the evening was spent in mirth and diversions of various kinds. Next morning they repaired betimes to the bonfire, where the situation of the stones was examined with much attention. If any of them were misplaced, or if the print of a foot could be discerned near any particular stone, it was imagined that the person for whom it was set would not live out the year. Of late years this is less attended to, but about the beginning of the present century it was regarded as a sure prediction. The Hallowe'en fire is still kept up in some parts of the Low country; but on the western coast and in the Isles it is never kindled, though the night is spent in merriment and entertainments."[2] In the Perthshire parish of Callander, which includes the now famous pass of the Trossachs opening out on the winding and wooded shores of the lovely Loch Katrine, the Hallowe'en bonfires were still kindled down to near the end of the eighteenth century. When the fire had died down, the ashes were carefully collected in the form of a circle, and a stone was put in, near the circumference, for every person of the several families interested in the bonfire. Next morning, if any of these stones was found to be displaced or injured, the people made sure that the person represented by it was *fey* or devoted, and that he could not live twelve months from that day.[3] In the parish of Logierait, which covers the beautiful valley of the Tummel, one of the fairest regions of all Scotland, the Hallowe'en fire was somewhat different. Faggots of heath, broom, and the dressings of flax were kindled and carried on poles by men, who ran with them round the villages, attended by a crowd. As soon as one faggot was burnt out, a fresh one was lighted and fastened to the pole. Numbers of these blazing faggots

1. Thomas Pennant, "Tour in Scotland, and Voyage to the Hebrides in 1772," in John Pinkerton's *Voyages and Travels*, iii. (London, 1809) pp. 383 *sq*. In quoting the passage I have corrected what seem to be two misprints.

2. John Ramsay, of Ochtertyre, *Scotland and Scotsmen in the Eighteenth Century*, edited by Alexander Allardyce (Edinburgh and London, 1888), ii. 437 *sq*. This account was written in the eighteenth century.

3. The Rev. James Robertson, Parish minister of Callander, in Sir John Sinclair's *Statistical Account of Scotland*, xi. (Edinburgh, 1794), pp. 621 *sq*.

were often carried about together, and when the night happened to be dark, they formed a splendid illumination.[1]

Nor did the Hallowe'en fires die out in Perthshire with the end of the eighteenth century. Journeying from Dunkeld to Aberfeldy on Hallowe'en in the first half of the nineteenth century, Sheriff Barclay counted thirty fires blazing on the hill tops, and saw the figures of the people dancing like phantoms round the flames.[2] Again, "in 1860, I was residing near the head of Loch Tay during the season of the Hallowe'en feast. For several days before Hallowe'en, boys and youths collected wood and conveyed it to the most prominent places on the hill sides in their neighbourhood. Some of the heaps were as large as a corn-stack or hayrick. After dark on Hallowe'en, these heaps were kindled, and for several hours both sides of Loch Tay were illuminated as far as the eye could see. I was told by old men that at the beginning of this century men as well as boys took part in getting up the bonfires, and that, when the fire was ablaze, all joined hands and danced round the fire, and made a great noise; but that, as these gatherings generally ended in drunkenness and rough and dangerous fun, the ministers set their faces against the observance, and were seconded in their efforts by the more intelligent and well-behaved in the community; and so the practice was discontinued by adults and relegated to school boys."[3] At Balquhidder down to the latter part of the nineteenth century each household kindled its bonfire at Hallowe'en, but the custom was chiefly observed by children. The fires were lighted on any high knoll near the house; there was no dancing round them.[4]

Hallowe'en fires were also lighted in some districts of the north-east of Scotland, such as Buchan.... Referring to this part of Scotland, a writer at the end of the eighteenth century observes that "the Hallow-even fire, another relict of druidism, was kindled in Buchan. Various magic ceremonies were then celebrated to counteract the influence of witches and demons, and to prognosticate to the young their success or disappointment in the matrimonial lottery. These being devoutly finished, the hallow fire was kindled, and guarded by the male part of the family. Societies were formed, either by pique or humour, to scatter certain fires, and the attack and defence were often conducted with art and with fury."[5] Down to about the middle of the nineteenth century "the Braemar Highlanders made the circuit of their fields with lighted torches at Hallowe'en to ensure their fertility in the coming year. At that date the custom was as follows: Every member of the family (in those days households were larger than they are now) was provided with a bundle of fir 'can'les' with which to go the round. The father and mother stood at the hearth and lit the splints in the peat fire, which they passed to the children and servants, who trooped out one after the other, and proceeded to tread the bounds of their little property, going slowly round at equal distances

---

1. The Rev. Dr. Thomas Bisset, in Sir John Sinclair's *Statistical Account of Scotland* v. (Edinburgh, 1793) pp. 84 *sq.*

2. Miss E. J. Guthrie, *Old Scottish Customs* (London and Glasgow, 1885), p. 67.

3. James Napier, *Folk Lore, or Superstitious Beliefs in the West of Scotland within this Century* (Paisley, 1879), p. 179.

4. J. G. Frazer, "Folk-lore at Balquhidder," *The Folk-lore Journal*, vi. (1888) p. 270.

5. The Rev. A. Johnstone, as to the parish of Monquhitter, in Sir John Sinclair's *Statistical Account of Scotland*, xxi. (Edinburgh, 1799) pp. 145 *sq.*

apart, and invariably with the sun. To go 'withershins' seems to have been reserved for curs-
ing and excommunication. When the fields had thus been circumnambulated the remaining
spills were thrown together in a heap and allowed to burn out."[1]

In the Highlands of Scotland, as the evening of Hallowe'en wore on, young people
gathered in one of the houses and resorted to an almost endless variety of games, or rather
forms of divination, for the purpose of ascertaining the future fate of each member of the
company. Were they to marry or remain single, was the marriage to take place that year or
never, who was to be married first, what sort of husband or wife she or he was to get, the
name, the trade, the colour of the hair, the amount of property of the future spouse —
these were questions that were eagerly canvassed and the answers to them furnished never-
failing entertainment.[2] Nor were these modes of divination at Hallowe'en confined to the
Highlands, where the bonfires were kindled; they were practised with equal faith and in
practically the same forms in the Lowlands, as we learn, for example, from Burns's poem
Hallowe'en, which describes the auguries drawn from a variety of omens by the Ayrshire
peasantry. These Lowlanders of Saxon descent may well have inherited the rites from the
Celts who preceded them in the possession of the south country.

...

In the northern part of Wales it used to be customary for every family to make a
great bonfire called *Coel Coeth* on Hallowe'en. The fire was kindled on the most conspic-
uous spot near the house; and when it had nearly gone out everyone threw into the ashes
a white stone, which he had first marked. Then having said their prayers round the fire,
they went to bed. Next morning, as soon as they were up, they came to search out the
stones, and if any one of them was found to be missing, they had a notion that the person who threw it would die before he saw another Hallowe'en.[3] A writer on Wales at the
beginning of the nineteenth century says that "the autumnal fire is still kindled in North
Wales, being on the eve of the first day of November, and is attended by many ceremonies; such as running through the fire and smoke, each casting a stone into the fire,
and all running off at the conclusion to escape from the black short-tailed sow; then sup-
ping upon parsnips, nuts, and apples; catching up an apple suspended by a string with
the mouth alone, and the same by an apple in a tub of water: each throwing a nut into
the fire; and those that burn bright, betoken prosperity to the owners through the following year, but those that burn black and crackle, denote misfortune. On the following
morning the stones are searched for in the fire, and if any be missing, they betide ill to
those who threw them in."[4] According to Sir John Rhys, the habit of celebrating Hal-

---

1. A. Macdonald, "Some former Customs of the Royal Parish of Crathie, Scotland," *Folk-lore*, xviii. (1907)
p. 85. The writer adds: "In this way the 'faulds' were purged of evil spirits." But it does not appear whether
this expresses the belief of the people or only the interpretation of the writer.

2. The Rev. John Gregorson Campbell, *Witchcraft and Second Sight in the Highlands and Islands of Scotland* (Glasgow, 1902), pp. 282 *sq.*

3. Pennant's manuscript, quoted by J. Brand, *Popular Antiquities of Great Britain* (London, 1882–1883),
i. 389 *sq.*

4. Sir Richard Colt Hoare, *The Itinerary of Archbishop Baldwin through Wales a.d. MCLXXXVIII. by Giral-
dus de Barri* (London, 1806), ii. 315; J. Brand, *Popular Antiquities*, i. 390. The passage quoted in the text
occurs in one of Hoare's notes on the Itinerary. The dipping for apples, burning of nuts, and so forth, are
mentioned also by Marie Trevelyan, *Folk-lore and Folk-stories of Wales* (London, 1909), pp. 253, 255.

lowe'en by lighting bonfires on the hills is perhaps not yet extinct in Wales, and men still living can remember how the people who assisted at the bonfires would wait till the last spark was out and then would suddenly take to their heels, shouting at the top of their voices, "The cropped black sow seize the hindmost!" The saying, as Sir John Rhys justly remarks, implies that originally one of the company became a victim in dead earnest. Down to the present time the saying is current in Carnarvonshire, where allusions to the cutty black sow are still occasionally made to frighten children.[1] We can now understand why in Lower Brittany every person throws a pebble into the midsummer bonfire.[2] Doubtless there, as in Wales and the Highlands of Scotland,[3] omens of life and death have at one time or other been drawn from the position and state of the pebbles on the morning of All Saints' Day. The custom, thus found among three separate branches of the Celtic stock, probably dates from a period before their dispersion, or at least from a time when alien races had not yet driven home the wedges of separation between them.

In Wales, as in Scotland, Hallowe'en was also the great season for forecasting the future in respect of love and marriage, and some of the forms of divination employed for this purpose resembled those which were in use among the Scotch peasantry. Two girls, for example, would make a little ladder of yarn, without breaking it from the ball, and having done so they would throw it out of the window. Then one of the girls, holding the ball in her hand, would wind the yarn back, repeating a rhyme in Welsh. This she did thrice, and as she wound the yarn she would see her future husband climbing up the little ladder. Again, three bowls or basins were placed on a table. One of them contained clean water, one dirty water, and one was empty. The girls of the household, and sometimes the boys too, then eagerly tried their fortunes. They were blindfolded, led up to the table, and dipped their hands into a bowl. If they happened to dip into the clean water, they would marry maidens or bachelors; if into the dirty water, they would be widowers or widows; if into the empty bowl, they live unmarried. Again, if a girl, walking backwards, would place a knife among the leeks on Hallowe'en, she would see her future husband come and pick up the knife and throw it into the middle of the garden.[4]

In Ireland the Hallowe'en bonfires would seem to have died out, but the Hallowe'en divination has survived. Writing towards the end of the eighteenth century, General Vallancey tells us that on Hallowe'en or the vigil of Saman, as he calls it, "the peasants in Ireland assemble with sticks and clubs (the emblems of laceration) going from house to house, collecting money, bread-cake, butter, cheese, eggs, etc., etc., for the feast, repeating verses in honour of the solemnity, demanding preparations for the festival, in the name of St. Columb Kill, desiring them to lay aside the fatted calf, and to bring forth the black sheep. The good women are employed in making the griddle cake and candles; these last are sent from house to house in the vicinity, and are lighted up on the (Saman) next day, before which they pray, or are supposed to pray, for the departed souls of the

---

1. (Sir) John Rhys, *Celtic Heathendom* (London and Edinburgh, 1888), pp. 515 *sq.* As to the Hallowe'en bonfires in Wales compare J.C. Davies, *Folk-lore of West and Mid-Wales* (Aberystwyth, 1911), p. 77.

2. See above, p. 183.

3. See above, p. 231.

4. Marie Trevelyan, *Folk-lore and Folk-stories of Wales* (London, 1909), pp. 254 *sq.*

donor. Every house abounds in the best viands they can afford: apples and nuts are devoured in abundance: the nut-shells are burnt, and from the ashes many strange things are foretold: cabbages are torn up by the root: hemp seed is sown by the maidens, and they believe, that if they look back, they will see the apparition of the man intended for their future spouse: they hang a smock before the fire, on the close of the feast, and sit up all night, concealed in a corner of the room, convinced that his apparition will come down the chimney and turn the smock: they throw a ball of yarn out of the window, and wind it on the reel within, convinced, that if they repeat the *Pater Noster* backwards, and look at the ball of yarn without, they will then also see his *sith* or apparition: they dip for apples in a tub of water, and endeavour to bring one up in the mouth: they suspend a cord with a cross-stick, with apples at one point, and candles lighted at the other, and endeavour to catch the apple, while it is in a circular motion, in the mouth. These, and many other superstitious ceremonies, the remains of Druidism, are observed on this holiday, which will never be eradicated, while the name of *Saman* is permitted to remain."[1]

In Queen's County, Ireland, down to the latter part of the nineteenth century children practised various of these rites of divination on Hallowe'en. Girls went out into the garden blindfold and pulled up cabbages: if the cabbage was well grown, the girl would have a handsome husband, but if it had a crooked stalk, the future spouse would be a stingy old man. Nuts, again, were placed in pairs on the bar of the fire, and from their behaviour omens were drawn of the fate in love and marriage of the couple whom they represented. Lead, also, was melted and allowed to drop into a tub of cold water, and from the shapes which it assumed in the water predictions were made to the children of their future destiny. Again, apples were bobbed for in a tub of water and brought up with the teeth; or a stick was hung from a hook with an apple at one end and a candle at the other, and the stick being made to revolve you made a bite at the apple and sometimes got a mouthful of candle instead.[2] In County Leitrim, also, down to near the end of the nineteenth century various forms of divination were practised at Hallowe'en. Girls ascertained the character of their future husbands by the help of cabbages just as in Queen's County. Again, if a girl found a branch of a briar-thorn which had bent over and grown into the ground so as to form a loop, she would creep through the loop thrice late in the evening in the devil's name, then cut the briar and put it under her pillow, all without speaking a word. Then she would lay her head on the pillow and dream of the man she was to marry. Boys, also, would dream in like manner of love and marriage at Hallowe'en, if only they would gather ten leaves of ivy without speaking, throw away one, and put the other nine under their pillow. Again, divination was practised by means of a cake called *barm-breac*, in which a nut and a ring were baked. Whoever got the ring would be married first; whoever got the nut would marry a widow or a widower; but if the nut were an empty shell, he or she would remain unwed. Again, a girl would take a clue of worsted, go to a lime kiln in the gloaming, and throw the clew into the kiln in the devil's name, while she held fast the other end of the thread. Then she would rewind the thread and ask, "Who holds my clue?" and the name of her future husband would come up from the depth of the kiln. Another way was to take a rake, go to a rick and

1. (General) Charles Vallancey, *Collectanea de Rebus Hibernicis*, iii. (Dublin, 1786), pp. 459–461.
2. Miss A. Watson, quoted by A.C. Haddon, "A Batch of Irish Folk-lore," *Folk-lore*, iv. (1893) pp. 361 *sq*.

Throwing the clue into the lime-kiln (circa 1910 postcard).

walk round it nine times, saying, "I rake this rick in the devil's name." At the ninth time the wraith of your destined partner for life would come and take the rake out of your hand. Once more, before the company separated for the night, they would rake the ashes smooth on the hearth, and search them next morning for tracks, from which they judged whether anybody should come to the house, or leave it, or die in it before another year was out.[1] In County Roscommon, which borders on County Leitrim, a cake is made in nearly every house on Hallowe'en, and a ring, a coin, a sloe, and a chip of wood are put into it. Whoever gets the coin will be rich; whoever gets the ring will be married first; whoever gets the chip of wood, which stands for a coffin, will die first; and whoever gets the sloe will live longest, because the fairies blight the sloes in the hedges on Hallowe'en, so that the sloe in the cake will be the last of the year. Again, on the same mystic evening girls take nine grains of oats in their mouths, and going out without speaking walk about till they hear a man's name pronounced; it will be the name of their future husband. In County Roscommon, too, on Hallowe'en there is the usual dipping in water for apples or sixpences, and the usual bites at a revolving apple and tallow candle.[2]

In the Isle of Man also, another Celtic country, Hallow-e'en was celebrated down to modern times by the kindling of fires, accompanied with all the usual ceremonies designed to prevent the baneful influence of fairies and witches. Bands of young men perambulated the island by night, and at the door of every dwelling-house they struck up a Manx rhyme, beginning

"*Noght oie howney hop-dy-naw,*"

that is to say, "This is Hollantide Eve." For Hollantide is the Manx way of expressing the old English *All hallowen tide*, that is, All Saints' Day, the first of November. But as the people reckon this festival according to the Old Style, Hollantide in the Isle of Man is our twelfth of November. The native Manx name for the day is *Sauin* or *Laa Houney*. Potatoes, parsnips and fish, pounded up together and mixed with butter, formed the proper evening meal (*mrastyr*) on Hallowe'en in the Isle of Man.[3] Here, too, as in Scotland forms of divination are practised by some people on this important evening. For example, the housewife fills a thimble full of salt for each member of the family and each guest; the contents of the thimblefuls are emptied out in as many neat little piles on a plate, and left there over night. Next morning the piles are examined, and if any of them has fallen down, he or she whom it represents will die within the year. Again, the women carefully sweep out the ashes from under the fireplace and flatten them down neatly on the open hearth. If they find next morning a footprint turned towards the door, it signifies a death in the family within the year; but if the footprint is turned in the opposite direction, it bodes a marriage. Again, divination by eavesdropping is practised in the Isle of Man in much the same way as in Scotland. You go out with your mouth full of water and your hands full of salt and listen at a neighbour's door, and the first name you hear will be the name of your husband. Again, Manx maids bandage their eyes and grope about the room till they dip their hands in vessels full of clean or dirty

1. Leland L. Duncan, "Further Notes from County Leitrim," *Folk-lore*, v. (1894) pp. 195–197.

2. H.J. Byrne, "All Hallows Eve and other Festivals in Connaught," *Folk-lore*, xviii. (1907) pp. 437 *sq.*

3. Joseph Train, *Historical and Statistical Account of the Isle of Man* (Douglas, Isle of Man, 1845), ii. 123; (Sir) John Rhys, *Celtic Folk-lore, Welsh and Manx* (Oxford, 1901), i. 315 *sqq.*

water, and so on; and from the thing they touch they draw corresponding omens. But some people in the Isle of Man observe these auguries, not on Hallowe'en or Hollantide Eve, as they call it, which was the old Manx New Year's Eve, but on the modern New Year's Eve, that is, on the thirty-first of December. The change no doubt marks a transition from the ancient to the modern mode of dating the beginning of the year.[1]

In Lancashire, also, some traces of the old Celtic celebration of Hallowe'en have been reported in modern times. It is said that "fires are still lighted in Lancashire, on Hallowe'en, under the name of Beltains or Teanlas; and even such cakes as the Jews are said to have made in honour of the Queen of Heaven, are yet to be found at this season amongst the inhabitants of the banks of the Ribble.... Both the fires and the cakes, however, are now connected with superstitious notions respecting Purgatory, etc."[2] On Hallowe'en, too, the Lancashire maiden "strews the ashes which are to take the form of one or more letters of her lover's name; she throws hemp-seed over her shoulder and timidly glances to see who follows her."[3] Again, witches in Lancashire used to gather on Hallowe'en at the Malkin Tower, a ruined and desolate farm-house in the forest of Pendle. They assembled for no good purpose; but you could keep the infernal rout at bay by carrying a lighted candle about the fells from eleven to twelve o'clock at night. The witches tried to blow out the candle, and if they succeeded, so much the worse for you; but if the flame burned steadily till the clocks had struck midnight, you were safe. Some people performed the ceremony by deputy; and parties went about from house to house in the evening collecting candles, one for each inmate, and offering their services to *late* or *leet* the witches, as the phrase ran. This custom was practised at Longridge Fell in the early part of the nineteenth century.[4] In Northumberland on Hallowe'en omens of marriage were drawn from nuts thrown into the fire; and the sports of ducking for apples and biting at a revolving apple and lighted candle were also practised on that evening.[5] The equivalent of the Hallowe'en bonfires is reported also from France. We are told that in the department of Deux-Sèvres, which forms part of the old province of Poitou, young people used to assemble in the fields on All Saints' Day (the first of November) and kindle great fires of ferns, thorns, leaves, and stubble, at which they roasted chestnuts. They also danced round the fires and indulged in noisy pastimes.[6]

1. (Sir) John Rhys, *Celtic Folk-lore, Welsh and Manx* (Oxford, 1901), i. 318–321.

2. John Harland and T.T. Wilkinson, *Lancashire Folk-lore* (Manchester and London, 1882), pp. 3 *sq.*

3. J. Harland and T.T. Wilkinson, *op. cit.* p. 140.

4. Annie Milner, in William Hone's *Year Book* (London, preface dated January, 1832), coll. 1276–1279 (letter dated June, 1831); R.T. Hampson, *Medii Aevi Kalendarium* (London, 1841), i. 365; T.F. Thiselton Dyer, *British Popular Customs* (London, 1876), p. 395.

5. *County Folk-lore* vol. iv. *Northumberland*, collected by M.C. Balfour (London, 1904), p. 78. Compare W. Henderson, *Notes on the Folk-lore of the Northern Counties of England* (London, 1879), pp. 96 *sq.*

6. Baron Dupin, in *Mémoires publiées par la Société Royale des Antiquaires de France*, iv. (1823) p. 108.

"Who Was Scared?"

From *The Complete Hallowe'en Book*, Elizabeth F. Guptill, 1915

As Halloween gained in popularity in America during the late 19th and early 20th centuries, educators began to explore ways to use the holiday in their classrooms — especially when Hallowe'en pranking became more and more destructive. Theater books began to include short Halloween plays, recitations, skits and exercises, and Hallowe'en books alternated party games and classroom activities. Also, many of the authors of the early Hallowe'en pamphlets were women who were also playwrights.

Elizabeth F. Guptill, like Martha Russell Orne (author of the 1898 *Hallowe'en: How to Celebrate It*), wrote primarily plays, and even one book on theatrical costuming. Guptill's 1915 *The Complete Hallowe'en Book* includes a number of short plays and skits for children, including this amusing one act play involving Halloween hijinx in a girls' boarding school. "Who Was Scared?" is also notable for focusing on prank-playing girls; although Halloween pranking was typically thought of as a practice for boys, Guptill shows us here that young ladies could be just as likely to indulge in a little Halloween mischief.

Who Was Scared?

A short play for girls.

CHARACTERS.

DOROTHY, KATHERINE, VIRGINIA, and LOUISE — school girls.
MISS FAIRLEE — one of the teachers. MADAME DESAUTELLE — the principal.

SCENE I.

A room in Madame Desautelle's boarding school. The room belongs to Dorothy and Katherine. Arrange room to suit fancy. The only really necessary thing about it is that there shall be a door, visible to the audience, and a drapery curtain, apparently over a wardrobe. The lack of a window may be supplied by a screen, around which the girls can come. Dorothy and Katherine seated, Katherine with a book, Dorothy working problems. Katherine rises, and tosses book across room.

The cover of *The Complete Hallowe'en Book.*

KATHERINE: Put up your book, my studious friend, and rejoice with me. The weary study hour is over, and recreation has begun. Didst not hear the bell, my busy room-mate?

DOROTHY: Oh, rest your mouth a minute or two more, Katherine, while I finish this problem. Do! that's a dear!

KATHERINE: Rest it! It's rested now till my jaw aches, and I absolutely must work it or have the lockjaw. Don't be a digest, Dorothy, it's a dreadful thing to be.

DOROTHY: But I can get it, I know, if you'll only let me alone five minutes.

KATHERINE: Can't do it, my lady fair. No conversation, no outside reading, no letter or note writing, no day-dreaming, no breathing, in study hour, young ladies! Conversely, no studying, no theme writing, no problem working after study hour. Do you wish me to report you to Madame, for breaking the solemn and important rules of this institution of learning — this home of the sciences — this charming prison, my dear room-mate?

DOROTHY: Oh, Katherine, don't! Let me alone, just a minute.

KATHERINE: Oh, Dorothy, do! Do stop studying just a minute! [*Katherine throws a sofa pillow, hits Dorothy, and a squabble ensues. Enter Louise and Virginia, laughing.*]

VIRGINIA: What's up?

KATHERINE: Dorothy's back.

LOUISE: What about?

KATHERINE: She wants to study.

VIRGINIA: Wants to study! Dorothy? Tell us something easier to swallow.

DOROTHY: But I was working on the very last problem, and might have finished it, if it hadn't been for Katherine.

VIRGINIA: There's another study hour coming, my dear. We haven't worked nearly to the last problem yet. We're much nearer the first one.

LOUISE: Don't waste good time discussing algebra. Talk of something worth while. I've thought of the greatest joke.

KATHERINE: Out with it. We're all ready to laugh.

LOUISE: Do you know what date it is?

DOROTHY: Sure. The thirtieth.

VIRGINIA: And that means that tomorrow is the thirty-first, and tomorrow night —

KATHERINE: Is the ghostly and mystical Hallowe'en.

DOROTHY: But don't you count on that, Louise. We don't celebrate that romantic holiday in Madame Desautelle's select boarding school for young ladies.

VIRGINIA: They don't? Why?

DOROTHY: Because such very young ladies as we should be thinking of our studies and not of our future mates. Besides, Tessie Morton had a surreptitious celebration in her room last year — your room, by the way — and managed to set it on fire —

LOUISE: The celebration?

DOROTHY: Certainly. The room, likewise. So Madame has strictly forbidden any notice being taken of Hallowe'en.

VIRGINIA: Oh, we'll take no notice. If we meet Miss Hallowe'en we'll turn our backs and say, haughtily, over our shoulders, "I haven't had the privilege of an introduction."

LOUISE: Oh, will we? I'm going to carry out my plan, if I do it alone. Sweethearts aren't allowed, either — teachers being included in the prohibition as well as pupils — yet Miss Fairlee has one.

KATHERINE: Miss Fairlee? Are you sure?

LOUISE: Sure as can be. She meets him every Wednesday evening at Dr. Finley's. Mrs. Finley is her cousin. I owe Miss Fairlee one. She gave me an impo last night.

DOROTHY: But you deserved it, you know.

LOUISE: That doesn't matter, my dear girl. I'm going to play ghost for Miss Fairlee — the ghost of her lover.

KATHERINE: But if he's alive —

VIRGINIA: This one is; but she had another, years ago.

KATHERINE: Not many years, I guess. She isn't very old.

VIRGINIA: And he was drowned. He will appear to her tomorrow night, and upbraid her with her unfaithfulness, and —

DOROTHY: "Tax her with faithlessness, claim her as bride. And bear her away to the grave." As the old song sayeth. But would you dare?

LOUISE: Of course. She'll shriek and faint away, and we will glide away to other scenes and places before she recovers her senses, or her sense.

KATHERINE: Let's all do it. We can take different corridors, and have great fun and excitement.

DOROTHY: But suppose we're caught?

LOUISE: We won't be. While excitement reigns upstairs, we'll slip down the back stairs, out the pantry window, round to this side of the house, and up the trellis to your window. That window explains why you are to be included in the Scarers, instead of the Scarees. Do you see?

DOROTHY: We do, and accept. It will be much more fun to *be* a ghost than to *see* one.

VIRGINIA: We'll slip in here after Madame goes the last rounds, and then ho, for some fun. At the witching hour, it must be.

LOUISE: Madame sleeps so soundly that she'll never hear, and Miss Fairlee will be ashamed of her fears in the morning, so she won't tell.

DOROTHY: Silence, then. Mum is the word. Not another mention of the plot till the time to carry it out arrives. Somebody'll be scared tomorrow night, I fear.

LOUISE: Be sure none of you gives it away.

KATHERINE: Sure. Not a soul shall know. We'll keep the dark and dreadful secret buried deep within our guilty breasts.

VIRGINIA: Let's go over to Maude's room, and talk up Hallowe'en and ghosts, in general. Maude's dreadfully superstitious.

GIRLS [*rising*]: So we will.

DOROTHY: Who else will be scared, I wonder? Of course, all the girls don't believe in ghosts.

LOUISE: Oh, there'll be enough of them scared to raise quite a breeze. Never you fear!

[*All pass out.*]

[*During this conversation, Miss Fairlee passes the door several times, unseen by the girls, but seen by the audience. After the girls have gone, she stops in doorway, and says, aloud, "Yes, who WILL be scared, I wonder?"*]

CURTAIN

SCENE II.

[*Same room as before. Enter Miss Fairlee, wearing a long, straight costume and mask of black, on which is outlined, in white paint, a skeleton. She closes the door, locks it, and removes the key, then stands in listening attitude.*]

MISS F.: And now for the last act in this little Hallowe'en drama. Who will be scared this time, I wonder? Let me see — behind that curtain, I think, will be a good place. I can reach the window easily, while they are busy at the door. Oh, the key! [*Steps back to door, picks up key from floor.*]

[*She steps to the curtain, stands listening a moment or two, then steps behind it. The girls enter, one at a time, through the window, or from behind the screen.*]

DOROTHY: Peek out, Louise, and see if the coast is clear. If it is, scoot, and get in to bed as quick as you can.

LOUISE [*trying door*]: It's locked.

KATHERINE: Of course it is, goosie, I locked it the last thing. Turn the key.

LOUISE: The key isn't there.

KATHERINE: Of course it's there.

VIRGINIA: Of course it isn't. What did you do with it?

KATHERINE: I didn't do anything with it — just left it there. Hurry up.

VIRGINIA: But it isn't here, Katie, truly.

KATHERINE: It must be.

DOROTHY: Maybe she pulled it out by mistake and dropped it. Look on the floor.

LOUISE: I've been looking there. It isn't anywhere.

KATHERINE: Nonsense! It must be!

[*All search. While they are thus occupied, Miss Fairlee glides from behind curtain, to window, which she closes and locks; or if there is no window, she glides behind screen and back again.*]

LOUISE: Well, of all the queer things!

VIRGINIA: Queer! I should say so! Real Hallowe'eny!

DOROTHY: Come, Katherine, give up the key. The joke's gone far enough, Madame may be here any minute.

KATHERINE: But I haven't it, truly! I locked the door, for I tried it afterwards, and the key was certainly in it.

DOROTHY: But no one could have taken it, when the door was locked!

KATHERINE: Well, it's gone.

LOUISE: Spirits! It's Hallowe'en.

VIRGINIA: It's queer, surely. What shall we do, Lou? It's no use to go back down the trellis. There's none at our window. And the doors are all locked inside.

DOROTHY [*looking towards window*]: That's queer, too. Girls, I came through that window last, and left it open, and it's shut and locked!

[*Girls look toward window, then huddle together.*]

LOUISE: I don't like it! There's no one here but us, and we've been here every minute, and not one of us has been near the window, yet it's shut and locked, and the door key's gone!

VIRGINIA: And it wasn't any fun, anyway, and now we're in a fix. Miss Fairlee was out for the night at the Finley's, and not a soul was scared, till we got to the kitchen. Funny, *none* of the girls believe in ghosts!

LOUISE: But they do! Maude does, and Geneva, and Ethelyn, anyway, and some of the others more than half believe in them.

DOROTHY: Yet every one of them knew who we were! There was a leak somewhere. Some one caught on to our plans and warned the rest, I'm sure.

KATHERINE: Well, Katy was scared enough, I'm sure.

DOROTHY: And so were we. We didn't expect to find anyone there, I'm sure.

LOUISE: And we got cheated out of the cats we meant to capture.

VIRGINIA: Seems to me Katy's beau stays pretty late.

[*All the girls have been glancing uneasily from the door to the window, and around the room.*]

LOUISE: Well, all we can do is camp here till morning, and then try our luck in getting out again unobserved.

DOROTHY: But George is almost always here and at work in the garden before the outer doors are opened.

VIRGINIA: We'll bribe George. I'm not afraid of anything that wears trousers. It's Madame that sends awe to my heart and soul. Hush! [*Raises forefinger, and all look at one another in consternation, as steps are heard, then the doorknob is turned.*]

MADAME [*outside*]: Dorothy! Katherine! [*All stand looking toward door. No one answers.*]

MADAME: Don't pretend to be asleep. Open this door instantly.

[*Dorothy seizes Katherine, and retreats behind screen to where bed is supposed to be, and leaves others still standing at door.*]

MADAME [*pounding loudly at door*]: Dorothy! Katherine!

DOROTHY [*behind screen, sleepily*]: What is it? Who's there?

MADAME: Open this door, instantly.

KATHERINE: We can't, Madame. Some one has played a trick on us, and stolen our key, after locking us in.

MADAME: No more nonsense, girls! Open this door.

DOROTHY: We can't, Madame, truly! We haven't any key.

MADAME: Very well, I will go and bring my keys. But do not try any tricks. If anyone tries to escape from this room, it will be the worst for her.

DOROTHY: We don't want to get out. We only want to sleep.

[*Girls listen a moment.*]

KATHERINE: She's gone. Off with our rigs, and into bed, long enough to muss it. Hide in the wardrobe, Lou and Virgie, till the storm blows over. Maybe you may get safely to your rooms yet.

VIRGINIA: My prophetic soul whispers that she has already discovered our absence and will haul us ignominiously from the dark depths of the wardrobe to immediate execution. But to leave no stone unturned, here goes.

[*Virginia and Louise throw back curtain, disclosing the skeleton. They scream, drop curtain, and run to door.*]

DOROTHY: What is it?

KATHERINE: What in the world ails you? Are you crazy?

LOUISE: Oh, the awful thing! The awful thing!

VIRGINIA [*rattling the door frantically*]: Oh, I want to get out! [*screams*].

DOROTHY [*shaking Virginia's arm*]: Virginia! Stop that noise this minute! What is the matter?

VIRGINIA: This room is haunted! I want to get out!

KATERINE: So did the starling.

DOROTHY: What did you think you saw? And where?

LOUISE [*pointing*]: In the wardrobe. Oh dear! If Madame would only come!

DOROTHY: There's nothing in the wardrobe, girls. Don't be foolish!

VIRGINIA: I tell you we saw it. Oh dear, oh dear!

KATHERINE: Look here, girls, we'll prove that there's nothing there. See! [*Katherine and Dorothy advance to wardrobe, lift curtain, discover skeleton, and run, screaming, to door.*]

DOROTHY: We must get out! Let's break it down.

KATHERINE [*screaming*]: Madame! Madame! [*All pound on door, and scream, with one eye on wardrobe.*]

LOUISE [*suddenly*]: Here she comes. Thank goodness! I thought she never would!

[*Madame unlocks and opens door. Virginia falls fainting into her arms; others try to crowd out, but Madame enters, pushes them back into room and locks door. While all are looking in that direction, Miss Fairlee slips from wardrobe, and out of sight behind screen. If window was used, she raises that and steps out.*]

MADAME: Bring some water.

[*Girls look toward wardrobe, but do not move. Madame lays Virginia down on floor, brings water herself, throws a little in V.'s face.*]

VIRGINIA [*sitting up*]: Oh, take it away! Take it away!

MADAME [*shaking her*]: Stop this nonsense at once, Virginia. Get up!

[*Virginia rises, slowly and unsteadily, helped by Louise.*]

MADAME: Now I want to know the meaning of this. Katherine, stop clinging so to me. Louise, stop crying! Dorothy, you usually have a little sense. Stop staring so at the other side of the room, and tell me what is the matter?

DOROTHY: It was something in the wardrobe.

VIRGINIA: It was a ghost, Madame.

MADAME: Indeed? A ghost? Well, young ladies, you may think you can frighten your mates, but you can not frighten me.

LOUISE: But we saw it, Madame, truly. Oh, please let us out. [*Sobs hysterically.*]

KATHERINE: We did see it, Madame, all of us. And the windows and doors act so mysteriously. They open and shut themselves. Oh! [*screams again.*]

MADAME: What utter foolishness. Come, now, I will show you that there is nothing there. [*She goes to wardrobe, raises curtain, sweeps it aside, and holds it so.*]

MADAME: See for yourselves. There is nothing here. [*Girls glance over, shudder, see nothing, step closer.*]

DOROTHY: Truly, Madame, there was something there.

MADAME: Indeed? What was it, a mouse?

LOUISE: A ghost.

MADAME: There is no such thing, as you know very well, Louise.

KATHERINE: It looked like a skeleton. Ugh! [*Shudders.*] It was horrid! But we did see it, all of us.

MADAME: Or you imagined you did! Now why do I find you, Louise and Dorothy, out of your room at this time of night? And why this masquerading?

VIRGINIA [*looking down as if just remembering her disguise*]: Why, it was Hallowe'en, and we thought we'd have a little fun.

MADAME: I see. And you tried to scare others, and so worked on your own nerves that you imagined you saw ghosts yourselves. Well, I think perhaps you have learned how pleasant such a shock really is, so no more punishment is necessary. You may remain here together the remainder of the night to think it over.

LOUISE: Oh, Madame, please!

VIRGINIA: Please let us go to our own room!

DOROTHY: And we'll take any amount of punishment, if you'll only let us sleep somewhere else.

KATHERINE: We can't sleep here, Madame. We'd be scared to death by morning.

MADAME: But surely you girls do not really believe that you actually saw a ghost?

DOROTHY: We did see it, Madame, truly!

MADAME: But there are no ghosts.

LOUISE: Well, we saw *something* and we've no desire to see it again. I won't stay. I'll jump out of the window and run away!

MADAME: As you came in, I suppose?

[*Girls look at one another, in surprise.*]

MADAME: Oh, yes, I know all about it, even to the ghost. [*Raises voice.*] Miss Fairlee!

[*Miss Fairlee comes into sight, still in the robe, but with mask removed.*]

MADAME: You see, girls, you were not the only Hallowe'en masqueraders tonight.

MISS FAIRLEE: You see, girls, I happened to overhear your kind plans to scare me, as well as your schoolmates, and while you were wondering just who would be scared, I wondered, too, that was all.

DOROTHY: And you told the other girls?

MISS FAIRLEE: I thought it only fair to let them know that if they saw ghosts tonight it would be some of their mischievous schoolmates. I thought, however, that Katy was to be away tonight, so I did not warn her. The rest, however, is only known to those now present. While Madame thought best to teach you a lesson, she did not wish to expose you to the ridicule of the entire school. But — who got scared, I wonder?

LOUISE: Oh, we did, all right. But you're a dear, Miss Fairlee, just the same, and so is Madame. We're really ashamed of ourselves, and I for one will never play ghost again.

VIRGINIA: Nor I.

KATHERINE: I'll try to keep the rules in future, Madame.

DOROTHY: If we get too smart, just say "Hallowe'en," and we'll be meek as Moses.

MISS FAIRLEE: No, say "Who'll be scared, I wonder?"

LOUISE: That would make us meek, I'm sure.

MADAME: And now, young ladies, I will say good night, or rather, good morning. We had better get what sleep we can before daylight. Come, Miss Ghost. Come, Louise and Virginia.

[*They pass out, with general "goodnights."*]

DOROTHY: Well, we know now who's afraid of ghosts, at any rate!

KATHERINE: I should say so! [*Girls turn toward wardrobe. Dorothy straightens curtain.*]
DOROTHY: I shall dream of ghosts, I know. If I scream, pinch me.
KATHERINE: With pleasure!

CURTAIN.

"In Brittany and France"

From *The Book of Hallowe'en,*
Ruth Edna Kelley, 1919

The Book of Hallowe'en, published in 1919, was the first book to take a serious look at the history of Hallowe'en. Unlike the popular pamphlets of the time that featured mainly party and school activities, Ruth Edna Kelley's 195-page book is detailed, illustrated, and even indexed.

Kelley was a librarian, and her book is actually more accurate than many books which came after; for example, she notes correctly that the Celtic word "Samhain" means "summer's end," and is not the name of a Celtic "Lord of Death," as many later books erroneously reported. One of the most unusual chapters in the book examines Halloween in Brittany and France; even now, few books provide detailed accountings of the celebration of the holiday outside of the British isles and America. Although the modern American version of Halloween was undoubtedly largely imported with Scotch and Irish immigrants, it's interesting to note the Bretons — like some modern Americans — focused less on playful divination and more on the holiday's darker aspects.

Chapter XI. In Brittany and France

The Celts had been taught by their priests that the soul is immortal. When the body died the spirit passed instantly into another existence in a country close at hand. We remember that the Otherworld of the British Isles, peopled by the banished Tuatha and all superhuman beings, was either in caves in the earth, as in Ireland, or in an island like the English Avalon. By giving a mortal one of their magic apples to eat, fairies could entice him whither they would, and at last away into their country.

In the Irish story of Nera (q.v.), the corpse of the criminal is the cause of Nera's being lured into the cave. So the dead have the same power as fairies, and live in the same place. On May Eve and November Eve the dead and the fairies hold their revels together and make excursions together. If a young person died, he was said to be called away by the fairies. The Tuatha may not have been a race of gods, but merely the early Celts, who grew to godlike proportions as the years raised a mound of lore and legends for their pedestal. So they might really be only the dead, and not of superhuman nature.

Engraving of Breton ossuary by George Wharton Edwards (from 1910's *Brittany and the Bretons*).

In the fourth century A.D., the men of England were hard pressed by the Picts and Scots from the northern border, and were helped in their need by the Teutons. When this tribe saw the fair country of the Britons they decided to hold it for themselves. After they had driven out the northern tribes, in the fifth century, when King Arthur was reigning in Cornwall, they drove out those whose cause they had fought. So the Britons were scattered to the mountains of Wales, to Cornwall, and across the Channel to Armorica, a part of France, which they named Brittany after their home-land. In lower Brittany, out of the zone of French influence, a language something like Welsh or old British is still spoken, and many of the Celtic beliefs were retained more untouched than in Britain, not clear of paganism till the seventeenth century. Here especially did Christianity have to adapt the old belief to her own ends.

Gaul, as we have seen from Caesar's account, had been one of the chief seats of Druidical belief. The religious center was Carnutes, now Chartrain. The rites of sacrifice survived in the same forms as in the British Isles. In the fields of Deux-Sèvres fires were built of stubble, ferns, leaves, and thorns, and the people danced about them and burned nuts in them. On St. John's Day animals were burned in the fires to secure the cattle from disease. This was continued down into the seventeenth century.

The pagan belief that lasted the longest in Brittany, and is by no means dead yet, was the cult of the dead. Caesar said that the Celts of Gaul traced their ancestry from the god of death, whom he called Dispater. Now figures of l'Ankou, a skeleton armed with a spear, can be seen in most villages of Brittany. This mindfulness of death was strengthened by the sight of the prehistoric cairns of stones on hilltops, the ancient altars of the Druids, and dolmens, formed of one flat rock resting like a roof on two others set up on end with a space between them, ancient tombs; and by the Bretons being cut off from the rest of France by the nature of the country, and shut in among the uplands, black and misty in November, and blown over by chill Atlantic winds. Under a seeming dull indifference and melancholy the Bretons conceal a lively imagination, and no place has a greater wealth of legendary literature.

What fairies, dwarfs, pixies, and the like are to the Celts of other places, the spirits of the dead are to the Celts of Brittany. They possess the earth on Christmas, St. John's Day, and All Saints'. In Finistere, that western point of France, there is a saying that on the Eve of All Souls' "There are more dead in every house than sands on the shore." The dead have the power to charm mortals and take them away, and to foretell the future. They must not be spoken of directly, any more than the fairies of the Scottish border, or met with, for fear of evil results.

By the Bretons of the sixth century the near-by island of Britain, which they could just see on clear days, was called the Otherworld. An historian, Procopius, tells how the people nearest Britain were exempted from paying tribute to the Franks, because they were subject to nightly summons to ferry the souls of the dead across in their boats, and deliver them into the hands of the keeper of souls. Farther inland a black bog seemed to be the entrance to an otherworld underground. One location which combined the ideas of an island and a cave was a city buried in the sea. The people imagined they could hear the bells of Ker-Is ringing, and joyous music sounding, for though this was a city of the dead, it resembled the fairy palaces of Ireland, and was ruled by King Grallon and his daughter Dahut, who could lure mortals away by her beauty and enchantments.

The approach of winter is believed to drive like the flocks, the souls of the dead from their cold cheerless graves to the food and warmth of home. This is why November Eve, the night before the first day of winter, was made sacred to them.

"When comes the harvest of the year
Before the scythe the wheat will fall."
BOTREL: *Songs of Brittany.*

The harvest-time reminded the Bretons of the garnering by that reaper, Death. On November Eve milk is poured on graves, feasts and candles set out on the tables, and fires lighted on the hearths to welcome the spirits of departed kinsfolk and friends.

In France from the twelfth to the fourteenth century stone buildings like lighthouses were erected in cemeteries. They were twenty or thirty feet high, with lanterns on top. On Hallowe'en they were kept burning to safe-guard the people from the fear of night-wandering spirits and the dead, so they were called "lanternes des morts."

The cemetery is the social center of the Breton village. It is at once meeting-place, playground, park, and church. The tombs that outline the hills make the place seem one vast cemetery. On All Souls' Eve in the mid–nineteenth century the "procession of tombs" was held. All formed a line and walked about the cemetery, calling the names of those who were dead, as they approached their resting-places. The record was carefully remembered, so that not one should seem to be forgotten.

"We live with our dead," say the Bretons. First on the Eve of All Souls' comes the religious service, "black vespers." The blessedness of death is praised, the sorrows and shortness of life dwelt upon. After a common prayer all go out to the cemetery to pray separately, each by the graves of his kin, or to the "place of bones," where the remains of those long dead are thrown all together in one tomb. They can be seen behind gratings, by the people as they pass, and rows of skulls at the sides of the entrance can be touched. In these tombs are Latin inscriptions meaning: "Remember thou must die," "To-day to me, and to-morrow to thee," and others reminding the reader of his coming death.

From the cemetery the people go to a house or an inn which is the gathering-place for the night, singing or taking loudly on the road to warn the dead who are hastening home, lest they may meet. Reunions of families take place on this night, in the spirit of the Roman feast of the dead, the Feralia, of which Ovid wrote:

"After the visit to the tombs and to the ancestors who are no longer with us, it is pleasant to turn towards the living; after the loss of so many, it is pleasant to behold those who remain of our blood, and to reckon up the generations of our descendants."

Fasti.

A toast is drunk to the memory of the departed. The men sit about the fireplace smoking or weaving baskets; the women apart, knitting or spinning by the light of the fire and one candle. The children play with their gifts of apples and nuts. As the hour grows later, and mysterious noises begin to be heard about the house, and a curtain sways in a draught, the thoughts of the company already centred upon the dead find expression in words, and each has a tale to tell of an adventure with some friend or enemy who has died.

The dead are thought to take up existence where they left it off, working at the same trades, remembering their old debts, likes and dislikes, even wearing the same clothes they wore in life. Most of them stay not in some distant, definite Otherworld, but frequent the scenes of their former life. They never trespass upon daylight, and it is dangerous to meet them at night, because they are very ready to punish any slight to their memory, such as selling their possessions or forgetting the hospitality due them. L'Ankou will come to get a supply of shavings if the coffins are not lined with them to make a softer resting-place for the dead bodies.

The lively Celtic imagination turns the merest coincidence into an encounter with a spirit, and the poetic temperament of the narrators clothes the stories with vividness and mystery. They tell how the presence of a ghost made the midsummer air so cold that even wood did not burn, and of groans and footsteps underground as long as the ghost is displeased with what his relatives are doing.

Just before midnight a bell-man goes about the streets to give warning of the hour when the spirits will arrive.

"They will sit where we sat, and will talk of us as we talked of them: in the gray of the morning only will they go away."

LE BRAZ: *Night of the Dead.*

The supper for the souls is then set out. The poor who live on the mountains have only black corn, milk, and smoked bacon to offer, but it is given freely. Those who can afford it spread on a white cloth dishes of clotted milk, hot pancakes, and mugs of cider.

After all have retired to lie with both eyes shut tight lest they see one of the guests, death-singers make their rounds, chanting under the windows:

"You are comfortably lying in your bed,
But with the poor dead it is otherwise;
You are stretched softly in your bed
While the poor souls are wandering abroad.
"A white sheet and five planks,
A bundle of straw beneath the head,
Five feet of earth above
Are all the worldly goods we own."

LE BRAZ: *Night of the Dead.*

The tears of their deserted friends disturb the comfort of the dead, and sometimes they appear to tell those in sorrow that their shrouds are always wet from the tears shed on their graves.

Wakened by the dirge of the death-singers the people rise and pray for the souls of the departed.

Divination has little part in the annals of the evening, but one in Finistère is recorded. Twenty-five new needles are laid in a dish, and named, and water is poured upon them. Those who cross are enemies.

In France is held a typical Continental celebration of All Saints' and All Souls.' On

October 31st the children go asking for flowers to decorate the graves, and to adorn the church. At night bells ring to usher in All Saints.' On the day itself the churches are decorated gaily with flowers, candles, and banners, and a special service is held. On the second day of November the light and color give way to black drapings, funeral songs, and prayers.

"Present-Day Mumming at Brooklyn"

From *English Pageantry: An Historical Outline,*
Robert Withington, 1920

This brief excerpt from Robert Withington's 1920 study of pageantry offers an account of several practices (Thanksgiving day house-to-house mumming and Hallowe'en costuming) that may be the beginnings of trick-or-treating; the Thanksgiving festivities in particular, with costumed children begging food, seems to be lacking only the actual "trick-or-treat" phrase (and the right holiday). The addition of the treat-demanding phrase itself probably occurred about fifteen years after the date of this piece.

A sporadical manifestation of what may be a survival of more elaborate holiday pageantry is found at Brooklyn (New York) on Thanksgiving Day.[1] This, like the mumming found on Hallowe'en and in connection with the Guy Fawkes' celebrations, is confined to children, dressed up in costume, whose buffoonery and hilarity find expression in their progress from house to house — rarely singly, often in groups of ten or twelve. They invade front lawns, court-yards, or hallways, and give a "performance," which is little more than a succession of antics, popular songs, and "movie" representations, to which each one in the group contributes his bit. The program ended, each collects what he can from the spectators, in the way of pennies, or cake, fruit, and other sweets (the edibles are more in demand than the money, and are often put into the basket, which is part of the holiday garb); after which, the group moves on to fresh fields and pastures new.

Often the girls will give exhibitions of folk-dancing, learned in the public school or at the recreation center: frequently Russian peasant dances, the Highland fling, some Irish jig, or Swedish dance is skillfully interpreted on the city pavement by youngsters often arrayed in a manner at least suggesting the national costume of the country in question. A convincing effect is often obtained by merely tucking up a skirt or rolling stockings down below the knee and cocking the hat on one side; the illusion is there, if not the detail.

1. I am indebted to Miss Helen L. Lieder, of Brooklyn, for the following information. Her account indicates that what goes on today is rather mumming than pageantry.

The boys usually prefer to dress up as "movie" heroes, and one often sees Charlie Chaplins and Bill Harts abroad; but pirates, Indians, cowboys and colored comedians, are not neglected. Of historical periods, the Revolutionary is perhaps the favorite; the blue and buff Continental uniform is somehow achieved — topped by a cocked hat, it is at least recognizable. The bouffante skirt of the period, with lace kerchief and cap, is an attractive costume sometimes encountered. Present-day uniforms, Red Cross costumes, the dress of the boy-scouts, have been in evidence for the past year or two; but on the whole, the hybrid costumes are commoner, and the attempt to approximate historical costumes is rare.

In many parts of America, children dress up on Hallowe'en and visit the neighbors, sometimes playing tricks, such as carrying off gates, turning signs around, changing house-numbers, or exchanging various articles — as witches, in the past, were supposed to play roguish, if not malicious, tricks. Perhaps such mumming as that at Thanksgiving in Brooklyn, was transferred from Hallowe'en; though it does not include any of the tricks sometimes found elsewhere. Professor Paul R. Lieder, whose boyhood was spent in Brooklyn, hazards the suggestion that if this mumming is not a legacy from the early Dutch settlers, it has come from New England. I may add that I have seen it on Hallowe'en in Bloomington, Indiana.

A youthful Hallowe'en mummer (1920 postcard).

Bibliography

Brine, Mary D. *Elsie's Hallowe'en Experience and Other Stories or Echoes from Story Land*, New York: Hurst, 1888.

Burns, Robert. *The Works of Robert Burns: With an Account of His Life, and Criticism on His Writings*, edited by James Currie, Philadelphia: Crissy and Markley, 1850.

Campbell, John Gregorson. *Superstitions of the Highlands & Islands of Scotland Collected Entirely from Oral Sources*, Glasgow: James MacLehose and Sons, 1900.

_____. *Witchcraft & Second Sight in the Highlands & Islands of Scotland: Tales and Traditions Collected Entirely from Oral Sources*, Glasgow: James MacLehose and Sons, 1902.

Chambers, R. *Chambers's Book of Days: A Miscellany of Popular Antiquities in Connection with the Calendar* (in two volumes), London and Edinburgh: W. and R. Chambers, 1869.

Elliott, Helen. "Hallowe'en," *Godey's Lady's Book and Magazine*, Vol. 81, No. 485 (November 1870).

Frazer, Sir James George. *The Golden Bough Part VII: Balder the Beautiful, Vol. I: The Fire-Festivals of Europe and the Doctrine of the External Soul*, 3rd edition, London: Macmillan, 1913.

Goodrich-Freer, A. "More Folklore from the Hebrides," *Folk-Lore*, Volume XIII (March 1902).

Gregor, Rev. Walter. *Notes on the Folklore of the North-East of Scotland*, London: The Folk-Lore Society, 1881.

Gregory, Lady. *Cuchulain of Muirthemne: The Story of the Men of the Red Branch of Ulster*, London: John Murray, 1902

_____. *Gods and Fighting Men: The Story of the Tuatha de Danaan and of the Fianna of Ireland*, London: John Murray, 1904.

Guptill, Elizabeth F. *The Complete Hallowe'en Book*, Lebanon, Ohio: March Brothers, 1915.

"Hallowe'en at Balmoral Castle," *Dundee Advertiser*, November 1869.

Hardy, Thomas. *The Return of the Native*, London: Smith, Elder, & Co., 1878.

Hazlitt, W. Carew. *Faiths and Folklore: A Dictionary of National Beliefs, Superstitions and Popular Customs, Past and Current, With Their Classical and Foreign Analogues, Described and Illustrated* Volume I, London: Reeves & Turner, 1905.

Hyde, Douglas. *Beside the Fire: A Collection of Irish Gaelic Folk Stories* ("Guleesh na Guss Dhu"), London: David Nutt, 1890.

Kelley, Ruth Edna. *The Book of Hallowe'en*, Boston: Lothrop, Lee & Shepard, 1919.

Montgomerie, Alexander. *The Poems of Alexander Montgomerie* (edited by James Cranstoun), Edinburgh and London: William Blackwood and Sons, 1887.

Newell, William Wells. "The Ignis Fatuus, Its Character and Legendary Origin," *The Journal of American Folklore*, Vol. 17, No. 65 (Jan.–Mar., 1904).

Orne, Martha Russell. *Hallowe'en: Its Origin and How to Celebrate It with Appropriate Games and Ceremonies*, New York: Fitzgerald Publishing Corporation, 1898.

Rhys, John. *Celtic Folklore: Welsh and Manx* (Volume I), Oxford: Clarendon, 1901.

Scott, Sir Walter. *Minstrelsy of the Scottish Border* (in 2 volumes), Edinburgh: Printed for Longman, Hurst, Rees, Orme, and Brown, London; And for Archibald Constable and Co., 1802.

Sharp, William. "Halloween: A Threefold Chronicle," *Harper's Monthly Magazine*, Volume 73, Issue 438 (November 1886).

Van Panhuys, Jonkheer L. C. "A European

Custom of Pagan Times Brought Over to America (Halloween at Chicago)" *Internationaler Amerikanisten-Kongress: Stuttgart 1904*, Stuttgart: W. Kohlhammer Druck und Verlag, 1906.

White, Corporal Charles Fred. *Plea of the Negro Soldier and a Hundred Other Poems*, Easthampton, Mass.: Enterprise Printing, 1908.

Wilde, Lady. *Ancient Legends, Mystic Charms, and Superstitions of Ireland* Vol. I, Boston: Ticknor, 1887.

Withington, Robert. *English Pageantry: An Historical Outline*, Volume II, Cambridge: Harvard University Press, 1920.

Woodman, Emma. "Hallowe'en," *The School Arts Book Volume Five*, Worcester, Mass.: Davis, 1906.

Index

Numbers in *bold italics* refer to pages with illustrations.